100 GREATS DONCASTER ROVERS
FOOTBALL CLUB

100 GREATS

DONCASTER ROVERS
FOOTBALL CLUB

PETER TUFFREY

TEMPUS

First published 2003

Tempus Publishing Limited
The Mill, Brimscombe Port,
Stroud, Gloucestershire, GL5 2QG

British Library Cataloguing in Publication Data.
A catalogue record for this book is available from the British Library.

ISBN 0 7524 2707 5

Typesetting and origination by Tempus Publishing Limited
Printed in Great Britain by Midway Colour Print, Wiltshire

This book is dedicated to Tony Bluff and Barry Watson for their untiring research work on Doncaster Rovers Football Club. Tony Bluff was kind enough to read through the final manuscript

Former player and manager Steve Wignall (left) pictured with the author, Peter Tuffrey, at Southport during the 2001/02 season.

Acknowledgements

I would like to express thanks to the following people: Tony Bluff, Syd Bycroft, Mrs Jack Haigh, Brian Kelly, Brian Makepeace, John Ryan, Laurie Sheffield, Steve Uttley and Barry Watson.

Introduction

I suppose books like this immediately create controversy as football fans will inevitably have in their own minds a list of players whom they would include in their 100 greats. The question also arises about what actually constitutes a great player, and what criteria might be used for their selection. Is it someone who has scored many goals, made spectacular saves, someone who did not play many games but thrilled the fans with their skills or a player with countless appearances? In compiling this book, I suppose I have 'played safe' in choosing a large number of players who would go into any Doncaster Rovers fan's 100 greats. Yet, I have selected the players who fall into all the categories just mentioned and have attempted to include greats from each decade, although the book is laid out in alphabetical, not chronological order. Having said all that, I know some fans will inevitably think that some players ought to have been chosen ahead of others. I knew that this was going to be a controversial book in some ways when I wanted to include someone who had won the Player of the Year award on one occasion. Yet a number of fans said that he was not worthy of a place!

Starting from the 1920s, Sammy Cowan was selected for his reliability and flair which he displayed between 1923/24 with Rovers. It is also interesting to learn of the illustrious career he had on leaving the club. Goalscorer Tom Keetley could not be left out from this decade and is someone that no Rovers fan would omit from a book of this nature because of his incredible goal-scoring ability. It is interesting to note that he left Belle Vue because of a dispute with the directors concerning the time he wanted to allocate to business interests outside of football. Reminiscent of today, some may argue. Players who won honours with the club in the mid-1930s championship-winning side are included from that decade. Then, of course, in the 1940s when Peter Doherty arrived, quite a number of individuals are included up until the time he left in 1957. And it was difficult to know who to leave out from that time, because it really comprised the halcyon years at Doncaster Rovers.

There were purple patches in following years: in the mid-1960s and the years under Lawrie McMenemy and Billy Bremner. From the mid-1980s until the fall from the Football League in 1998, it cannot be underestimated how difficult times were. Trying to establish a criterion for choosing choosing greats from this period was difficult to say the least. But that is not to say that greats did not don Rovers shirts at this time. Darren Moore, Mark Rankine and Rufus Brevett all played through these troubled years. But, of course, it was sad to see players leaving because of non-payment of wages and escalating troubles off the field.

Whilst languishing in the Conference, Rovers have been fortunate enough to attract former great players, and it has been refreshing to see that they have not just turned out in the club's colours to bask in their former glory. Former Liverpool favourite Steve Nicol only played a few games, but thrilled both young and old with his skills. Mark Atkins won a Premiership title medal with Blackburn, but also played with pride and commitment whilst with Rovers.

The club's great days were undoubtedly when Doherty was at the helm and, for a time, under Billy Bremner. Players came through like Alick Jeffrey and the Snodin brothers, although all too often they left to further their careers at clubs in higher divisions. Let all Rovers fans hope players of their undoubted abilities can be home-grown once more, and that the good times are only round the corner once again – in the Football League at least.

Peter Tuffrey, February 2003

100 Doncaster Greats

Jack Ashurst
Mark Atkins
Dave Bentley
John Bird
Colin Booth
Willie Boyd
Gary Brabin
Ian Branfoot
Rufus Brevett
Albert Broadbent
John Buckley
Dizzie Burton
Syd Bycroft
Colin Clish
Tony Coleman
Sammy Cowan
Colin Cramb
Dave Cusack
Gerry Daly
Brian Deane
Jim Dobbin
Ronnie Dodd
Peter Doherty
Colin Douglas
Mike Elwiss
Fred Emery
John Flowers
Brian Flynn
Paddy Gavin
Bobby Gilfillan
Eddie Gormley
Len Graham
Harry Gregg
Jack Haigh

Alfie Hale
Kenneth Hardwick
David Harle
Ray Harrison
John Haselden
Jack Hodgson
Glenn Humphries
Archie Irvine
Alick Jeffrey
Mike Jeffrey
Dave Jones
Graeme Jones
Clarrie Jordan
Tom Keetley
Brian Kelly
Peter Kitchen
Joe Laidlaw
Kit Lawlor
Tony Leighton
Steve Lister
Alan Little
Eddie McMorran
Brian Makepeace
Dave Miller
Ian Miller
Johnny Mooney
Darren Moore
Steve Nicol
John Nicholson
Willie Nimmo
Brendan O'Callaghan
Brendan Ormsby
Bill Paterson
Dennis Peacock

Dave Penney
Daral Pugh
Chris Rabjohn
Mark Rankine
Neil Redfearn
Graham Ricketts
Stuart Robertson
Fred Robinson
Les Robinson
Billy Russell
John Schofield
Laurie Sheffield
Glynn Snodin
Ian Snodin
Barry Staton
John Stiles
Cec Stirland
Jack Teasdale
Bert Tindill
Paul Todd
Lee Turnbull
Brian Usher
Steve Uzelac
Alan Warboys
Willie Watson
Jim Watton
Dick White
Steve Wignall
Russ Wilcox
Harold Wilcockson
Charlie Williams
John Wylie

The top twenty, who appear here in italics, occupy two pages instead of the usual one.

John (Jack) Ashurst
Centre half 1988-1992

Football League
Appearances: 139
Goals: 2

FA Cup
Appearances: 7
Goals: 0

FL Cup
Appearances: 3
Goals: 0

Total appearances: 149

Jack, a vastly experienced centre-back, was signed by Dave Mackay from Leeds for £15,000 in November 1988, to add experience, strength and organise the Rovers' defence and that's exactly what he did. It was also hoped that he would set an example to younger members of the side, including Raven, Raffell and Beattie. His signing ended weeks of patient negotiations for the thirty-four-year-old six-footer, which had begun when Billy Bremner was sacked as manager at Elland Road. Ashurst had been the first-choice central defender under Bremner, but played once only as substitute after Howard Wilkinson took over. Mackay said: 'We've had to wait a long time before clinching the deal because other clubs were interested, but we are delighted he has chosen to come to us.'

Jack was born in Renton on 12 October 1954. Initially, he was an apprentice with Sunderland and signed pro for them in October 1971. He made his debut as a teenager in the same season that the Roker Park team won the FA Cup. He went on to make 129 appearances for them (11 as substitute) and scored 4 goals. He moved to Blackpool during October 1979 and his record there was 53 outings and 3 goals. Thereafter, he moved to Carlisle United (194 appearances, 2 goals) and Leeds United (88 appearances, 1 as substitute and scored 1 goal) before coming to Belle Vue under Dave Mackay.

He made his first-team debut in the Fourth Division home game against Peterborough United on 12 November 1988. His fellow defenders that day included R. Robinson, Beattie, Raven and Turnbull, with Malcolm in

goal. During this season, Jack was playing against a backdrop of the club announcing that it was losing £3,000 a week and was £500,000 in debt. Jack was eventually made captain and won the supporters' club Player of the Year for the 1988/89 season. This was a remarkable achievement, as he had only been at the club since November. During this season, he made 30 League appearances and scored 1 goal. He was presented with an inscribed wrist watch and the Eddie Ward Memorial Trophy by supporters' club president, Dr William Erskine, at the last game of the season. This was no small reward for a player who had earned a reputation as a solid, dependable defender with plenty of pace. In the same season, Jack had also shared the honour of winning the Bob Nellis Award for the Player of the Month on three occasions with Les Robinson.

He was released in May 1990, after reputedly turning down a new contract to concentrate on his business interests, and started playing for non-League Bridlington Town. However, he rejoined the fold during the first week of November 1990. Billy Bremner needed somebody to cover because defender Andy Holmes was on the long-term injury list, and Colin Douglas, Brendan Ormsby and Rufus Brevett were all receiving treatment. Manager Billy Bremner said: 'He agreed to come and help us out on a non-contract basis and we will see how things develop from there. Jack has kept himself quite fit but he may need a few days to sharpen up.' Jack eventually left Rovers for Rochdale on a non-contract basis in August 1992.

Mark Nigel Atkins

Defender/Midfield 1999-2001

Football Conference
Appearances: 36 (+2 as substitute)
Goals: 4

FA Cup
Appearances: 2
Goals: 0

Total appearances: 40

Mark was born in Doncaster and, in recent times, is probably one of the town's most successful players, having played for England at Youth level and won a Premiership title medal with Blackburn Rovers. He was born on 14 August 1968 and did well at school, gaining nine O-levels and two A-levels.

Mark started his career at Scunthorpe, signing for them during July 1986 and turning out for them on 45 occasions – 5 as substitute – and scoring 2 goals. From there he joined Blackburn Rovers in June 1988, and enjoyed much success with them, playing alongside players such as Alan Shearer. He once said that the biggest break in his career was when he switched from playing as a full-back to adopting a midfield role. He made 224 appearances at Blackburn, 33 as substitute, and scored 35 goals. Mark said one of the highest compliments that he was paid was Kenny Dalglish saying that he did not look out of place with the top players.

Mark moved to Wolverhampton Wanderers in September 1995, making 100 appearances, 11 as substitute, and scoring 8 goals. A move to York City followed in 1999, with 10 appearances and 2 goals. He joined Rovers under Ian and Glynn Snodin towards the end of 1999 after training for a while at Belle Vue. He made his Rovers debut in the Nationwide Conference away game against Sutton United on 6 November 1999. Rovers lost the match 1-0, in front of a crowd of 1,097. A short time afterwards, manager Ian Snodin said: 'I do not like to single out individuals but I feel I must comment on the way that Mark Atkins has settled in and the influence he has had on the side. His experience and ability encourages others to play football the way we believe in and gives us options on formation more freely.'

Standing 6ft tall, Mark played well in defence or midfield for Rovers and always endeavoured to get on the score sheet. He listed Glenn Hoddle as one of his favourite players. When the Snodins were sacked in April 2000, Dave Penney and he took over at the helm for a while. He moved to Hull City in March 2001 and has since moved to Shrewsbury Town.

David Alwyn Bentley
Midfield 1977-1980

Football League
Appearances: 87 (+2 as substitute)
Goals: 4

FA Cup
Appearances: 2
Goals: 0

FL Cup
Appearances: 7
Goals: 0

Total appearances: 98

Dave was born in Worksop on 30 May 1950 and started his career at Rotherham United, signing for them in July 1967. While at Millmoor, he played 242 games (7 as substitute) and scored 14 goals. He had a spell on loan at Mansfield Town in 1972 (1 game, 3 as substitute and 1 goal) then moved to Chesterfield (53 outings, 2 as substitute and 4 goals) in June 1974. He arrived at Belle Vue under Stan Anderson in July 1977 for a period on loan. Chesterfield had given him a free transfer. During this period at Belle Vue, he played in the pre-season friendly games against Chesterfield and Coventry City, and it was reported that he showed poise and style. After the Chesterfield game, the *Doncaster Evening Post* had the following to say: '[T]he new man who made the biggest impression was Dave Bentley ... [he] showed the class that made him a fine prospect at Rotherham a few years ago with some precision passing and fitted in well.'

Towards the end of the loan period, Dave had impressed Stan Anderson sufficiently to be offered a full-time contract. Stan thought that Dave was shaping up well, and added: 'Dave has played extremely well in our two friendlies. He has shown good vision and has shown himself to be a good ball-player in midfield. He is what I have been looking for, a left-sided midfield player.' Dave made his debut in the Fourth Division home game against Newport County on 20 August 1977, the first fixture of

the 1977/78 season. His team-mates on that day included Hemsley, Reed Taylor, Owen, Laidlaw and Olney.

In the 1977/78 season, Rovers finished twelfth and Dave made 28 League appearances. He became a member of the coaching staff at the end of the 1979/80 season but he was still sometimes called upon to play when needed. The *Doncaster Evening Post* of 14 February 1980 reported: 'Doncaster Rovers' reserve and youth coach Dave Bentley is coming out of retirement to try and help the team end their depressing run of 11 matches without a win. Twenty-nine-year-old Bentley, who quit playing to join the coaching staff before Christmas, has answered Billy Bremner's call and will be in the side for Saturday's home match against Scunthorpe. The player, whose retirement coincided with the arrival of Alan Little from Barnsley, agreed that Rovers' main need at that time was experience.'

Bremner added: '[Dave's] a great pro and a good friend who is prepared to do things for you and he agreed to play again ... I'm hoping that David will help us out of a sticky situation ... I think he can be just the steadying influence we need.' But Bremner defended his decision to 'retire' Dave and make him reserve and youth team coach. 'It was one of the best decisions I've made in my life. He's the ideal man for the job and at the time it looked as though we could manage without him on the field ... '

John Charles Bird

Centre half 1967-1971

Football League
Appearances: 48 (+2 as substitute)
Goals: 3

FA Cup
Appearances: 2
Goals: 0

FL Cup
Appearances: 3
Goals: 0

Total appearances: 55

John Bird became known as a 'utility man' while playing in defence for Rovers. It is also recorded that it took a lot of persuading for him to leave his intended career in surveying for the less safe and stable world of professional football. But the thrill of playing in League soccer had always been at the back of his mind, and he once admitted he knew that he had made the right choice as soon as he made his League debut for Rovers.

He was born in Rossington on 9 June 1948 and he played for Don Valley Boys' under-11 side. He then joined Doncaster United, before moving across to Belle Vue – first as a part-timer and then as a full-time professional in March 1967. Other clubs had been after the promising youngster, and he had the chance of trials with Nottingham Forest, Mansfield and Rotherham before finally throwing in his lot with his home-town team. He made his Rovers debut on 14 November 1967 in the Fourth Division game against Workington Town. It was a match attended by 1,873 and was drawn 2-2. He was captain of the Doncaster team that finished as runners-up in their excursion abroad during his time at Belle Vue.

He was transferred to Preston North End in March 1971. The *Doncaster Evening Post* of 12 March 1971 reported that Doncaster Rovers figured in the last of the season's transfer deals when they sold John Bird to Preston for about £8,000. Officials at League headquarters at Lytham St Anne's were looking at the clock as the registration arrived only thirty seconds before the deadline. Manager Lawrie McMenemy drove John to Preston on the previous day, and arrived at Deepdale at 4.25 p.m. Preston boss Alan Ball, the club's assistant secretary and a director were waiting on the doorstep. They all bundled into a car, with Alan Ball and John discussing details on the way to Lytham. McMenemy said that, at twenty-two, John was not a regular first-teamer and was 'a bit dissatisfied with the situation'. It was added that John had been on offer for a while and had always done his best when called upon to step into the side – usually in Stuart Robertson's absence –and 'he certainly never let anyone down'.

John played 166 times for Preston and was on the score sheet on 9 occasions. From there he had a stay at Newcastle United (84 appearances, 3 as substitute and scoring 5 goals). His League career ended at Hartlepool United (139 outings, 2 as substitute and 16 goals). Thereafter, he was manager at Halifax Town for a period and was then a coach at Belle Vue. Apart from soccer, John has arguably a rather unusual hobby for a footballer – oil and watercolour painting. For quite some time now he has sold small limited edition prints of his work.

Colin Booth
Inside forward 1962-1964

Football League
Appearances: 88
Goals: 57

FA Cup
Appearances: 8
Goals: 3

FL Cup
Appearances: 5
Goals: 2

Total appearances: 101

Inside forward Colin Booth was born in Manchester on 30 December 1934, and joined Wolverhampton Wanderers as a junior in January 1952. He was at Wolves for nearly eight years, scoring 26 goals in 78 appearances. Whilst he was at Molineux, he made one appearance for the England Under-23 team.

In October 1959, he moved to Nottingham Forest for a fee of £20,000. His stay at Forest was successful, scoring 39 goals in just 87 League games. Therefore, it was amazing that Rovers were able to snap up this proven goal-scorer for just £12,000 in August 1962. There was a rush to sign him before the first game of the 1962/63 season, but a stubbed toe sustained in a Nottingham Forest training session was still worrying the inside forward, who decided that it would be safer to wait until Rovers' next fixture. The fee for him – described by Tom Garnett, the Rovers general manager, as a record for the club – was believed to be just under £10,000. This exceeded the £8,000 paid to Cardiff City for Danny Malloy during the previous season. Only a year before, Middlesbrough and Forest agreed on a fee approaching £20,000, but Colin declined to move to the North East.

He made his Rovers debut in the away game against Chesterfield on 20 August 1962 and scored the only goal in the 3-1 defeat. He was bought to add bite to the forward line, and his fellow attackers on that day included Hale, Windross, Sambrook and Robinson. In a review of the game, it was noted: 'Rovers' latest capture was still finding his feet in a new set-up, but after the interval he came into his own and his well-taken goal inspired him to better efforts. He brought the best out of Powell with a searing drive which the 'keeper did well to turn round the post for a corner.'

During Colin's first season at Belle Vue, he rattled in 34 League goals (in 45 appearances) and 4 in the Cup. He usually played in the inside-right, number eight position, although occasionally at centre forward. In the following season, he formed a good striking partnership with John Nibloe, and especially with Alfie Hale, Colin netting 23 times and Alfie 20. Some fans claim that their finest hour came in the 10-0 demolition of Darlington on 25 January 1964, when they scored six goals between them.

The most goals he ever scored in a game was a hat-trick. One time when he was at Belle Vue, it was reported that a Second Division club had made a 'fantastic' offer to secure his services, but this was subsequently declined. Yet, surprisingly, at the end of the 1963/64 season, a local paper dismissed Colin's efforts in that second season as a 'bitter disappointment', and said that a change of clubs would be beneficial to the player. This was alarming criticism for a striker who had scored 57 goals in just 88 League appearances. Whether this adverse criticism had any effect on his decision to put in a transfer request is unknown, but Colin did just that in early May 1964, citing the fact that he wanted to move to a club further south than Belle Vue. Oxford United came in for him a few weeks later and their bid of just £7,000 was accepted, although it was the only one on the table. Whilst he was with the U's he scored 22 goals in 48 games.

William Boyd

Goalkeeper 1974-1984

Football League
Appearances: 104
Goals: 0

FA Cup
Appearances: 7
Goals: 0

FL Cup
Appearances: 4
Goals: 0

Total appearances: 115

Whilst hampered by injury problems during a ten-year stint at Belle Vue, Willie was nevertheless a very agile, impressive and popular figure between the posts for Rovers. He was born in Hamilton on 18 October 1958. During his early youth, he played for the Scottish Youth side. He was an apprentice at Hull City before signing for them during October 1977. He came to Belle Vue under Billy Bremner in February 1980. This was just before the departure of Dennis Peacock to Bolton Wanderers for £70, 000 – although he had spent three months on loan from his former club, Hull City, the previous year.

His first Rovers' game was in the Fourth Division away match against Peterborough United on 22 March 1980. He played 104 times for Rovers. This was in front of a crowd of 4,107 and Rovers lost the encounter. The Rovers back line on this day included Russell, Lister, Dowd, G. Snodin and Lally. Recalling details about his debut sometime later, Willie said: 'I was a bit nervous before the match – which ended in a 3-2 win for Peterborough United – but once I'd gone out there and had an early couple of touches, I got on with the job. Since then, I don't get quite as nervous, but I do know when I've played badly – I don't need anyone to

tell me that. The funniest comment from the terraces that I've heard was when I let one soft shot go through my legs in our Group Cup match against Grimsby at the start of this season. Quick as a flash from the crowd came the comment: "No buts, it's got to be butter" – referring, I think, to my handling.'

Willie wasn't normally superstitious, but he did have one match-day ritual. 'I never [shaved] on a match day,' he said adamantly 'and never [will] do.' After his debut appearance, Willie held his place in the first team until the end of the season, playing 11 League games, keeping a clean sheet on 4 occasions. During the following season, he only missed one game.

In subsequent years, he shared the goalkeeping position with Dennis Peacock. His last appearance for Rovers was in the away game in the FA Cup at Mansfield Town on 19 November 1983. He had his career tragically cut short by a serious knee injury. A testimonial game was held for him on 8 August 1984, when Rovers played West Bromwich Albion. He played non-League football for Grantham and Kettering for a short spell after leaving Rovers. During March 1988, he returned to Belle Vue, working with the Football in the Community scheme for while.

Gary Brabin
Midfield 1994-1996

Football League
Appearances: 58 (+1 as substitute)
Goals: 11

FA Cup
Appearances: 2
Goals: 0

FL Cup
Appearances: 2
Goals: 0

Total appearances: 63

Gary Brabin (nicknamed 'Sumo') was a steady and reliable force in midfield during the turbulent mid-1990s at Belle Vue. He was born in Liverpool on 9 December 1970 and started his career in the youth team at Stockport County, signing for them in December 1989. While there, he only played 1 game, plus 1 as substitute, and came to Doncaster after a spell with Runcorn in July 1994. He was new manager Sammy Chung's first major signing. Rovers succeeded in landing the Vauxhall Conference club's Player of the Season, where the likes of Oxford United and Lincoln City – both reported to have put in a competitive bid – failed. Runcorn were reluctant to part with Gary, who played an influential role in their successive Wembley appearances in the FA Trophy.

Sammy Chung regarded Gary as an important capture in his efforts to build a side capable of bidding for promotion during the 1994/95 season. Sammy said: 'I think he is the sort of player who the fans will like. He is a hard-tackling player, but I think he can also play a bit as well. What I like about him is the fact that he is an honest and dedicated player. He is also very brave and is not afraid to go in where it hurts.'

Gary accepted that Rovers had signed him for his defensive qualities, but stated: 'I would like to think that I have also got other strings to my bow.' Gary, a stocky player at 5ft 11in, made his debut soon after signing. During his time at

Belle Vue, he made 58 outings (1 as substitute) and scored 11 goals. In March 1996, he was transferred to Bury (5 appearances). The deal was done only days after Rovers chairman Ken Richardson had been arrested for the alleged arson attack on Rovers' main stand. This, and other worrying matters shrouding Belle Vue, obviously caused unrest amongst the players and Gary was one of the first to leave.

In the press, manager Sammy Chung blamed poor attendance on skipper Gary's move. 'Neither I or Ken Richardson wanted Gary to go,' said Sammy in the *Doncaster Star* of 29 March 1996. 'But Gary has been disappointed for some time at the failure of the town to get behind the club this season. Gary is ambitious and would have stayed with the club had he thought he could realise his ambitions with us. But he doesn't see much of a future for the club unless attendance picks up.' It was reported in the newspaper that Sammy Chung had stressed Gary's departure had nothing to do with Ken Richardson's much-publicised personal problems. Apart from Bury, Gary's clubs have included Blackpool (50 appearances, 13 as substitute and 5 goals), Lincoln City (3 appearances and 1 as substitute), Boston United (1 appearance), Torquay United and Chester City. He has played for the England semi-professional side 4 times.

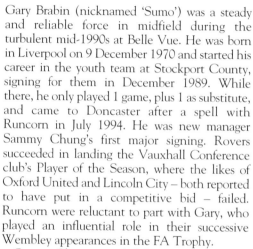

Ian Grant Branfoot

Right-back 1969-1973

Football League
Appearances: 156
Goals: 5

FA Cup
Appearances: 6
Goals: 0

FL Cup
Appearances: 4
Goals: 1

Total appearances: 166

Ian Branfoot came to Belle Vue under Lawrie McMenemy during December 1969, along with Archie Irvine from Sheffield Wednesday. It was a player deal without any fee involved and which took Harold Wilcockson to Hillsborough. The *Doncaster Evening Post* of 17 December reported that less than an hour after reporting at Belle Vue, Branfoot and Irving, who were both twenty-two, took part in their first Rovers training session. It was envisaged that Branfoot would take the place of Wilcockson at right-back.

Ian and Archie did not sign the transfer forms until after the training session on the Sandall Beat Road pitches. 'I did not want to hold the rest of the players up. The training session was more important. Signing was only a formality', said manager Lawrie McMenemy. Although no cash was involved, the three players were to receive signing-on fees in accordance with their valuations by the clubs. After the deal had been completed, McMenemy said 'I know the two Sheffield players very well and feel that they will fit into our set-up. I first came across Branfoot when I was at Gateshead and sent him to Wednesday.' The Rovers boss believed that the two players would not take too long to settle in and make an impact at Belle Vue. 'The exchange deal with Rotherham [in February 1968] was a springboard from the Fourth Division to the Third. I believe this transfer can be a springboard into the Second. Both Branfoot

and Irvine are First Division players and they are only twenty-two. They could still be looked on as prospects for the First Division.'

Ian was born in Gateshead on 26 January 1947 and joined Sheffield Wednesday during July 1965. Between 1966 and 1969, he made 33 appearances (3 as substitute) before arriving at Belle Vue. He played his first game in the Third Division home encounter with Rotherham United, on 26 December 1969. The crowd on that local derby day swelled to 19,742. In the back line with him were Clish, Flowers, Robertson, Haselden and Ogston in goal.

Under Maurice Setters in July 1973, Ian was transferred for a reported £8,000 to Lincoln City, managed by Graham Taylor. Ian had been in dispute with Rovers over his contract and talks with Maurice Setters had ended in deadlock. Ian had also been the subject of bids from other clubs, including Grimsby Town. Maurice Setters said: 'I have always told my players that if they are not happy, I will not stand in their way. Ian is a good pro and he has been a good player here. But Lincoln made a good offer and both parties are happy about it. We need the money towards our team-building plans for next season.' It was also speculated that Southend United's Ray Ternent was to be signed as a replacement for Ian. At Sincil Bank, Ian made 106 appearances, scored 11 goals and was part of the team that won the Fourth Division Championship in the 1975/76 season.

Rupis (Rufus) Brevett
Left-back 1987-1991

Football League
Appearances: 106 (+3 as substitute)
Goals: 3

FA Cup
Appearances: 4
Goals: 0

FL Cup
Appearances: 5
Goals: 0

Total appearances: 118

Rufus worked his way through the youth team and signed for Rovers during June 1988. He was born in Derby on 24 September 1969. Recalling his early footballing days, Rufus said 'I started playing football at the age of ten years, with a team in Derby by the name of Normanton. I played with them for three years and got recognised and started playing for Derby Boys. I signed schoolboy forms for Derby County when I was fourteen and at the end of my two-year contract I was only offered a non-contract, which was no good to me. I then got in touch with Steve Beaglehole and came down to train at Belle Vue and played a couple of games in the juniors and he asked me to sign. Steve helped me more than anyone in football. Coming to Doncaster was the best thing I have ever done.'

A resilient full-back, standing 5ft 8 ins tall, Rufus made his debut on 29 August 1987, six weeks after leaving school, in the Third Division home game against Sunderland. It was a match Rovers lost 2-0 in front of a crowd of 2,740. In the back line with him on that day were Stead, R. Robinson, Flynn, Cusack and Rhodes in goal.

He moved to Queen's Park Rangers in February 1991 for a club record fee of £275,000. He had been watched by several clubs all season, but no bids had been forthcoming until Rangers' boss Don Howe – the former England coach – made Rovers an offer they could not refuse. Despite their dramatic improvement in form and a ten-match unbeaten home run in the League, Rovers' gates were scarcely adequate. The club also had a six-figure tax bill to clear, which had built up from the past. Manager Billy

Bremner admitted that they could not afford to reject the QPR offer. He said 'Obviously I am very sorry to lose him because he has been absolutely outstanding this season, but at the end of the day it was a financial deal which the club needed to survive. We can't cope without selling in our position – that's the name of the game until we become more established.'

Bremner also said that the club could not stand in the way of Brevett's chance of First Division football. 'It's a great opportunity for him. I rate him highly and I think he is capable of improving and getting into the England Under-21 side this year. There have been a few clubs interested in him but this was the only offer we received, and I'll bet one or two managers will be kicking themselves for not moving in sooner when they see how he performs,' he added.

Rufus said: 'I'm still in a bit of a daze at the prospect of moving into the First Division, but it was an opportunity I just could not pass up.' He said that the move was tinged with regret and added: 'I wanted to win a championship medal with Doncaster first. I'm sorry to be leaving and I hope Rovers don't just go up but that they win the League as well.' Rufus played 141 games for QPR (11 as substitute) and scored 1 goal before being transferred to Fulham in January 1998.

Albert Henry Broadbent
Left wing 1959-1966

Football League
Appearances: 206
Goals: 40

FA Cup
Appearances: 15
Goals: 2

FL Cup
Appearances: 10
Goals: 2

Total appearances: 231

Albert (nicknamed 'Yogi') Broadbent was one of those players who had two spells at Belle Vue during his career. He signed in 1959, then again in 1963, with a spell at Lincoln during the intervening years. Albert was born at Dudley on 20 August 1934 and kicked off his career with non-League Dudley Town. He attracted the attention of Notts County and was signed by them in March 1952. In time, he made 31 League appearances and scored 11 goals.

A move to Sheffield Wednesday followed in July 1955, and he turned out 81 times for the Owls until moving to neighbours Rotherham United in December 1957 (48 appearances and 13 goals). He arrived at Belle Vue for his first period with the club in June 1959. The *Yorkshire Evening Post* of 5 June 1959 told a tale behind Albert's signing. 'A dramatic dash to the side of a dam near Bradfield, Sheffield, where a footballer was fishing, had its sequel at Millmoor today when the Rotherham United and former Sheffield Wednesday and Notts County forward, Albert Broadbent, signed for Doncaster Rovers. The fee is believed to be about £2,000. The Rovers, who had received permission from United to approach the player who was 'on offer' by the Millmoor club, wired Broadbent yesterday that secretary-manager Jack

Crayston and team manager Mr Jackie Bestall were coming to see him. But when they arrived at Broadbent's Sheffield home, they found him out – he had gone fishing before the telegram arrived. "A friend of the family kindly volunteered to take us to the spot where Broadbent was likely to be," said Mr Bestall. "There was a lot of people there, but we finally located him and had a frank talk with him ..." '

Albert's debut was in the Fourth Division home game against Torquay United on 22 August 1959. Leading the attack with him on that day were Walker, Fernie, Chappell and Sharp. He went on to make 100 appearances and score 20 goals in that first period. He was noted as featuring in the Rovers' early League Cup years. He found the net in the 1961 giant-killing victory over Second Division Grimsby which Rovers won 3-2.

Albert moved to Lincoln City during November 1961, and it was said that the signing ended a long search by Lincoln for a thrusting inside forward. It was pointed out that in the previous season he was the only ever present in the Rovers' side, and he was second highest scorer with 13 goals, no fewer than 11 of which were registered at Belle Vue. He had been a regular in the team for the first part of the subsequent season and gave a

particularly brilliant display in the 5-1 victory at Exeter. At Lincoln, he made 38 outings and scored 4 goals.

He returned to Belle Vue under manager Oscar Hold in January 1963, in a player-exchange deal which took Bobby Rooney to Lincoln. No money was involved. Tom Garnett, Rovers' general manager, said: 'Broadbent is a big strong player, who we hope will be able to work in midfield, and make the openings for Colin Booth.' No games were played during January due to adverse weather conditions, so Albert made his debut in this second term with Rovers on 9 February 1963, in the Fourth Division match against Stockport County. Thousands of tons of snow were removed by players and fans before the game went ahead.

In attack, he played alongside Hale, Booth, Nibloe and Purvis. Albert stayed at Belle Vue until joining Bradford Park Avenue in October 1965. Rovers received around £4,500 for him. It was reported that he had twice asked for a transfer during his second stay at Belle Vue – once because he was selected for the wing instead of his more favoured inside position. It was alleged that the last request was because he was not satisfied with the basic pay at Belle Vue, even though it probably matched or was greater than that of the majority of footballers in the lower divisions. It was understood that Albert was looking ahead to a time when loss of form or injury would put him out of the first team.' Tom Garnett said: 'The club wish to emphasise that they did not want to transfer the player ... it was the player who wanted to go.' At Bradford, Albert made 56 apperances and scored 11 goals. A final move saw him sign for Hartlepool United in February 1967.

John William Buckley

Right winger 1984-1986, 1987

Football League
Appearances: 85 (+5 as substitute)
Goals: 11

FA Cup
Appearances: 5
Goals: 0

FL Cup
Appearances: 3
Goals: 0

Total appearances: 98

Many people will remember John for the horrific injury he suffered in a game, which left him on a life-support machine. He was lucky to survive and never played football again. This was a sad end to his career as he was a very clever, tricky winger who was a favourite with many fans. John was born in East Kilbride on 10 May 1962. He had a spell with Partick Thistle, before Rovers manager Billy Bremner brought him to Belle Vue during July 1984. At the time, it was reported that Scottish sources expressed surprise that Rovers had managed to capture a player regarded as one of the best young wingers north of the Border.

Partick had finished third in the Scottish First Division in the previous season, and John was chosen for a team representing the League in an international tournament held in Italy. Newcastle, Hearts and Hibernian were interested in signing John, and Leeds United were understood to have offered cash and a player in exchange. But Rovers beat them to the punch with a straight cash bid. Bremner commented: 'He can play on either wing, is very quick and he loves to take on defenders. It's another piece in the jigsaw and I believe he is a player who could really excite the crowds.'

John's debut was in the Third Division away game at Preston North End on 25 August 1984. He followed manager Billy Bremner to Elland Road in June 1986. John had been persuaded to sign a new contract with Rovers, but there was a proviso that he would be allowed to leave if a club from a higher division moved in for him. Meanwhile, Bremner commented that he was excited about his new signing. 'John is a talented young player with a rare ability to go past defenders, and he could be a sensation with the fans at Leeds', he said.

However, John could not make his mark in the first team (6 appearances, 4 as substitute, and 1 goal) and went on loan, first to Leicester City in March 1987 (1 appearance and 4 as substitute) and then to Belle Vue in October 1987. Manager Cusack stated: 'John's no stranger to the camp and we all know what he can do. He has the ability to entertain people and we are grateful to him for agreeing to help us out, because he has turned down approaches from other clubs.' From Doncaster, John went to Rotherham United in November 1987 (85 appearances, 20 as substitute and 13 goals), Partick Thistle, Scunthorpe United in August 1991 (39 appearances, 4 as substitute, and 8 goals) and then returned to Rotherham during February 1993 (2 appearances and 2 as substitute).

Stan 'Dizzie' Burton

Right winger 1933-1938

Football League
Appearances: 196
Goals: 50

FA Cup
Appearances: 6
Goals: 2

FL Cup
Appearances: 0
Goals: 0

Total appearances: 202

Stan's footwork and cleverness on the right wing made him a favourite with the supporters, who gave him the nickname of 'Dizzie'. And all this was in spite of having severe hearing problems, which he never allowed to bother him. He was born in Wombwell, South Yorkshire in December 1912, and arrived at Belle Vue from Thurnscoe Victoria, a Sheffield Association League club, during the 1932/33 season and developed rapidly.

Dizzie made his first-team debut on 30 March 1933, in a home win over Halifax Town. On that day, the forward line included Burton, Waterson, R. Smith and Parker. He scored his first goal for the club in the next match, and played in all the remaining 11 games of the season, notching 3 goals. It was noted that he also played in 5 Midland League games and scored once.

In his first full season for the Rovers, he played 33 times and scored 10 goals. In time, Stan was useful, along with his opposite number on the left wing, Albert Turner, in helping Rovers to win their first major honour by taking the championship of the Third Division (North) in the 1934/35 season. He

was a dangerous player, never afraid to take on a full-back, and possessed a terrific shot. His finest performance was probably in the Second Division away game at Hull City on 19 October 1935, where he scored his first career hat-trick, which was enough to beat the home side 3-2.

Stan played 42 games, plus 1 in the FA Cup during the 1935/36 season in the Second Division, and scored 15 goals. He played so well throughout the remainder of the 1930s that his first-team place was always assured. But, shortly after the start of the 1938/39 season, he moved to Wolverhampton Wanderers. Details of the transfer fee were not divulged but it was understood to be a club record. The previous highest transfer fee received by Rovers was said to be for Gladwin, the half-back who went to Manchester United. He was replaced by George Little. Stan's stay at Wolverhampton was brief, although he did stay long enough to feature in the 1939 FA Cup final where Wolves lost to Portsmouth at Wembley. Dizzie concluded his League career with a single League appearance at West Ham United in the same season. He died in Sheffield in February 1977.

Sydney Bycroft

Centre half 1935-1952

Football League
Appearances: 333
Goals: 2

FA Cup
Appearances: 20
Goals: 0

FL Cup
Appearances: 0
Goals: 0

Total appearances: 353

At the time of writing, Syd Bycroft has just cele-brated his ninetieth birthday. He played his last League game for Rovers at thirty-nine, in December 1951, and was involved with the club for a total of sixteen years. It has been speculated that if the Second World War had not stopped the League for six seasons, he might have become the holder of the largest number of League appearances for the club. He was born in Lincoln in 1912, and played as a goalkeeper and a striker in his younger years. He had several trials with League clubs before joining Grantham Town, and in time he came to Belle Vue. He joined Rovers for a reported fee of £251. The odd quid, Syd recalled, was to pay for the boots Grantham had recently bought him.

He played one game as a centre forward for the reserves and was then moved to centre half. He made his debut on 1 February 1936 in the Second Division away game against Swansea. Rovers suffered a defeat in that game. The person he was marking on this occasion was also making his initial first-team appearance for Burnley, and this turned out to be seventeen-year-old Tommy Lawton who, like Syd, was destined to become a football legend. Syd, with his shiny, slick black hair and dark good looks,

earned a reputation throughout the football world for being hard and uncompromising in the centre-half position. Michael Parkinson, the television personality, declared in an article recalling footballers of the past that Syd Bycroft 'had a tackle like a bear trap'. When asked about his reputation, Syd commented: 'While I was on a football field, I had an intense hatred for members of the opposing team and I was deter-mined nobody was going to beat me, although I never lost my temper. I had a job to do and was only sent off twice.'

Syd's hard tackling did, however, cause problems during Rovers' away games. On one occasion, Syd went too far with the away crowd. After a game at Wrexham, a group of irate fans waited outside the Rovers dressing room, jostling and jeering, anxious to 'get Bycroft'. Syd cleverly avoided them by leaving the dressing room and boarding the team coach, hidden in a big wicker basket containing the players' kit. When the coach had travelled a 'safe' distance away from the Wrexham ground, Syd emerged from the basket.

Although he was barracked and booed by away crowds, Syd was immensely popular with

Syd pictured during his coaching days.

Rovers fans. He even had a fan club, which was run by a strong nucleus of supporters from Epworth. The clashes between Syd and Rotherham United's centre forward, Wally Ardron, were the ones enjoyed most by the Rovers crowd. Local derby games between Doncaster and Rotherham United were built up in the press as grudge contests between Wally and Bycroft. Syd commented: 'The crowds loved this and they all thought the two of us were paid to kick lumps off each other. Of course, Wally and me were deadly enemies on the field, but after the games at Doncaster, he would come to my house for tea.' Syd's role as a successful 'stopper' was frequently declared in the press, and he had several opportunities to leave Doncaster and join more glamorous clubs. Syd, however, could not be prised away from Doncaster.

During the Second World War, he joined the police and was frequently recognised on point duty in Doncaster's busy town centre. After the cessation of hostilities, Syd continued his career with Rovers, despite being thirty-four. He continued to give loyal service, seeing Rovers go through the good and the bad times: the team winning the

Third Division (North) Championship during 1946/1947, then being relegated the following season and winning again in 1949/50. By the early 1950s, his fitness and form were beginning to slip and young Scot Bill Paterson was challenging him for the number five shirt. Syd's last game was at Goodison Park on Boxing Day 1951, a game in which he was sent off. Although he retired at the end of the season, he stayed at Belle Vue, taking up training and coaching duties. In 1948, he had qualified as an FA coach from Birmingham University. Amongst the young Rovers' players he coached was the club's Under-23 international, Alick Jeffrey. Later on, Bycroft took the job as manager along with Jack Hodgson. He finally left Belle Vue in 1959.

His grandson, Richard Cooper, played for Sheffield United, Lincoln City and Exeter City. When asked if he would rather have played now than in the past, Syd replied: 'No, I enjoyed my own footballing era. The high wages and the glamour of the game today don't really interest me. Also, I got away with a lot in my playing days. I don't think it would be the same today. Bodily contact is frowned upon now.'

Colin Clish

Left-back 1967-1972

Football League
Appearances: 99 (+1 substitute)
Goals: 4

FA Cup
Appearances: 7
Goals: 0

FL Cup
Appearances: 4
Goals: 0

Total appearances: 111

Colin was born in Hetton-le-Hole on 14 January 1944. He came from a musical family. His mother, father and brother have all appeared in operatic shows, and Colin himself – along with his father and brother – were members of a male voice choir which made an LP recording. Not only was the family musical, but they were sporting as well, with another member of the Clish clan being an England Grammar Schools soccer international and a professional cricketer in Durham.

In his younger days, Colin captained Durham County Schoolboys at both football and cricket, and went on to play for England Schoolboys at cricket. He was also a member of the Durham County Colts when they played against Yorkshire Colts. Colin didn't get international honours at football, but he did get as far as a trial for the England Schoolboys team. He was only fifteen when he joined Newcastle and he turned professional in January 1961. He made 20 appearances at St James' Park and captained Newcastle United Youth team to their first success when winning the FA Youth Cup, beating Manchester United in the semi-final and Wolves in the final. There were 25,000 people in St James' Park that night, he

recalled, a night he would never forget.

He signed for Rotherham United in December 1963. Whilst at Millmoor he broke his leg, but he still managed 128 appearances and scored 4 goals. He joined Rovers in February 1968 as part of the deal which brought Harold Wilcockson, Chris Rabjohn and himself (plus around £8,000) to Doncaster and sent Graham Watson and Dennis Leigh to Rotherham. It is worth noting that the Millers had turned down a bid of £50,000 for each of them only a year earlier. The *Doncaster Evening Post* of 8 February 1968 said 'Clish is the most experienced of the trio, joining Rotherham from Newcastle United for a fee of about £8,000 in 1962.'

Colin made his Rovers debut in the Fourth Division home game against Brentford, on 10 February 1968, with 7,183 in attendance. The defence on that day included Gavan (in goal), Robertson, Flowers, Wilcockson and Gray. Colin played his part in the Rovers side that won the Fourth Division Championship during the 1968/69 season under Lawrie McMenemy. After breaking his leg again in an away game at Shrewsbury, he subsequently retired from the game and joined the British Transport Police.

Anthony George Coleman
Forward 1965-1967

Football League
Appearances: 58
Goals: 11

FA Cup
Appearances: 2
Goals: 0

FL Cup
Appearances: 4
Goals: 0

Total appearances: 64

It is unfortunate that most people will possibly only remember Tony Coleman for one crazy incident whilst he was at Belle Vue. This was the occasion when he took a swipe at the match referee on 6 May 1965 before leaving the field during the Notts County home game.

He was born in Liverpool on 2 May 1945 and took his first step on the football ladder as an apprentice with Stoke City. In October 1962 he moved to Tranmere Rovers, playing just 8 times for them. A move in May 1964 took him to Preston North End, but this was brief, resulting in only 5 appearances and 1 goal. From there, it was to on Non-League Bangor City and eventually his talents were spotted by one of Rovers' scouts.

He arrived at Belle Vue in November 1965, making his debut in the Fourth Division game against Port Vale on 19 November 1965. Bob Gilfillan also made his debut in this match. Coleman's pace and tenacity was much admired by the Rovers fans. Unfortunately, though, he was easily riled, and opposition players and fans played on this. The worst example of his unpredictable temperament occurred on 6 May 1966, in Rovers' last home game of the season, against Notts County. He had been sent off for blatantly kicking an opponent, and whilst on his way to the dressing room, he suddenly turned, ran back to referee Mr Pickles of Stockport and punched him. Although unconfirmed, it has often been alleged that Pickles swore at Tony and that the player reacted to this abuse. For the offence, Tony was banned for 28 days by the FA, which was a relatively light sentence, considering what had happened.

Tony was one of just a handful of players that performed well in the desperate 1966/67 season. And before it was over he moved to Manchester City, in March 1967, although the fee of £12,000 was less than most thought he was worth. The *Doncaster Evening Post* of Friday 17 March 1967 reported that Tony was one of the last League footballers to be transferred before the sell-and-buy deadline of the previous day and was to make his debut for Manchester City at Elland Road, Leeds, the following day. Tony signed for the First Division club at Maine Road only a few hours after the Rovers board of directors received his alleged third transfer request of the season.

On that Friday, the deal had taken a turn not even Tony could have expected. Mike Summerbee, City's regular outside right, was travelling to London to see a Harley Street specialist about a persistent thigh injury. Tony had been chosen to replace him in the number seven shirt, where he was to be partnered by Irish international Johnny Crossan with Colin Bell switching to inside left.

The loss of a player of Tony's power was obviously going to be felt, but Rovers' chairman, Hubert Bates, said: 'As far as the board is concerned, we have taken a price which we consider fair.' Tony had been a regular in the side since he had signed in November 1965, and it was stated that he felt defeat more than most and had been unhappy with a struggling team for some time.'

The *Doncaster Evening Post*'s sports correspondent, Joe Slater, had the final word on the transfer on 18 March 1967. He said 'Coleman for the last few matches was a 90-minute player ... even with all his hanging-on-too-long faults (and I expect this was largely due to the lack of confidence in his colleagues), Coleman was one of those characters of the game who MUST be missed when they leave for another club. His departure will leave another gap too, and that is the job of taking Doncaster Rovers penalties, Coleman's duty since Laurie Sheffield missed one or two at the end of last season.'

Whilst at Maine Road, Tony won many of the game's top honours, but a further move followed to Sheffield Wednesday, in October 1969. The stay here was very brief and he went on to play for a number of other clubs, including Blackpool, Southport and Stockport.

Sammy Cowan
Central defender 1923-1924

Football League
Appearances: 48
Goals: 13

FA Cup
Appearances: 3
Goals: 1

FL Cup
Appearances: -
Goals: -

Total appearances: 51

Sammy Cowan made his League debut for Doncaster Rovers in Third Division (North) in the first match of the 1923/24 season – on 25 August 1923 against Wigan Borough. This was Rovers' first match back in the Football League and Rovers' manager was Dick Ray, the former secretary-manager of Leeds United. The game, watched by 10,923, ended in a 0-0 draw. During his first season, Sammy played in the number five shirt 33 times and scored 9 goals. He was a strong and fearless centre half, who went on to play in the FA Cup final and made several England international appearances.

According to the *Doncaster Chronicle* of 19 December 1924, Sammy was a product of local football. He was born in Chesterfield in 1901. He first played football with Adwick Juniors in the Doncaster Palace League. He then had one season with Bullcroft in the Sheffield Association League, and one with Denaby United, with whom he scored many goals, earning a reputation as a penalty kicker, before joining Rovers. A well-built player, standing nearly 6ft tall and weighing about 13st, Sammy made good use of his physique. He was a good spoiler of opposing forwards and also took a big share in attack. He was not a pretty dribbler, but his passing was neat and accurate. It was said that he was 'able to head the ball almost as far as he could kick it'. He soon attracted the attention of more affluent and successful clubs. Before he moved on, he notched up 48 appearances and scored 13 goals – all of which were bagged at Belle Vue. In one match during the 1924/25 season, he played at centre forward.

This was in an away match against Walsall on 20 September. However, Rovers lost 4-0.

Yet, on many occasions, Sammy pulled the Rovers out of a tight corner. He shares with Tom Keetley the distinction of being the only pair of Rovers players to score three goals each in the same League game. This was in the 7-0 thrashing of Halifax Town at Belle Vue on 22 March 1923.

Sammy played his last game for Rovers on 13 December 1924 in the FA Cup match against Southport. He signed for Manchester City for around £2,000 and his career soon flourished. The transfer was a great blow to the Rovers supporters, among whom Sammy was a great favourite. Yet the Rovers directors were unanimous in feeling that it would be unfair to stand in the way of Sammy's advancement. He played in the FA Cup final, although City were beaten by Bolton. However, despite this and the fact that City were relegated during his first season, his summer was brightened when he gained his first full England cap.

Over the following years, he had further success with Manchester City, in a career that spanned 350 games. With his career entering its twilight years, he moved to Bradford City in October 1935, and then non-League Mossley in 1937. He managed Manchester City briefly post-war, and thereafter became a physiotherapist, dying in October 1964.

Colin Cramb

Striker 1995-1997

Football League
Appearances: 60 (+1 as substitute)
Goals: 25

FA Cup
Appearances: 1
Goals: 1

FL Cup
Appearances: 2
Goals: 1

Total appearances: 64

One of the good points about the mid-1990s at Belle Vue was that fans saw striker Colin Cramb beat the 20 goals a season barrier, which hitherto had not been surpassed for twenty years. Colin (nicknamed 'Baresi') was born in Lanark on 23 June 1974 and began his career at Hamilton. He was rated as one of the brightest prospects in Scottish football when he made a sensational start, scoring twice on his First Division debut at the age of sixteen, in a 4-0 win over Morton. Southampton splashed out £75,000 to sign him at the age of eighteen after he had notched 10 goals in 29 starts for the Accies. But after making his Southampton debut at Everton (later claiming that was his best moment in football), he failed to settle and returned to the Scottish Premier League with Falkirk, scoring in his second home game in a 2-1 win over Aberdeen.

The move to Hearts quickly followed, but after making 6 first-team appearances during the 1994/95 season, he had been unable to regain his place in the side in the 1995/96 campaign, despite scoring 17 goals in 19 reserve games. And from there he came to Belle Vue for an alleged five-figure deal in December 1995. Manager Sammy Chung commented: 'He has already packed a lot into his career and now he is looking to settle down here and prove his worth.'

He made his debut on 16 December 1995 in the home game against Leyton Orient. His co-striker in this game was Graeme Jones, and Chung said about Colin after the game: 'He did

well. He showed some lovely touches when bringing other people into play ... I think he will be a real asset to the side once he settles in.'

Despite having a fiery temperament, which sometimes got him into trouble on the field, he scored a number of memorable goals. Colin once mentioned that the players he admired were Ally McCoist ('the man's a legend') and George Weah. He was regularly reported in the columns of local newspapers as giving an impressive all-round show.

On 2 July 1997, the *Doncaster Star* reported: 'Rovers' top scorer during the 1996/97 season has become the second big name to leave the cash-strapped Division Three club this summer when he agreed to join Division Two Bristol City last night.' Colin was a free agent after turning down the offer of an improved contract at the end of the previous season. With Rovers committed to cutting the wage bill, it was inevitable that Colin – the highest earner behind player-manager Kerry Dixon – would leave. Bristol City manager John Ward said: 'Colin has a lot of potential. He is not a bustling type of forward, but he has something about him. He has a lot of skill and can score goals from tight angles. I know Sunderland were interested, but I managed to persuade him that, at this stage of his career, he would be better off with us, where he would be in the shop window, rather that possibly getting lost at a bigger club.'

David Stephen Cusack
Defender 1985-1988, 1989-1990

Football League
Appearances: 101
Goals: 4

FA Cup
Appearances: 4
Goals: 0

FL Cup
Appearances: 8
Goals: 0

Total appearances: 113

Dave was born at Thurcroft, near Rotherham, on 6 June 1956. He joined Sheffield Wednesday from being an apprentice in June 1974. He played 92 games for the Owls (3 as substitute) and scored 1 goal. He was transferred to Southend United in September 1978, making 186 appearances and finding the net on 17 occasions.

He was a dominant figure in the Southend team which won the Fourth Division Championship, only conceding 6 home goals in 1981. But when the Roots Hall club ran into financial difficulties, he moved to Millwall during March 1983, making 98 appearances and scoring 9 goals. The 6ft 2in defender found his way to Belle Vue in July 1985, under Billy Bremner, after Doncaster paid Millwall, managed by George Graham, around £40,000 for him. During 1985, he had been named as the top centre half in the Third Division in the PFA awards. Several other clubs were interested in the player, but Bremner said 'I am happy that he will be joining us. Everything is starting to fall into place. This is a very important signing for us because Dave is dominant in the air and he has the experience to be a commanding influence in the back four. He is a player I have been after for some time.' Billy also added that the signing of Dave would complete his defensive rebuilding.

Cusack's contract with Millwall had terminated during July, and although he was offered improved terms by George Graham, who was keen to keep him at the Den, Dave decided to return to South Yorkshire. Dave made his first-team debut on 24 August 1985 in the Third Division home game against Bolton Wanderers, with 2,990 in attendance. Rovers drew the match 1-1. When Billy Bremner was asked to take the hot seat at Elland Road in 1985, Dave became player-manager at Belle Vue. The *Doncaster Star* of 5 November 1985 stated: 'Rovers chairman Ian Jones confirmed Dave Cusack's appointment as the club's new manager following a board meeting last night ... At twenty-nine, Cusack will be the youngest manager in the Football League.'

Whilst playing with Rovers in the first period, he made 100 appearances and scored 4 goals. He was dismissed as manager in 1987 and replaced by Dave Mackay. He then performed a player-manager role at Rotherham United, signing for the Millers during December 1987. He made 18 appearances whilst at Millmoor, before being transferred to Boston United, where he made 47 outings and scored 1 goal. He rejoined Rovers during August 1989, playing 1 game as a non-contract player. After finishing with Rovers, he had a further stint as a player-manager. He rejoined Boston United in 1990 in this role, turning out for them on 29 occasions, including 2 as substitute. Later, he went on to manage Kettering Town and Dagenham & Redbridge. Towards the end of 1999, he was involved in a serious car crash. He is currently involved in running his own private company.

Gerald Anthony Daly

Midfield 1988-1989

Football League
Appearances: 37 (+2 as substitute)
Goals: 4

FA Cup
Appearances: 1
Goals: 1

FL Cup
Appearances: 1
Goals: 0

Total appearances: 41

Gerry came to Rovers after a long and distinguished career with a number of prominent clubs, including Manchester United, Derby County, Coventry City and Leicester. He also gained 47 caps for the Republic of Ireland. He was born in Dublin on 30 April 1954. He started out with Bohemians before moving to Manchester United in April 1973. At Old Trafford, he made 107 appearances (4 as substitute) and scored 23 goals.

He came to Belle Vue under Dave Mackay in July 1988, and said he had complete faith in the latter's ability to bring the club success. Mackay had staked his reputation on Rovers winning promotion during the season ahead (1989/90), and was relieved and delighted when Gerry agreed to sign. Gerry turned down other offers, including a couple of lucrative moves abroad, to join up with a team of which it was said 'he clearly respects'. He said 'I've known Dave a long time, but when he approached me, I needed a while to think it over because, obviously, I wasn't keen on a drop down a couple of divisions. I think I have a good few years left playing, but there seems to be a great deal of potential here with all the fine young players and that was something that appealed to me.' But he added: 'There is no way I would have joined any other Fourth Division club – the only reason I am here is because of Dave Mackay.'

Gerry made his debut in the League Fourth Division away game at Rotherham United on 27 August 1988. Lining up alongside him on that day were Douglas, R. Robinson, Turnbull, Raven and Raffel, with Malcolm in goal. The game, which Rovers lost 3-0, was attended by a crowd of 4,489. The remainder of the season was quite turbulent off the field, to say the least, and must have been quite unnerving, not only for a player of Gerry's calibre, but for all the other players too. In December, the club was issued with a winding-up petition over a tax debt of £86,000. In March, Dave Mackay resigned, and the club made a statement saying it was £500,000 in debt and losing £3,000 a week. Later in the month, it was announced that Joe Kinnear had been appointed as manager, but youth-team coach Steve Beaglehole resigned. Dave Bentley subsequently became youth development officer and reserve coach. Just before the end of the season, Doncaster Council was trying to recover an outstanding balance of £52,000 from the club.

During Gerry's only season at Belle Vue, he made 39 appearances (2 as substitute) and scored 5 goals. He was given a free transfer, even though he had a year remaining on his contract. Rovers finished twenty-third in the Fourth Division during the 1988/89 season. During his career, he made 457 appearances (15 as substitute) and scored 88 goals.

Brian Christopher Deane
Striker 1985-1988

Football League
Appearances: 59 (+7 as substitute)
Goals: 12

FA Cup
Appearances: 2 (+1 as substitute)
Goals: 1

FL Cup
Appearances: 3
Goals: 0

Total appearances: 72

It now seems odd that Brian Deane should slip through the net in his home town of Leeds and begin his career at Doncaster before returning there later on. He was born in Leeds on 7 February 1968 and came to Belle Vue as a junior, signing during December 1985. He stood 6ft 3in tall, and the *Doncaster Star* made comments under the heading 'Rovers call up goal kid', when he was included in the first-team squad, aged seventeen. They said 'Deane [is] a tall young striker who joined Rovers earlier in the season [1985/86], and scored 14 goals in 17 matches with the junior team. Player-manager Dave Cusack has not yet decided whether to throw the youngster in for his debut, but he said "He has the knack of scoring goals which is something we are lacking at present".'

Brian made his debut on 4 February 1986 in the League home game against Swansea, in front of a small crowd of 2,029. He played for Rovers over just three seasons. In the 1985/86 campaign, he made just 2 appearances, but this improved during the following year when he made 15 League appearances, 6 as substitute, and scored 3 goals. During 1987/88, he made 47 appearances, 1 as substitute, and found the net on 10 occasions.

He joined Sheffield United in July 1988 in a £40,000 deal. United had been relegated during the 1987/88 season and aimed to bounce back

at the first attempt. They paid Rovers £30,000 for twenty-one-year-old Brian, and were to pay a further £10,000 after he had played 40 games. Although Rovers boss Dave Mackay said he was sad to see Brian – who had refused to sign a new contract – leave, he said it had been on the cards for several weeks. Said Mackay, on 15 July 1988: 'We have been expecting him to be going because we have had one or two clubs after him. That is why we signed Paul Dobson for £35,000 earlier this week.'

Although Brian was Rovers' top scorer during the 1987/88 season, he had scored just 10 goals. Mackay, however, still believed he had the potential to do well in the game wherever he went. 'I think he is a very good player. He worked while he was here and I hope he does well at Sheffield United. I know he didn't score a lot of goals for us last year, but we had a poor season and we didn't get the ball into the box for him often enough.'

Whilst at Sheffield United, Deane made 197 outings and scored 82 goals. A move to Leeds United followed in July 1993 (131 appearances, 7 as substitute, and 32 goals). He returned to Bramall Lane in July 1997 (24 appearances, 11 goals), before going first to Benfica, and later joining Middlesbrough for £3 million. He made his international debut for England in 1991 in the game against New Zealand.

James Dobbin

Midfield 1984-1987, 1997-1998

Football League
Appearances: 84 (+11 as substitute)
Goals: 13

FA Cup
Appearances: 3
Goals: 0

FL Cup
Appearances: 5
Goals: 1

Total appearances: 103

Jim played for Rovers on 2 occasions, the last one being during the fateful season when the club fell from the Football League. Jim aired his views quite strongly about the predicament at the club during its last year in the League in the TV documentary *Changing Places*. He was born in Dunfermline on 17 September 1963, and early in his career played for the Scottish Youth side.

Dobbin joined Rovers under Billy Bremner from Celtic in March 1984 for a £25,000 fee. It was reported that he had made 3 first-team appearances for Celtic, scoring on each occasion, but was unable to command a regular place with the Premier League side. He also hit 9 goals for the Scotland Youth team and received offers from Dundee United and Motherwell, but decided to join Rovers instead. Jim said 'Everyone has been asking: What do you want to join Doncaster for? But I'm very impressed with the club. Mr Bremner has offered me the chance to try and establish myself in English football and now it's up to

me. Doncaster may be in the Fourth Division now, but they seem very ambitious and don't intend to be in the lower regions for long.'

He made his League debut in the Third Division home game against Burnley on 31 August 1984. Lining up with him at the back on that occasion were: Gregory, Russell, Humphries, I. Snodin and Yates. Against a background of the club trying to cope with a massive overdraft, several players were transferred during the summer of 1986. Even at the start of the 1986/87 season, the flood continued, with John Philliben leaving at the end of August and Jim going to Barnsley for £35,000 at the end of September. At Oakwell, Jim made 116 appearances, 13 as substitute, with 12 goals. He then moved on to Grimsby in July 1991 (154 outings, 10 as substitute, 21 goals) and Rotherham United in August 1996 (17 appearances, 2 as substitute). He rejoined Rovers in August 1997, playing 28 times (3 as substitute) before moving first to Scarborough and then to Grimsby.

Ronald Dodd

Inside forward 1933-1937

Football League
Appearances: 68
Goals: 38

FA Cup
Appearances: 1
Goals: 0

FL Cup
Appearances: -
Goals: -

Total appearances: 69

Ronnie was born in 1913 and joined Rovers from Usworth Colliery, a north-eastern club, shortly before the start of the 1933/34 season. It was said that the season before he came to Rovers, he scored 63 goals. He was described as a foraging raider and an accurate marksman. He was just over 5ft 10in, weighed 12st and made his debut at centre forward in the Third Division home game against Walsall on 9 September 1933. Joining him in the forward line that day were Matthews, R. Smith, Beresford and Parker. During his first season, he made 34 appearances and scored 24 goals. He was a strong, bustling type of leader, and a favourite with the Belle Vue crowd. The most goals he ever scored in a game was 4 and this was in the home fixture against Gateshead – who had once given him a trial – on 16 December 1933. He was a member of the Third Division (North) championship side in 1934/35.

Ronnie left in 1937 and played with New Brighton and Walsall. The *Yorkshire Evening Post* of 6 May 1937 said the fee 'was a substantial one'. It also mentioned 'In his 26 appearances in the Midland League [Reserve] team, he has notched 20 goals. In the two recent Sheffield Invitation Challenge Cup rounds, he performed the hat-trick on each occasion ... He is the nephew of the international winger, Sam Crookes.'

During the Second World War, a newspaper report stated that Ronnie was home from North Africa with serious injuries. His left arm had been amputated at the elbow and his left foot shattered. 'It means the end of my football career', he commented. Ronnie had landed in North Africa with the Royal Armoured Corps – attached to the First Army – early in the Tunisian campaign, and was soon in the thick of the fighting. Although also trained as a tank driver and gunner, he was employed as a lorry driver. It was while driving the leading lorry of a convoy carrying supplies to the front lines that he received his wounds. A mortar shell struck his truck. When he regained consciousness two days later, he was in hospital. He had high praise for the medical services out there. 'They almost brought the dead back to life', he said.

Dodd worked at Pilkington's Glass Works and died suddenly, aged forty-four, in December 1955. He left a wife and seven children. His widow, Constance, commented shortly after his death: 'The children will be heartbroken. He used to leave each of them three pennies on the mantelpiece each night before he went to bed.' Connie was refused a War Widow's pension, and in 1956 her plea went to appeal. She lost and her plight came to the attention of Rovers' manager Peter Doherty, who arranged a benefit match. 'The match raised nearly £700, which was a large sum in those days. I shall never forget Doncaster Rovers' kindness in my darkest hour', said Constance.

Peter Dermot Doherty

Forward 1949-1953

Football League
Appearances: 103
Goals: 55

FA Cup
Appearances: 7
Goals: 3

FL Cup
Appearances: -
Goals: -

Total appearances: 110

Peter Doherty was regarded as one of the best footballers to emerge from Northern Ireland. He was born in Magherafelt, Co. Londonderry, on 5 June 1913. As a youth he played for Glentoran, and was a member of the team that won the Irish Cup in 1933. When he was nineteen, Blackpool paid £2,000 for him, his midfield skills having attracted the attention of a number of top English clubs. He also gained his first full cap for Northern Ireland in 1935, playing against England at Goodison Park. Manchester City splashed out a large fee for him in 1936, and he won a championship medal with them a year later.

After the cessation of hostilities in 1945, he joined Derby County, where Raich Carter was also playing, and they were both in the cup-winning side of 1946. From there, Peter had a short spell with Huddersfield Town from 1946 before joining Rovers as player/manager, in June 1949 for a fee of around £8, 000. He made his debut in the Third Division (North) away game against Bradford City on 21 August 1949. Rovers won 2-1 in front of a crowd of 21,338, Peter getting on the score sheet himself.

During the 1949/50 season, Peter led the team admirably and his play was superb. He made 35 League appearances and scored 27 goals. He also made 4 FA Cup appearances and scored 3 times. At the end of the 1949/50 campaign, Rovers won the Third Division (North) championship. Whilst being relatively new to football management, Peter knew the importance of a sound youth policy, which he put into place at Doncaster. He introduced 'feeder clubs' to develop young players. It was Peter who discovered and nurtured the talents of Alick Jeffrey, arguably Rovers' greatest ever player. He also maintained his links with Northern Ireland, and signed a number of players from clubs over there.

In the following season, Rovers finished midway up the Second Division, with an average attendance of 23,000 – which would be very pleasing if this were the same today. He broke his leg in January 1950, in the home match against Swansea, which sidelined him for the rest of the season, but he still managed to be the top scorer, as in the previous year. Peter's international career was impressive too. He won 16 caps, and one of these (against Scotland) was acquired during his time at Belle Vue. Under Peter, the Rovers were a respectable Second Division outfit, but they could not make that final push up to dizzier heights. Another position he held whilst at

Peter Doherty is on the extreme left (holding the football).

Doncaster was that of Northern Ireland team manager, although he retired from playing at the end of the 1952/53 season. He remained as Rovers' manager until 1958. The *Doncaster Gazette* of Thursday 23 January revealed 'The resignations of Doncaster Rovers' manager Peter Doherty, honorary secretary Mr Geoff Dickinson and director and honorary surgeon Mr J.P. Semple came on Monday as a dramatic climax to the three-week-old controversy at Belle Vue, concerning the manager and another director, Mr Hubert Bates.'

Peter's resignation was handed to the club chairman, H.A. Butler, before the previous Saturday's League game, but the first the public heard about it was two days later. Peter made the following statement: 'As the director concerned has failed to comply with the wishes of the board to resign, and as the club is greater than either of us, I gracefully tender my resignation.' In a statement, Hubert Bates said that he had allegedly offered to meet with Peter and resolve their differences, and had offered to tend his resignation at the next annual meeting of the club. But it was all too late, and Peter was subsequently installed as manager of Bristol City. Administration of the playing side was to be carried out by the trainer, Jack Hodgson, and coach Syd Bycroft.

The *Doncaster Gazette* of 30 January 1958 said that it was rather ironic that Peter should leave at a time when Rovers were reaping their richest harvest from the youth policy which he had decided to adopt eight or nine years earlier. It added: 'Rovers, in fact, are likely to enjoy the fruits of Mr Doherty's labours for a few years to come, for there is no doubting the fact that the current crop of youngsters playing together in the Northern Intermediate, North Midlands Combination and Midland League are the most promising Rovers have ever had the good fortune to come across. Having built up strong connections with many junior clubs, not only in South Yorkshire but also in other parts of the country, Mr Doherty leaves a profitable legacy at Belle Vue.' Peter died at home in Blackpool in 1990.

Colin Douglas

Centre forward/Right-back 1981-1985, 1988-1993

Football League
Appearances: 384 (+20 as substitute)
Goals: 53

FA Cup
Appearances: 18
Goals: 4

FL Cup
Appearances: 22 (+1 as substitute)
Goals: 3

Total appearances: 445

Colin 'Duggie' Douglas played over two periods for Rovers and notched up over 400 appearances. He was a totally committed player on the field, which earned him immense popularity with fans. He was born in Hurlford, Glasgow on 9 September 1962. He started his career with Glasgow Celtic, and first signed for Rovers in November 1981. His first appearance in a Rovers shirt came on 5 September 1981 in the Third Division away game against Bristol City, when he came on as a substitute. His first full game was the home fixture on 11 September against Exeter City, in front of a crowd of 4,369.

During his first period at Belle Vue, he played 202 times, 10 as a substitute, and scored 48 goals. He was voted Player of the Season for 1983/84. He signed for Rotherham in July 1986, but the fee was disputed for a time. Colin was originally listed at £20,000, but the Millmoor club believed that they had reached an agreement with Rovers over a much lower fee a fortnight earlier. The situation became complicated when Scunthorpe came in with a cash offer of around £15 000, which was attractive to hard-up Rovers because it was to be paid in one go rather than in the usual instalments. Whereas Colin had played much of his time for Rovers in midfield, Rotherham boss Norman Hunter intended to use him chiefly in attack: 'I

believe that's his best position. He's a hard-working player with an ability to score goals and I think he will do well for us.'

At Belle Vue, Colin was a model of consistency, barely missing a match after signing from Celtic. He even turned out with cracked ribs on one occasion. Commenting on the Rotherham move, Colin said: 'I would have been happy to stay at Doncaster if they had been able to sort out a better contract.' Rovers manager Dave Cusack said: 'We are sorry to be losing Colin but we were unable to match his terms. We have to work to a strict budget and run a tight ship next season because of the financial difficulties.' In the wake of Colin's departure, hard-up Rovers launched a '50p appeal' to the people in the town, to help them hang on to their better players.

Colin returned to Rovers in August 1988 for £15,000. He was signed by manager Dave Mackay, who commented: 'The beauty of it is that he can play anywhere. He is a very important signing because every club needs a player like that on their books.' Colin refused to state whether he preferred to play in attack or defence: 'I don't mind, as long as I'm in the team.'

He was voted Player of the Season for the 1989/90 and 1990/91 campaigns. Later, he played for Armthorpe Welfare and has recently become player-manager at Hatfield Main.

Michael Walter Elwiss
Striker 1971-1974

Football League
Appearances: 96 (+1 as substitute)
Goals: 30

FA Cup
Appearances: 8
Goals: 3

FL Cup
Appearances: 3
Goals: 1

Total appearances: 108

Mike developed his talents in Rovers Juniors, joining the club under Maurice Setters straight from Danum Grammar school, despite the interest of other clubs, including Coventry City, Sheffield United, Manchester City, Derby County and Hull City. Elwiss was born in Doncaster on 2 May 1954, making his debut on 16 October 1971 in the Fourth Division away game at Newport County, where he scored 2 goals. The side during this period was a mixture of youth and experience and included his fellow youth-team team-mates, Stan Brookes and Steve Uzelac. Mike's total of 15 goals from 35 League appearances at the end of his first season (1971/72) went some way to help the club finish twelfth in the table, having been relegated from the Third Division during the previous campaign. Whilst at Belle Vue, Mike notched up 96 appearances (1 as substitute) and scored 30 goals.

Early in 1974, Mike was the subject of much talk when it was rumoured that Liverpool were considering a £70,000 bid for him. Bill Shankly even came to Belle Vue, paid at the turnstile and sat incognito in amongst regular supporters, watching him play in the game against Rotherham United. There was great hope amongst the board members that the deal would come off, as the club was nearly £70,000 in the red. Liverpool and the Rovers board were said to have been in discussions about the player for some time. They had made an offer after the Liverpool-Rovers FA Cup tie, but this was turned down as being too low. The obvious potential of the player – he was big and strong and only nineteen years of age – caused Liverpool to think again and their 'improved' offer was accepted by the Belle Vue board.

'It is up to Liverpool', said Rovers' chairman, Ben Rayner, adding: 'The move could make him an England player in two years. We have a duty to the player. In my opinion, he is good enough to be an international if he joins a top club ... The money involved could put the club on its feet and we would be able to spend some money on the team.'

In time, however, Liverpool called off the move and Mike was transferred to Preston North End, under Bobby Charlton, in February 1974 for a club record fee of around £80,000. In his last three months at Belle Vue, he had seen the team play indifferently and plummet to the bottom of the table. From Preston, Mike moved to Crystal Palace in July 1978 where, after a while, he picked up a serious injury. This restricted his appearance total to just 19 (1 as substitute) and he netted 7 goals. Mike spent a period on loan to Preston (8 appearances, 2 as substitute and 3 goals) in March 1980, but eventually retired through injury at the end of the 1979/80 season. Whilst at Deepdale, he married the chairman's daughter and, for a period, was employed as a dairy manager on the outskirts of Preston.

Fred Emery

Defender 1924-1936

Football League
Appearances: 417
Goals: 30

FA Cup
Appearances: 20
Goals: 1

FL Cup
Appearances: -
Goals: -

Total appearances: 437

Fred Emery has the honour of holding the Rovers record for most appearances. He played 437 times over a twelve-year period. He was born in Lincoln in May 1900 and joined his home-town team, before eventually making his League debut with Bradford City during the 1923/24 season. After playing a few games there, he came to Belle Vue under manager Dick Ray, shortly before the start of the 1924/25 season. Other players added to the squad at that time included Jimmy Hanwell, Tom Gascoigne, Fred Horsman, Joe Bowman and Harold Keetley – brother of goal-scorer Tom. In the previous season, Rovers had finished ninth in the Third Division (North).

Fred first appeared in Rovers' colours, at left-back, in the Third Division (North) home game against Hartlepool United on 6 December 1924. His usual position was left half, but he did have stints in a number of defensive positions, and in time he became club captain. He also stepped up on occasions to take penalties. He scored his first goal for Rovers in the 8-1 thrashing of Coventry City at Belle Vue on 23 January 1926.

During his time as a player at Belle Vue the team won the Third Division (North) championship in the 1934/1935 season for the first time. He formed part of the defence that conceded only 44 goals, whilst the attack netted 87. In that season, he played 38 times out of a possible 42 and scored twice. Having gained experience as captain, he became player-manager in February 1936 when David Menzies left his duties at Belle Vue and moved to accept the manager's position at Hull City. Fred played his last game away at Tottenham Hotspur on 25 April 1936.

Unfortunately, his first full season as manager brought no luck, the team being relegated to the Third Division (North), conceding 84 goals and bagging only 30. There were some successes in the following years, however, the team finishing second in the Third Division (North) on two occasions. Fred finally parted company with Rovers during the summer of 1940. Three years later, he became Bradford Park Avenue's team manager, spending time there before another managerial move in 1951 to Carlisle United. He enjoyed a seven-year stay there and died a year later.

John Edward Flowers

Wing half 1966-1971

Football League
Appearances: 162 (+2 as substitute)
Goals: 4

FA Cup
Appearances: 13
Goals: 0

FL Cup
Appearances: 9
Goals: 0

Total appearances: 186

John Flowers was the younger brother of Ron, the Wolves and England international. He was born in Edlington, near Doncaster, on 26 August 1944. He joined Wolverhampton Wanderers in 1959, when he was fifteen years of age, but he was only there a season before moving to Stoke City in September 1961. John made his First Division debut for Stoke in a team which also included Sir Stanley Mathews, and he toured South America and Europe with the team. However, it is alleged he once stated that none of these experiences equalled the thrill of playing for his home-town team, Doncaster Rovers.

Recalling the team in which he broke into the big time, John remembered that the half-back line read Clamp, Stewart and Flowers, exactly the same as the Wolverhampton half-back line a year or so earlier – except that on the first occasion, Flowers was John's brother, Ron. He once played with the Stafford Cricket Club, which also included fellow ex-Rover, Keith Mottershead. John arrived at Belle Vue in August 1966, costing the club £10,000. It was a summer where hopes were high for the season ahead in the Third Division. Several players had left the club, including Colin Grainger, Keith Ripley and Fred Potter, and amongst the newcomers were Martin Ferguson (Alex's

brother), Keith Webber and John himself.

Flowers played his first Rovers' game in the Third Division on 20 August 1966, the opening match of the 1966/67 season, away at Peterborough. The hopes for the season, as we all know now, were dashed following the death of captain John Nicholson and the injuries sustained to Alick Jeffrey, leading to his long lay-off. Rovers' defensive record for this season was appalling, with 117 goals being scored against them. No wonder then that they dropped straight back to the Fourth Division.

Whilst John only made 11 appearances in the Rovers back line during this unforgettable first season, he was a regular in the team for the next four years. He played a useful role under manager Lawrie McMenemy when promotion was gained from the Fourth to the Third Division during the 1968/69 campaign. During this period, the defence only conceded 38 goals, which was quite a turnaround from two years earlier. John left the club (and football) at the close of the 1969/70 season to run a hotel, but was back in September 1970, playing on a part-time basis. During the following year, he made 32 appearances (1 as substitute) before he was transferred to Port Vale in August 1971. During his time there, he made 34 appearances.

Brian Flynn

Midfield 1985-1986, 1987-1988

Football League
Appearances: 45 (+6 as substitute)
Goals: 1

FA Cup
Appearances: 1 (as substitute)
Goals: 0

FL Cup
Appearances: 4
Goals: 0

Total appearances: 56

Brian was born in Port Talbot on 12 October 1955. One of the smallest players in League Football, he was with a number of clubs before coming to Belle Vue. He played in the First Division for Burnley (115 appearances, 5 as substitute, 8 goals) as a teenager, before signing for Leeds United (152 appearances, 2 as substitute, 11 goals) in November 1977 for £175,000. The diminutive midfielder then rejoined Burnley on loan (2 appearances), and signed again for them (76 appearances, 4 as substitute, 11 goals) in a £60,000 deal. He then signed for Cardiff City (32 appearances) for £20,000 two years later.

He was signed by Dave Cusack in November 1985, on a free transfer, shortly after the latter took control, and subsequently became captain of the side. It was said that Brian had talked with Rovers before opting to join Cardiff, but had regretted the move and was keen to return north. On signing Brian, manager Cusack said: 'I cannot believe we've got him for nothing ... Brian's been around for so long that people think he is older than he is – but he's certainly no has-been. He's a quality player who I rate highly. He's a little fellow with a big heart, and I'm sure the fans will like him.' Brian revealed

that he had talked with several other clubs, including Second Division Bradford City, before deciding to join Rovers. Brian said 'I was very impressed with the way Doncaster played at Cardiff last week. They seem good, honest lads who work very hard, and that's the way I like to play.'

Brian made his debut in the Third Division home game against Bournemouth on 23 November 1985. At the time, Brian was one of the most capped players in Welsh history, making 66 international appearances between 1974 and 1984. His wealth of experience helped the team pick up points over the following games, but by the end of the season they could only finish in eleventh position, albeit in their highest Third Division place in sixteen years. Brian moved to Bury during July 1986, when Rovers were really struggling to survive financially and under intense pressure to reduce their debts to the bank. During May, all the playing staff, with the exception of Dave Cusack and Micky Stead, had been put on the transfer list. But Brian rejoined Rovers on a non-contract basis from Limerick in August 1987. He then moved to Wrexham in February 1988.

Patrick Joseph Gavin
Full-back 1953-1960

Football League
Appearances: 147
Goals: 5

FA Cup
Appearances: 9
Goals: 0

FL Cup
Appearances: -
Goals: -

Total appearances: 156

Born in Drogheda, Ireland on 6 June 1959, for a time Gavin played with League of Ireland side Dundalk, before joining Rovers in June 1953. He came at a time when a free transfer had been given to winger Alf Calverley, and Jack Hodgson (full-back) had been appointed as coach. Two other players who arrived around the same time were Johnny Mooney and Reece Nicholson. He made his debut in the Second Division home game on 13 February 1954 against Bury. Rovers lost the game 1-0, with 16,175 in attendance. In the defence with him on that day were Makepeace, T. Brown, Paterson and Teasdale, with Hardwick in goal. Paddy was comfortable playing in the defensive positions of right-back, left-back or left half.

He announced that he was leaving Belle Vue at the end of the 1959/60 season. A headline in the *Yorkshire Evening Post* on 22 April 1960 announced 'Paddy Gavin is to quit football.' It was explained that the Irish full-back had dropped a bombshell at Belle Vue that day by telling secretary-manager Jack Crayston: 'I'm quitting at the end of the season. I can't see any future for me in football … Football's a grand life but it is usually a

short one. I'm thirty now and there comes a time when you have to weigh up what is best. I've been offered a good position with my father-in-law's ice-cream firm at Chesterfield, and I'm going to take it.'

Paddy had given up his managerial ambitions. A few weeks earlier, he had been in the running for a post with Yeovil Town. 'I think I could have had that job, but the terms did not suit me. It would have been all right whilst I was playing, but after that they would not have wanted me. Only the top players get the good managerial positions, and even then the life is not too secure.' The hard-tackling Irishman was obviously reluctant to quit football. 'I shall miss the boys at Belle Vue,' he said. 'They are a good crowd, but I shall have to go.' Paddy stressed that he had no quarrel with the Rovers. His retirement was solely for future security. He was to become an under-manager with his father-in-law's firm, and there were excellent prospects.

Paddy would be the last to pretend that he was a brilliant player, but he was always above average, dependable and loyal. The Rovers were losing a fine clubman.

Inside forward 1965-1971

Football League
Appearances: 178 (7 as substitute)
Goals: 34

FA Cup
Appearances: 10
Goals: 2

FL Cup
Appearances: 11
Goals: 1

Total appearances: 206

Bob Gilfillan made his Rovers' debut on 9 November 1965 in a friendly game against the West German side Wormatia Worms. He was signed by Rovers manager, Bill Leivers, along with Tony Coleman and Terry Stanford, for a total bill of £8,000. A reported £5,000 of this was for Gilfillan himself. He was born in Cowdenbeath on 29 June 1938 and at seventeen signed for his home-town side, who were in the Scottish Second Division. Bob's father had played for Dunfermline. His cousin, also called Bob Gilfillan, was a winger with Blackpool and had Stanley Mathews as a team-mate. Bob's uncle Jock played in goal for Hearts and Portsmouth and managed to win one international cap.

Bob was also a trained turner, serving his apprenticeship in NCB Workshops at Cowdenbeath. In his spare timem he played in a skiffle group called the Red Hawks and played the drums and washboard as well as doing some of the vocals. The group was quite successful and appeared on Scottish television in a programme called *Dance Party Roof*. They were also invited to appear on the well-known BBC rock 'n' roll programme *6.5 Special*.

When he reached twenty-one, Bob left Scotland and signed for Newcastle United in a £5,000 deal. After a number of games in the Magpies' reserves, he played centre forward in the first team's First Division game against Bolton Wanderers. He stayed for fifteen months at St James' Park and only made 7 first-team appearances, scoring 2 goals. In 1961, he signed for St Johnstone in a £4,000 deal, but he found himself at Raith Rovers some ten months later. After several turbulent years there, he travelled across the Border once more and signed for Southend in July 1963. This was quite a successful period for him as he played 67 first-team games for the Roots Hall side and found the net 33 times.

Rovers manager Bill Leivers approached Bob to sign for Rovers after Southend's game at Mansfield, where they lost 6-1. It was Leivers' intention that Bob should not only be a goalscorer when the chances arose, but also a goal provider for the strike partnership of Alick Jeffrey and Laurie Sheffield. Bob's debut was in a friendly, but his League debut was a Fourth Division game against Port Vale on 19 November 1965. Tony Coleman, who had

signed for Rovers at the same time as Bob, also made his debut in this game and together they added an extra sharpness to the attack. Bob was an integral part of the successful 1965/66 promotion-seeking side, his inspirational play being a joy to watch. Consequently, hopes were high for the following season in the Third Division. But this was not to be, the side dropping straight back into the Fourth Division, though Bob managed 38 League appearances and 9 goals. Bob was retained for the 1967/68 season and he played his part once more in the side that won promotion to

the Third Division during the 1968/69 season. He was also in the brave Rovers team that met Liverpool at Anfield in the third round of the FA Cup in January 1969. The match was played in front of 48,330. After being released by Rovers at the end of the 1970/71 season, Bob signed for Northern Premier Club Northwhich Victoria. From there, he moved back across the Pennines to play for Retford Town in the Midland League, eventually blowing the whistle on his career at the end of the 1972/73 season.

Football League
Appearances: 110 (+8 as substitute)
Goals: 16

FA Cup
Appearances 5
Goals: 1

FL Cup
Appearances: 4 (+1 as substitute)
Goals: 0

Total appearances: 128

Eddie Gormley was born in Dublin on 23 October 1968. Initially, he played for Bray Wanderers, before joining Tottenham Hotspur in November 1987. He made no first-team appearances whilst at White Hart Lane and for a period went on loan to Chesterfield. He also played for the Irish Under-21 side. Whilst at Saltergate, he made 4 outings before Rovers' manager Billy Bremner brought him to Belle Vue on a free transfer in July 1990. He joined Rovers at the same time as Brendan Ormsly and Andy Holmes.

Eddie's debut was in the Fourth Division away game at Carlisle United on 25 August 1990. On that day, his colleagues included Stiles, Muir, D. Jones and Noteman. In his first season, he managed 32 League appearances, 8 as substitute, and scored 5 goals, the team finishing in eleventh position.

The next couple of seasons were played against a backdrop of troubles, both on and off the field. The Inland Revenue served the club

with a winding-up order, the PFA were called in to pay their players' wages, there was a change of manager and of ownership of the club and, at one point, the team plummeted to the bottom of the League. Despite all this, some players shone through and Eddie was one of them.

On 19 August 1993, the *Doncaster Star* reported that Eddie looked set to join Irish club Drogheda United on a permanent basis. At that time, Eddie was on loan with the Irish side, but wanted to join them on a permanent basis at the end of the month. The player and his wife had become keen to return to their home country following the birth of their first child earlier in the year. Steve Beaglehole said: 'There is no point trying to persuade Eddie to come back if his mind is set. He has not signed a new contract and in effect is a free agent. We could hold on to his registration and prevent him from playing, but that would be silly.'

William George Leonard Graham

Left-back 1949-1959

Football League
Appearances: 312
Goals: 3

FA Cup
Appearances: 20
Goals: 0

FL Cup
Appearances: -
Goals: -

Total appearances: 332

Len is one of Rovers' greats because he is the club's most capped player, turning out 14 times for Northern Ireland. He was born in Belfast on 17 October 1925. He played with Brantwood FC of Northern Ireland before manager Peter Doherty brought him to Belle Vue in September 1949. The *Yorkshire Evening Post* of 30 September 1949 said: 'The outlook has never been brighter at Belle Vue than it is just now. The first team are maintaining their strong position in the League. Mr Peter Doherty, the player-manager, is back in training and hopes to be playing again in a fortnight ... an important addition has been made to the playing strength ... the coming of Leonard Graham, another Irishman, will help to strengthen the defence, where more than one player will have to be rested from time to time if Rovers are to get the best out of them. Leonard has the ideal build for the job.'

The *Yorkshire Evening Post* on Monday 12 December 1949 informed: 'Negotiations have been successfully completed for the transfer of twenty-three-year-old Leonard Graham of Brantwood FC, Ireland, to Doncaster Rovers. Graham is now in the Rovers' Midland League side again after absence through injury. When he came to Belle Vue in September, the terms were that if he did not settle in English football, the Rovers would be prepared to release him. He is quite happy here and he is now a Rovers player. Graham stands 5ft 10in and weighs 12st.' Len's first outing was in a Third Division (North) home game against Wrexham on 18 March 1950. Rovers won the game 2-0 in front of a crowd of 15,114. In defence with Len on that day were

Hainsworth, Hodgson, Bycroft and Goodfellow, with Hardwick in goal. During his first season at Belle Vue, Rovers won promotion to the Second Division, where they stayed until the 1958/59 season – Len enjoyed some good times.

There came a time when his international commitments clashed with those at Rovers. In October 1952, he put in a transfer request, partly because it was suggested that the Rovers board would not release him for international duty. Rovers' chairman said: 'Some time ago we agreed that our manager should be allowed to take charge of the Irish team and at that time we expected Graham might be selected. What we did not know then was what our position would be regarding injuries and our lowly position in the League. When the request for Graham came, it meant us being without two good players ... We felt in fairness to our supporters and to the public we could not let Graham go ...'

There was no doubt that Len was a gifted, polished performer. He made over 300 appearances for Rovers before his transfer to Torquay United in November 1958. The *Yorkshire Evening Post* of 6 November 1958 reported: 'Mr Crayston [Rovers' manager] said a fee was involved, but he would not disclose the amount. ... It is expected that Graham will receive the accrued share of his benefit money, which would have been £1,000 had he stayed with the Rovers another year. By joining a Fourth Division side, Graham, who played for Ireland earlier this season, is probably giving up his chance of playing for his country again. [He] is a fully qualified FA coach.'

Len made 20 appearances for Torquay and later took up coaching full-time at Blackpool.

Henry (Harry) Gregg

Goalkeeper 1952-1958

Football League
Appearances: 94
Goals: 0

FA Cup
Appearances: 5
Goals: 0

FL Cup
Appearances: -
Goals: -

Total appearances: 99

It may surprise some to learn that Doncaster Rovers once transferred a goalkeeper for a world record fee. This was Henry (Harry) Gregg, one of a number of Irish players capped by his country whilst at Belle Vue during the 1950s. At the time, it was stated that no fee was disclosed, but it was thought to have been around £25,000.

Born in Derry in October 1932, Harry played for Coleraine before moving to Belle Vue in October 1952. He was described as a big lad, standing 6ft 1in and weighing 13st 7lb. He came with an impressive record too. He held 5 schoolboy international caps, 8 youth international caps, 1 amateur international cap and 2 inter-league caps. He had represented Ireland in youth internationals on the Continent and was capped for Ireland in the amateur international against England during the previous season. Also in that period, he had played for the Irish League against the English and Scottish Leagues. He will probably never forget his entry into big-time soccer when he saw 9 goals go past him when playing for the Irish League against the English League in Belfast.

It was in a junior game in Linfield that Peter Doherty first spotted Harry playing in goal around 1946, and even then he was able to detect great potential in the well-built fourteen year old. When Peter became Rovers' manager, one of the first things he did was to return to Ireland in the hope of persuading Gregg to sign for the club. Harry made his Rovers League debut at home to Blackburn on 24 January 1953. Understudying Ken Hardwick at Belle Vue was not an enviable job, and Harry almost began to despair when, in his first League game, he dislocated his elbow and broke his arm. This would have shattered the confidence of many a young 'keeper but it was not so in the case of Harry. He started weightlifting to strengthen his right arm and to keep his body in perfect condition.

It has been stated that quite a number of supporters did not think the young raw-boned Harry would make the grade – how wrong they would be. In his first term, Harry made 11 League appearances, keeping a clean sheet on 3 occasions. The following season, Harry was capped for the first time in Northern Ireland's game against Wales. However, he only made 2 first-team outings in the 1953/54 campaign (and both times Rovers lost), Ken Hardwick being the preferred goalkeeper. He did not command a regular Rovers position until Peter Doherty made him his first-choice goalkeeper for the 1956/57 season.

Harry missed just 2 league games during this season, and was attracting the interest of the top clubs with his impressive displays at club and international level. One of Peter Doherty's last managerial duties was to sanction Harry's transfer to Manchester United in December 1957, for £23,500. At that time it was a world record fee for a goalkeeper. This represented good business for the Rovers, with Harry having played just 93 league games for the club. Harry commented: 'It's a dream come true. I naturally wanted to rise to the top and now I've got there. I can hardly believe it, especially when [at one point] the negotiations between Rovers and Manchester United had broken down. I was deeply disappointed ... Mind you, I had reconciled myself to staying at Belle Vue, where I'd been very happy with everybody, but I still had that sneaking feeling that to join the League Champions would be just the thing for me. Looking back, I realise I've had a lot to thank Doncaster Rovers for, especially Mr Doherty. We've had our quibbles and arguments, but I've found he's always been right and I've always been wrong. I'm a very happy man and no one could have arranged a better Christmas present than this.'

The day of his signing was certainly one of dramatic developments at Belle Vue and it ended with Rovers obtaining the services of Sheffield United's goalkeeper, Ted Burgin, for around £4,500. Harry enjoyed an impressive career at Old Trafford, with 210 League appearances for the Red Devils as well as 25

full caps for Northern Ireland. He was also lucky to escape the horrors of the Munich air disaster, which claimed the lives of so many of his team-mates. He left United in December 1966 to join Stoke City, yet played only 2 League games for the Potters before bringing his playing career to a close. Thereafter he went into football management, first at Shrewsbury Town, and then with Swansea City, Crewe Alexandra and Carlisle United, before leaving the game.

John (Jack) Haigh

Inside forward 1960-1962

Football League
Appearances: 72
Goals: 6

FA Cup
Appearances: 3
Goals: 0

FL Cup
Appearances: 4
Goals: 1

Total appearances: 79

Jack was the subject of several unsuccessful transfer bids by Rovers before he eventually came to Belle Vue under the management team of Jack Crayston and Jackie Bestall in July 1960. The pair were convinced that Jack had the ability and the organisational skills in midfield to make the Rovers worthy of challenging for promotion over the ensuing campaign.

Jack had been watched by Rovers during the previous three seasons. Scunthorpe manager Dick Duckworth had rejected a bid from Rovers in June, but accepted one reported to be around £5,000 the following month. Rovers had beaten an offer from Blackpool, who had supposedly offered £8,000 for Jack's services, but a move to Doncaster may have been more favourable to him, because he had married a girl from a suburb of the town. A report in the local press gave the following description of him: 'Haigh is a fast and powerful runner and very hard to dispossess. Scunthorpe have been using him at wing-half, where he has proved to be a solid, effective tackler.'

Before arriving at Doncaster, he had made 340 League appearances over an eleven-year period, playing first at Liverpool and then Scunthorpe. Jack was born in Thornhill, Rotherham, not far from Millmoor, Rotherham United's ground, on 10 September 1928. Hopes were high for Rovers as they started the 1960/61 season. In the previous campaign, Rovers had finished seventeenth. Many thought that if Jack could forge a partnership with Albert Broadbent, together they could feed the hungry goal-scoring skills of both Tony Leighton and Jim Fernie, thus giving the team a good chance of promotion.

Jack made his debut in the Fourth Division home game against Southport on 23 August 1960, and the season had hardly begun when the club appointed ex-Sheffield Wednesday full-back Norman Curtis as player-manager. But, as time passed, many injuries and indifferent performances forced Norman to reorganise the side. Jack was moved into the forward line, making a number of fans unhappy, as they thought his best position was at half-back. Jack scored his first goal for

Rovers in the home game against Oldham Athletic on 19 November 1960. He accepted a pass from Albert Broadbent and rifled in a shot from 25 yards, bringing a hearty cheer from the 3,400 in attendance. Older fans submit that his best goal was scored on 15 April 1961 in the 4-3 home victory against Workington. In this game, he sent a powerful drive into the net from 35 yards.

At the end of the season, the club finished in eleventh position – an improvement on the previous term's efforts, Jack making 45 appearances and scoring 5 goals. In his second term with Rovers, under new player-manager Danny Malloy, it was said that Jack made a number of impressive displays and also inspired some of the younger members of the team. Jack, who was considered to be one of the best players in the Fourth Division, played

regularly up until December, when a knee injury forced him to miss a number of games. Prior to this, he had turned in a large number of consecutive appearances. Some argued that this had a detrimental effect on the team's performance, and he only managed 27 outings that season, the team finishing in twenty-first position. They had to apply for re-election to the League – the first time this had occurred since 1905.

Jack left the club in the summer to join ex-Rovers manager Norman Curtis, who was in charge of Midland League side Buxton. He played there for two seasons before deciding to retire from the game. He is best remembered by Rovers fans for his gritty, inspiring performances during the post-Doherty years, when the club was in free-fall and trying to steady itself.

Inside forward 1962-1965

Football League
Appearances: 119
Goals: 42

FA Cup
Appearances: 9
Goals: 2

FL Cup
Appearances: 7
Goals: 0

Total appearances: 135

Alfie Hale was another player capped for Republic of Ireland during his time at Belle Vue. He was born in Waterford on 28 August 1939 and played for his home team before a brief spell at Aston Villa, joining them in June 1960 for £4,500. His brother Richard, better known as 'Dixie', had moved from Waterford to Swansea Town a year earlier. He joined Rovers under manager Oscar Hold, just before the start of the 1962/63 season. He won his first cap for his country against Austria, shortly before moving to Belle Vue.

Alfie was only 5ft 6in tall, but a clever and tricky inside forward. His strength lay in his quickness off the mark. He made his debut in the Fourth Division home game against Brentford on 18 August 1962, with 8,247 in attendance. In the forward line with him on that day were Windross, Sambrook, Robinson and Johnson. He notched up 9 goals in his first season, but netted 20 times the following season. In time, he formed a useful partnership with Colin Booth. Alfie scored four memorable goals in Rovers' 10-0 thrashing of Darlington on 25 January 1964.

In January 1963, it was announced that Rovers were open to offers for the transfer of Alfie and had circulated information to clubs to that effect. The player asked for a transfer because he preferred to play at inside forward instead of on the wing, and because he did not command a regular place in the first team. In any event, Alfie did not leave and, in the 1964/65 season, he formed a successful strike partnership with the legendary Jeffrey, who returned to this country and found a place in Rovers' first team in December 1963. Together, they notched up almost 50 League goals, with Alick ending the season as the leading goalscorer in the Football League.

The 1964/65 season was Alfie's last one at Belle Vue before moving to Newport County. The Rovers board had earmarked Newport County's Laurie Sheffield as a new target for the coming season and, in August 1965, Alfie was on his way to south Wales in a player exchange deal, with a further £5,000 going to County. Many Rovers fans welcomed the arrival of Laurie Sheffield, but they were also sad to see the departure of Alfie, who had earned much respect and popularity whilst at Belle Vue. At Newport, he found the net 21 times in 34 matches. Later in his career, he returned to Waterford and played with them for a number of years. He played 13 times for the Republic of Ireland between 1962 and 1971. Whilst Alfie was at Belle Vue, he was capped for his country against Iceland and Spain (twice).

Kenneth Hardwick
Goalkeeper 1947-1957

Football League
Appearances: 307
Goals: 0

FA Cup
Appearances: 24
Goals: 0

FL Cup
Appearances: -
Goals: -

Total appearances: 331

Between 1947 and 1958, goalkeeper Ken Hardwick made an impressive 308 League appearances for Doncaster Rovers. Some people have even argued that he was Rovers' finest ever goalkeeper. Yet early in his career, it was reported that he wanted to be a centre forward.

A native of West Auckland, he was born in January 1924. He moved to Rossington, south of Doncaster, at an early age and eventually played for Doncaster Boys and the Rossington Colliery side. On joining the armed forces, he guested for Huddersfield Town before arriving at Belle Vue in April 1945.

Ken had played 26 times for Rovers during the Second World War. He made his League debut on Boxing Day 1947, in Rovers home win over Nottingham Forest. His back line on that day included Swallow, Bycroft, Squires, Corbett and McFarlane. Ken had pushed out Archie Ferguson, who had been injured at Southampton, and Ken's subsequent form was so impressive that Archie never regained his place. Ken was a brave and consistent 'keeper and when the Rovers took the Third Division (North) championship in 1949/50, their 'goals against' total of just 38 gave some indication of his contribution to the side's success. Over the next two seasons, he missed only a handful of League games, but Harry Gregg's arrival in October 1952 would provide him with a keen rival over the next few years.

At one point, Hardwick was chosen to play for the England Under-21 side, until the selectors discovered he was thirty! During the 1956/57 season, Gregg became Rovers' first-choice goalkeeper. Ken only made 2 League appearances during the 1956/57 season – the away fixture at Sheffield United on November 1956, unfortunately a 4-0 defeat, was his last in a Rovers jersey. The *Yorkshire Evening Post* of 18 April 1957 reported 'Negotiations for the transfer of Ken Hardwick to the Northern Section Club Scunthorpe United were taking place at Belle Vue today ... [Ken] who [has] turned out to be one of the most reliable goalkeepers in the Second and Third Divisions, expressed a wish to leave Belle Vue four months ago. The Rovers turned down his request but decided to place him on offer. It was early last season when Hardwick had a temporary loss of form and asked to be seconded to the Midland League side. Irish international goalkeeper Harry Gregg stepped in and has kept his place ever since. The Rovers has been Hardwick's only League club and he has given them fine service for the past ten years.'

On moving to Scunthorpe United, he made a further 96 appearances over a two-and-a-half year period, before ending his long career at Barrow in 1960. Ken died in June 1977, still in his early fifties.

David Harle

Midfield 1979-1982, 1983-1986, 1989-1992

Football League
Appearances: 167 (+22 as substitute)
Goals: 23

FA Cup
Appearances: 10 (+1 as substitute)
Goals: 2

FL Cup
Appearances: 8
Goals: 0

Total appearances: 208

David has played for Doncaster Rovers during three separate periods. He was born in Denaby, near Doncaster, on 15 August 1963. He played for the England Youth team and first joined Rovers in 1979, making his debut in the Fourth Division away game at Port Vale on 3 May 1980. This was the last game of the season, when Rovers finished third and were promoted to the Third Division.

In his first full season playing in the first team, Rovers finished nineteenth. He formed a formidable midfield partnership with Ian Snodin. Although they were both just seventeen years old, both were first-team regulars in the side which won promotion in 1980/81. David joined Exeter City in July 1982, making 42 appearances (1 as substitute) and scoring 6 goals before returning to Belle Vue in September 1983. He played a prominent part in the team, which finished as Fourth Division runners-up in 1984.

One of the highlights of his career was scoring the memorable eightieth-minute goal in the FA Cup 1-0 home win against Queens Park Rangers on 5 January 1985. The *Doncaster Star* of Monday 7 January 1985 commented: 'Billy Bremner's babes came of age on a day when hearts were pounding and eyes were moist among the joyful Belle Vue fans ... Twenty-one-year-old David Harle grabbed the glory – and rightly so – for his twenty-yard match-winning volley. But it was a collective effort – an outstanding team performance which paved the way for a memorable victory.'

However, during the 1984/85 season, he had a poor disciplinary record, being sent off 3 times and booked on 11 occasions. On 17 December 1985, the *Doncaster Star* revealed that the ex-

England Youth international had been placed on the transfer list at his own request. Player-manager Dave Cusack said: 'I only want players who want to play for Doncaster Rovers and his name will be circulated among other clubs as available for transfer.' David had signed a new two-year contract during the summer, but had been unsettled since the departure of former manager Billy Bremner to Leeds United in October.

Despite having earlier bids turned down, Leeds United signed David in December 1985, but he only managed 3 first-team appearances whilst at Elland Road. There followed moves to Bristol City in March 1986 (23 appearances, 2 goals), Scunthorpe United in November 1986 (88 appearances, 1 as substitute and 10 goals) and Peterborough in March 1989 (21 appearances, 1 as substitute and 2 goals), before a return to Belle Vue under Billy Bremner in March 1990. The fee was reported to have been £12,500. Bremner commented: 'Dave will be a reliable asset and I've signed him because I know what to expect from him. When you're in a battle, you want battlers alongside you and David is one of those guys who will get up and be counted.' David said: 'I've travelled about a bit but you can't beat playing for your home-town club and it's great to be back.'

In January 1992, David moved out on a month's loan to Vauxhall Conference side Stafford Rangers. Rovers had been taking drastic steps to try and meet debts and cut their wage bill. In his final term with Rovers, David made 39 outings (6 as substitute) and scored 3 goals.

Raymond William Harrison

Centre forward 1949-1954

Football League
Appearances: 126
Goals: 47

FA Cup
Appearances: 9
Goals: 3

FL Cup
Appearances: -
Goals: -

Total appearances: 135

Ray was over thirty when he joined Rovers from Burnley in January, but that did not restrict him in any way from leading the forward line of a team that won the Third Division (Northern) championship during the 1949/1950 season. During that period, Ray netted 8 goals in 20 appearances. 'He's a trier,' commented player manager Peter Doherty, speaking just after he had signed Ray from Burnley at a record fee for the club.

Ray was born in Boston on 21 June 1921 and his father at one time was reported as playing for Boston United. The *Yorkshire Evening Post* of 29 July 1954 informed that he started his football career at twelve years of age with his school team and a year later was playing at inside left for Boston Town Boys. He played in amateur football after leaving school and developed his football skills further in the RAF. When he was stationed in Germany with the British Army of the Rhine (BAOR), he was chosen to play against Portsmouth. Ray was also involved in the D-Day landings in France.

He went to Burnley straight after demobilisation and became a professional. He got his chance and took it when regular centre forward Jack Billingham was injured, and he got two of the goals in Burnley's 5-1 victory over Aston Villa in the first round of the FA Cup. His greatest thrill was his goal which took Burnley to the final of the FA Cup – the only one of the game – in 1947, but they were beaten by Charlton. In four seasons playing for Burnley's first and second teams, he had

scored 70 goals in 121 appearances.

Ray was just over 5ft 9in tall and weighed 10st 10lb. It was stated that Burnley were reluctant to part with him, being described as a tireless worker who was always harassing the opposing defence. Both Middlesbrough and Brentford were interested in him. In a general comment on the signing, Peter Doherty said: 'We shall sign at any time, any player who is in the star class and who we think will help us. We are always trying to remedy any weaknesses we have and, in my opinion, the signing of Harrison is one of the answers.'

Ray made his first-team debut in the Third Division (North) home game against Southport in front of a crowd of 21,941. Rovers won the game, trouncing the Seasiders 5-1, and Ray got himself on the score sheet with one goal and made two of the others. In time, it was quickly realised by the Rovers crowd that Ray was not afraid to have a shot at goal and worked just as hard to create scoring opportunities for his inside forwards.

During the 1953/54 season, Ray lost his place in the Rovers first team to Arthur Adey, a move which caused some controversy amongst Rovers supporters. Then he was

placed on the transfer list at the end of the season. He had asked to be put on the list in March 1954. His reasons for this were, he said, the fact that he had been made a scapegoat for the results of two previous Rovers games and that he felt a change of team would benefit his play. During July 1954, Ray considered joining non-League Yeovil Town, but it was stated that he would have to give serious thought to the move. If he left League football, it meant that he lost his chance of an accrued share of benefit – amounting to over £600 – by signing.

Later in July, Ray signed for Grimsby Town 'at an undisclosed fee'. Rovers manager Peter Doherty commented: 'Everybody should be pleased at getting a fee for one of their transfer-listed players, even if it is not as much as they anticipated: Grimsby are getting a leader of their attack who is quite fit and who has plenty of football in him; and the player is signing for a League club after a period of anxiety during which he has several times contemplated joining a non-League club.' It was also pointed out that Ray would be pleased to join a Lincolnshire club, for he was a native of the county. For many years, Ray had a sports shop in the town. He died in June 2000.

John James Haselden
Central defender 1968-1974

Football League
Appearances: 168 (+4 as substitute)
Goals: 20

FA Cup
Appearances: 11
Goals: 0

FL Cup
Appearances: 4
Goals: 0

Total appearances: 187

John James Haselden was born in Maltby on 3 August 1943. He supported Rovers as a young boy and always wanted to play for them. John was an old boy of St Peter's School – now at Cantley, Doncaster – and captained the school team. As he got older, he began playing for local clubs – Crompton Parkinsons in the Bentley League at fifteen, Brodsworth Main at sixteen, and then Denaby in the Midland League. As Rovers dropped from the Second to the Fourth Division, he eventually signed for Rotherham in February 1962.

According to the record books, John Haselden is six feet tall, but he remembered the time he felt exactly three inches tall. The setting was Villa Park, the game a League match between Aston Villa and Rotherham United, with more than 20,000 fans present. John was playing at right half, with Laurie Sheffield making his debut for Rotherham in the forward line. Rotherham, playing in a dark-blue strip, were building up an attack nicely, and the ball was at John's feet with plenty of time to make good use of it. Laurie moved into a good position down the right wing and John was just about to pass the ball to him when, out of the corner of his eye, he caught a glimpse of what he thought was right-back Harold Wilcockson making an overlapping run. So he pushed the

ball to him, only to find that the 'overlapper' was the linesman running along the touchline to keep up with the play. The ball, of course, went out of play; Laurie looked amazed, the crowd just laughed and poor old John wished the ground would open up and swallow him.

He remembers, particularly, playing in some thrilling cup games with Rotherham. One example was at Manchester United, which ended in a goalless draw, before Matt Busby's men won in extra time at Millmoor in the second leg. Another was the one against Leicester City, again a draw, with City winning the replay.

Haselden signed for Rovers in September 1968, three of his former Rotherham team-mates – Colin Clish, Harold Wilcockson and Chris Rabjohn – having arrived at Belle Vue earlier in the year. When required, John played up front, and during his time at Belle Vue, he found the net on 20 occasions. His first game for Rovers was as a substitute against Chesterfield in the Fourth Division game on 28 September 1968. His first full game was at home against Darlington on 4 October 1968 in front of 22,268 people. In 1972, he spent a period on loan at Mansfield Town. Later, he was a trainer-coach at the club, earning his full FA coaching badge in 1969. In subsequent years, he held a trainer-coach position at Sheffield Wednesday.

John Venner Hodgson

Left-back 1947-1952

Football League
Appearances: 95
Goals: 2

FA Cup
Appearances: 5
Goals: 0

FL Cup
Appearances: -
Goals: -

Total appearances: 100

John (known as Jack) Hodgson was born on 30 September 1913 at Seaham, County Durham. Jack's father was Brian Hodgson, who played for Askern Welfare, Grimsby Town and Workington Town. Jack's brother, Sam, had spells with Sunderland, Grimsby and Mansfield. As a youth, Jack played for Durham County Schoolboys in addition to gaining an England international Schoolboys trial. After joining Seaham Colliery Welfare team at sixteen, scouts from League clubs began to take notice of him. He had trials with Wolverhampton Wanderers and Bradford Park Avenue before joining Grimsby Town during 1931/32. He played his first League game for them during the following season, against Plymouth Argyle. Between 1932 and 1948, he played 212 times for Grimsby, including 2 FA Cup semi-finals.

He came to Belle Vue in January 1948, and the *Yorkshire Evening Post* of Saturday 31 January noted the following: 'Hodgson is regarded as a sound and safe player. He has had long service at Blundell Park, he was there during the time of Mr Bestall [the manager] ... He started out as a centre half. He played well in that position before he developed into a full-back.' He signed during the same week as Walter Bennett, who was from Barnsley. Dave Miller had signed a couple of weeks earlier.

Jack made his debut in the Second Division home game against Chesterfield on 31 January

1948. Rovers won 1-0, with 23,527 in attendance. The back line on that day consisted of Hardwick, Hodgson, Bennett, Sterland, Archer and Squires. Jack never missed a game for the remainder of his first term at Belle Vue, playing 16 League games, but Rovers were relegated to the Third Division. Two seasons later, he made 35 League appearances and saw the team leap back into the Second Division.

Hodgson gained a reputation as a very consistent player and was eventually dislodged from the side by Len Graham. Jack played until the end of the 1951/52 season. After that, he became trainer until February 1958, when he was appointed joint manager with coach Syd Bycroft, after the departure of Peter Doherty to Bristol City. However, both men were to continue as club trainer and coach in addition to their joint managerial duties. It was the first time in the history of the club that joint managers had been appointed, and it was a system of management comparatively new to English football. Jack and Syd had worked together as trainer and coach at Belle Vue for five years. When Jack's playing career finished, he spent a lot of time with the Doncaster Senior League teams and Yorkshire League teams at Belle Vue, up to his appointment as trainer in succession to Jack Martin. Jack and Syd were relieved of their duties at the end of the 1957/58 season. Jack died in 1970.

Glenn Humphries
Central defender 1981-1988

Football League
Appearances: 174 (+6 as substitute)
Goals: 8

FA Cup
Appearances: 9
Goals: 0

FL Cup
Appearances: 12 (+1 as substitute)
Goals: 1

Total appearances: 202

Born in Hull on 11 August 1964, Glenn Humphries played for the England Youth team. He came to Belle Vue as an apprentice and signed on his eighteenth birthday, in 1982, when Billy Bremner was the manager. He joined the club following several rave reports from Humberside scout John Nicholson, and appeared regularly in the junior and reserve teams.

Humphries made his first appearance as a substitute in Rovers' last appearance in the Fourth Division during the 1980/81 season. However, it didn't last long, as he went off the field after two minutes to have stitches in a nasty gash, following a collision with a Mansfield player before he'd even touched the ball. Glenn made his first-team debut on 17 October 1981 in the Third Division home game against Millwall. His colleagues in defence on that day were Lister, Dowd, Lally, Russell and Dawson, with Boyd in goal. In his first season, he played 12 League games (2 as substitute). Amongst his many attributes, Glenn became known for his remarkable heading ability.

He was loaned to Lincoln City during March 1987 and stayed there for a period. In March 1987, he was placed on the transfer list at his own request. It was reported that Glenn had been unsettled for some considerable time and had first asked for a transfer almost two years earlier, under boss Billy Bremner, because he felt a move would benefit his career.

Competition for the centre-back positions had become intense following the acquisition of Stuart Beattie. The *Doncaster Star* of 25 March 1987 said that Glenn had joined Fourth Division strugglers Lincoln 'in a surprise switch today after turning down the chance to join promotion-chasing Wigan Athletic'. Both clubs wanted to sign him on loan until the end of the season, with a view to a permanent deal. Glenn seemed set to go to Wigan after speaking on the telephone to their manager, Ray Mathias, but then changed his mind and opted for Lincoln on loan instead. Rovers boss Dave Cusack said: 'I don't really know what the deciding factor was, but Glenn has a young family and if he had gone to Wigan it might have meant living away in digs, so that could have had something to do with it.'

Whilst at Lincoln, he made 9 appearances, and then was transferred from Rovers to Bristol City in October of the same year. City had been watching Glenn for some time, and boss Terry Cooper had played alongside the defender during a spell at Rovers some five years earlier. At Bristol, Glenn made 81 outings (4 as substitute). In March 1991, he moved to Scunthorpe United (71 appearances, 1 as substitute and 5 goals). Later, he joined Hull City (9 appearances, 3 as substitute). Glenn's older brother, Stephen, made 13 appearances in goal for Rovers in the early 1980s.

Archibald Irvine

Midfield 1969-1975

Football League
Appearances: 220 (+8 as substitute)
Goals: 16

FA Cup
Appearances: 12
Goals: 0

FL Cup
Appearances: 6 (+1 as substitute)
Goals: 3

Total appearances: 247

Archie Irvine, Rovers' former midfielder, was the fans' Player of the Year for the 1971/72 and 1972/73 seasons. He was born at Coatbridge, Scotland on 25 June 1946. He kicked off his career at Airdrieonians and then moved south to Sheffield Wednesday in 1968. He made 25 League appearances for the Owls, in addition to 4 as substitute, and scored 1 goal.

Standing 5ft 5in and weighing 10st 4lb, he arrived at Belle Vue under Lawrie McMenemy in December 1969, along with Ian Branfoot. It was an exchange deal, which saw Harold Wilcockson travel in the opposite direction. In the previous season, Rovers had won promotion to the Third Division. He made his first-team debut in the Third Division home game against Rotherham United on 26 December 1969. This was played in front of a bumper crowd of 19,742. The Rovers team on that day was: Ogston, Branfoot, Wilcockson, Clish, Flowers, Robertson, Haselden, Briggs, Johnson, Usher, Irvine (substitute), Gray.

From December until the end of the season, Archie played in 23 games (1 as substitute) and scored 1 goal. This latter, his first for the club, was in the away fixture at Stockport on 21 February 1970. Rovers made a reasonable return to the Third Division, finishing in eleventh position, having been in sixteenth place in February. However, in the following campaign, Rovers were relegated and Archie spent much the rest of his time with Rovers playing in the Fourth Division; he did not see them finish higher than twelfth. He played in both FA Cup games against Liverpool in January 1974. He also featured in the Football League Cup second round home game against Newcastle United on 8 October 1973.

During his time at Belle Vue, Archie carved out opportunities for such forwards as Elwis, Kitchen and O'Callaghan. He was a consistent performer and, for two seasons running, he made 44 League appearances.

During July 1975, he moved to Scunthorpe United. He played for the Iron 22 times, plus 1 as substitute, and scored 1 goal.

Alick James Jeffrey
Inside forward 1954-1957, 1963-1969

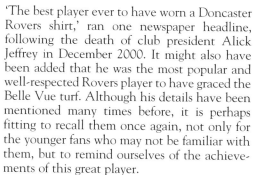

Football League
Appearances: 261 (+1 as substitute)
Goals: 129

FA Cup
Appearances: 22 (+1 as substitute)
Goals: 8

FL Cup
Appearances: 9
Goals: 3

Total appearances: 294

'The best player ever to have worn a Doncaster Rovers shirt,' ran one newspaper headline, following the death of club president Alick Jeffrey in December 2000. It might also have been added that he was the most popular and well-respected Rovers player to have graced the Belle Vue turf. Although his details have been mentioned many times before, it is perhaps fitting to recall them once again, not only for the younger fans who may not be familiar with them, but to remind ourselves of the achievements of this great player.

Alick was born in Rawmarsh on 29 January 1939, the son of a colliery blacksmith. None of his family had any previous football connections. He showed an early ability in many sports, but as school-leaving age approached, he was expected to follow his father to the pit. However, he was playing for Rotherham, Yorkshire and England Boys, and it quickly became apparent that he would follow a football career. At fifteen, he scored twice for England Schoolboys against Scotland, one headline proclaiming: 'Jeffrey, Hammer of the Scots.'

Just before leaving school, Alick had met Matt Busby, and Manchester United were favourites to sign him. He had even participated in a five-a-side game at the club, and the great Duncan Edwards had lent him a pair of boots. Yet, Alick chose to become a member of the groundstaff of Doncaster Rovers, where the great Irish legend Peter Doherty was manager. This may seem a strange choice today, but it has to be remembered that in the mid-1950s, Rovers were a team to be reckoned with in the old Second Division and were amongst the First Division promotion contenders.

Alick made his first appearance for Rovers aged only fifteen, and a fortnight after his sixteenth birthday scored two goals against Aston Villa to win an FA Cup replay. As the season progressed, Alick buzzed, attracting the attention of all the top clubs. Newcastle United legend Jackie Milburn described him as the best youngster he had ever seen and, after an appearance for the England amateur side, Stanley Mathews said that the boy showed genius.

In one England game, Alick was proud to take the place of the injured Johnny Haynes, but disaster was to follow. Shortly before the Under-23 England international game with France in October 1956, Alick had further talks with Matt Busby, where the great man said: 'You'll be a Manchester United player very soon.' Sadly, during the game with France, Alick broke his right leg in two places. Complications followed, side-lining him from football for many months. A complete recovery didn't seem to be on the cards and the FA eventually awarded him compensation early in 1959, for receiving a career-threatening injury while on international duty.

Rovers chairman John Ryan with Alick Jeffrey.

A little later in the year, Alick was taken under the wing of George Rayner, the former Swedish World Cup coach who was manager of Skegness Town. Under Rayner, Alick appeared to make a complete recovery. Yet, not long after, Alick broke his other leg. However, this was not as serious as the previous injury, and it was not long before Alick professed that he was ready to try again. Doncaster Rovers, now minus Doherty and languishing in the Fourth Division, were happy to take him back, but the FA refused to allow him to register unless he paid back the compensation.

In frustration, and wanting to make a fresh start, Alick emigrated to Australia and played football there. Yet, missing English football, he made enquiries about coming back and, to his delight, the FA relented over the compensation issue. On playing in his first come-back League game for Rovers, he was welcomed with open arms by the fans, even if he did take some time before scoring his first goal. In time, the goals flowed, and during the 1964/65 season, he scored 36. Everyone remembers him for the unique goal-scoring partnership he formed with Laurie Sheffield in the 1965/66 promotion season, the pair of them netting 50 goals between them.

However, disaster was looming in the shadows once more for Alick. A little way into the 1966/67 season, club captain John Nicholson and himself were involved in a crash in the early hours on Sheffield Road, Warmsworth. John was killed and Alick was out of action for several months. Although he continued to score on his return, things were never quite the same. Not long after the appointment of Lawrie McMenemy as manager in 1969, Alick was transferred to Lincoln City, remaining there for a season.

Michael Richard Jeffrey

Striker 1991-1994

Football League
Appearances: 48 (+1 as substitute)
Goals: 18

FA Cup
Appearances: 0
Goals: 0

FL Cup
Appearances: 4
Goals: 0

Total appearances: 53

The *Doncaster Star* of Friday 6 March 1992 revealed that Rovers had signed twenty-year-old striker Mike Jeffrey on a month's loan from Bolton Wanderers. He was to make his debut in the Fourth Division away game at Hereford on 7 March 1992. Mike was Bolton's leading scorer in the Central League, with 38 goals in the previous two seasons, and he had been watched closely by Rovers. The young striker had made a handful of first-team appearances, and Bolton were allowing him to go to Belle Vue for more experience. Because Rovers had no money to spend, the deal was arranged in conjunction with a number of local firms, who were to finance the player's wages during his spell at the club. Manager Steve Beaglehole said: 'We have struggled to score goals recently and I hope Mike can help us out in that respect ... he is an enthusiastic young player who wants to do well and, because of the way the deal has been done, he is not costing us a penny.'

Mike was born in Liverpool on 11 August 1971, and initially joined Bolton Wanderers during February 1989. He played 9 first-team games for them and 6 as substitute, but perhaps surprisingly never scored any goals. After eventually signing for Rovers for £20,000, Mike made a further 11 appearances during the remainder of

the 1991/92 season and scored 6 goals. In the 1992/93 campaign, he made 31 appearances (1 as substitute) and found the net 11 times.

During the following year, before he was transferred to Newcastle United in October 1993, he made 8 appearances and scored 1 goal. The transfer of Mike to St James' Park was reported as being a six-figure player-exchange deal, which brought highly-rated midfielder David Roche to Belle Vue. Manager Steve Beaglehole acknowledged that some fans might be disappointed at Mike leaving, and added: 'I'm not entirely happy about it either, but we have to look at the overall picture. We need to bring two or three players in and the money was not available to do that. We have had to generate our own cash, and I hope and believe the deal will turn out to be in the best interests of the club as a whole.' Before signing for Newcastle, he had been on trials with other big clubs. A hernia operation proved a big set-back but Newcastle continued to keep tabs on him and stepped in when Rovers advertised his availability.

At Newcastle, he made only 2 appearances before a move to Rotherham United in June 1995 (22 outings and 5 goals). In time, he went to Kilmarnock and Grimsby Town (5 appearances with 3 as substitute).

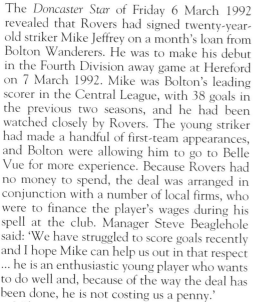

David Jones

Striker 1989-1991

Football League
Appearances: 34 (+6 as substitute)
Goals: 14

FA Cup
Appearances: 2
Goals: 0

FL Cup
Appearances: 2
Goals: 1

Total appearances: 44

Born in Harrow on 3 July 1964, Dave had a succession of clubs including Chelsea, Bury, Leyton Orient, Burnley and Ipswich before joining Rovers in November 1989.

The *Doncaster Star* of Friday 10 November 1989 announced that Rovers could have a new strike force at Rochdale the next day, after clinching a double signing breakthrough with the acquisition of Leeds United's Kevin Noteman and Ipswich Town's David Jones. It was revealed that the latter had accompanied vice-chairman Peter Wetzel to Rovers' match at Huddersfield earlier in the week. Said the *Star*: 'The massive twenty-five-year-old target man, who is 6ft 3in tall and built like Frank Bruno, agreed terms on Wednesday, but then asked for time to consider the move.' Rovers kept the deal under wraps because other clubs were interested in the player, who was a free transfer because he was only on a month-to-month contract at Ipswich. At first, it did not look as if he was going to sign, but general manager Dave Blakey contacted him again and he agreed to join the club.'

Dave had been unable to force his way into the first team of the Second Division side, although on occasions he had forced himself on to the substitutes' bench. It was said that Dave could play in attack or defence. Assistant boss Steve Beaglehole said: 'It was vital that we increased the competition for places at the club.' At this time, Rovers were near the foot of the Fourth Division table. He added that the signings enabled Rovers to consider a number of permutations.

Known as 'Bruno', Dave was a typical bustling centre forward and became popular with the crowd. Dave made his debut in the Fourth Division home game against Rochdale on 11 November 1989 and scored a hat-trick. This was the last hat-trick scored by a Rovers player in the 1980s. Whilst at Belle Vue, he sustained a serious neck injury which sidelined him for a while. He was transferred to Bury during September 1991. Whilst he was there, he appeared as a substitute on 9 occasions. He then moved to Hull City in February 1993 (11 appearances, 1 as substitute and 1 goal). Dave currently earns a living as a television cameraman.

Graeme Anthony Jones
Forward 1993-1996

Football League
Appearances: 80 (+12 as substitute)
Goals: 26

FA Cup
Appearances: 2 (+1 as substitute)
Goals: 2

FL Cup
Appearances: 4 (+1 as substitute)
Goals: 1

Total appearances: 100

Graeme was born in Gateshead on 13 March 1970. Standing 6ft tall, he was signed by Steve Beaglehole from Bridlington Town in August 1993. In the previous season, 1992/93, the team had finished in sixteenth position, scoring only 42 goals, so it was hoped that Graeme could increase the tally. He made his debut in the Division Three home game against Chester City on 14 August 1993. During the 1993/94 campaign, he made 25 appearances and scored 4 goals. The first of these was taken on 2 October 1993, in the home game against Rochdale.

That year, the team finished in fifteenth position. In the following year, he made 25 appearances (1 as substitute) and netted on 13 occasions. In his final year, it was 11 goals from 25 appearances (with 1 as substitute). He was Rovers' leading goalscorer for two seasons running.

He went on the transfer list at his own request towards the end of the 1995/96 season, after becoming unsettled at Belle Vue. On returning after the summer break, Graeme said 'I have not had a change of heart over the summer and I still want to leave … I am disappointed to still be here because I had hoped to have got myself fixed up with another club by now.' He was linked with a number of clubs and, during July 1996, he was transferred to Wigan Athletic. After signing for the Lancashire outfit, he commented: 'I will be sad to leave Rovers, but the set-up at Wigan is tremendous and I need a fresh challenge.'

The *Doncaster Star* of 4 July 1996 said: 'The size of the fee has not been revealed, but it is believed to be a club record for Wigan.' Manager Sammy Chung said: 'We are sorry to see Graeme go, but you can't keep players against their will and we wish him well in the future.' At Wigan, he made 67 appearances (6 as substitute) and scored 40 goals. In November 1999, he signed for Scottish Premier Division club St Johnstone.

Clarence Jordan

Inside forward 1946-1948

Football League
Appearances: 60
Goals: 48

FA Cup
Appearances: 5
Goals: 2

FL Cup
Appearances: 0
Goals: 0

Total appearances: 67

Centre forward Clarence (Clarrie) Jordan was born in South Kirkby on 20 June 1922. He left school at fourteen and worked at South Kirkby Colliery. Remarkably, he continued to work at the colliery until he left Rovers to join Sheffield Wednesday. Early in his football career, Clarrie played at left-back for South Kirkby Juniors, but later switched to centre forward and in his first full season scored 117 goals.

Rovers' scout at the time, Jimmy Geary, was instrumental in getting him to sign part-time forms. He signed only a few weeks before the start of the Second World War, and did not make his Football League debut until 1946. However, he first played for Rovers in the East Midland Division of the wartime League at Bramall Lane at the end of the 1939/40 season. His first Rovers goal came several weeks later, when he scored at Blundell Park against Grimsby Town in the same competition.

Throughout the 1940/41 season, Clarrie mainly appeared in the Rovers' reserves. He was paid 12s 6d for each reserve match and £1 10s for a first-team appearance. In the following season, he largely turned out for

South Kirkby Colliery FC. Clarrie also made guest appearances for several other clubs during the wartime years. These included Birmingham City, Leeds United, and Derby County – where offers were made for him to play full-time after the war, but he turned them all down to stay at Belle Vue. He also played for Aldershot under the name of Brookes, and became a favourite with the Shots, until a local sports writer discovered his true identity, after which he quickly returned to Doncaster.

As the war drew to a close, Clarrie settled himself into the Rovers side and found the back of the net with amazing alacrity. At the end of the 1944/45 season, Clarrie led the Rovers' goal-scoring jointly with Harold Bodle, both having 27 goals. Towards the end of the war, Rovers were managed by Billy Marsden, who later handed over to Jackie Bestall the foundations of a good team, which eventually won promotion to the Second Division.

During the 1945/46 period, Clarrie was on top of the list again with 24 goals. Clarrie once stated that the goal he enjoyed scoring most was at Haigh Avenue against Southport on 19 April 1947, in a 5-0 victory. It was a

first-time volley from twenty yards out that barely left the ground. Clarrie is remembered most of all for the 42 goals he scored during the 1946/47 season. The tally was 44, counting the goals he scored in the FA Cup. To score this amount of goals in one season is quite a feat. It is worth mentioning that during 1946/47 season, Clarrie failed to score in 14 of the 42 games, and therefore his 42 goals came in 28 games, giving the amazing average of 1.5 goals per match. He scored 4 hat-tricks and 2 goals, during 6 different occasions.

Previously, Tom Keetley had held the Rovers goal-scoring record, with 43 goals in the 1928/29 season. Interestingly, at the end of the 1946/47 season, Clarrie had his photograph taken shaking hands with Tom Keetley, whose record he had broken by two goals. The only other Rovers player who came close to beating Clarrie's record in subsequent years was Alick Jeffrey, with 39 League and cup goals. Rovers struggled during the 1947/48 season and Clarrie was allowed to leave Belle Vue to join Sheffield Wednesday. This was unpopular with the fans, many of whom idolised Clarrie, but,

just before the transfer, Clarrie had stated that he was ready for a change. In the deal, Rovers received £6,000 and inside forward Arnold Lowes. Meanwhile, Sheffield Wednesday were hoping that Clarrie was the centre forward they had been looking for.

At Hillsborough, Clarrie became a full-time professional and made 92 appearances, scoring 32 goals. Clarrie ended his football career in the summer of 1955 and went into the licensed trade, first as steward at the South Kirkby Coronation Working Men's Club, until he became manager of the White Rose public house at Rossington fourteen months later. From there, he became landlord of the Schoolboy pub at Norton, where he stayed for many years, dying in 1992.

Tom Keetley

Inside forward 1923-1929

Football League
Appearances: 231
Goals: 180

FA Cup
Appearances: 10
Goals: 5

FL Cup
Appearances: -
Goals: -

Total appearances: 241

A player who figures highly in an account of the club's history is Tom Keetley, born in 1899 at Normanton near Derby. Standing at 5ft 7in and weighing 11st, he was one of twelve brothers, four of whom – Frank, Harold, Joe and Tom himself – played for Rovers in the League. Tom, Frank and Harold played in the same forward line. In 1925/26, when Tom was top scorer with 24 goals, Harold was second to him with 17, and three years later, when Tom was leading scorer with 40, Frank was next with 13.

Tom played for Victoria Ironworks, a local Derby side, before joining Bradford Park Avenue in 1919. But with few opportunities to command a regular first-team place, he was transferred to Rovers in 1923. He made his first appearance in the Third Division (North) home game against Wigan Borough on 25 August 1923. He scored his first Rovers goal in the home game against Ashington on 3 September 1923. Over the next six seasons, he bagged 180 goals. In one match, at Ashington on 16 February 1929, he found the back of the net six times in Rovers' 7-4 hammering of the home side. The most goals he scored during a season came during 1928/29 with 40, the record eventually being broken by Clarrie Jordan's 42 in the 1946/47 season.

There was a surprise for Rovers fans in October 1928, when Tom was placed on the transfer list at his own request. Apparently, there was a problem over his benefit terms. Some time previously, he had received offers from American clubs, and wanted Rovers to give a clear commitment about a benefit for him. The club agreed and guaranteed him a certain sum from a match to be played on 10 September against Heart of Midlothian. But disagreement arose, and this had prompted him to seek a transfer. However, in time, it was seemingly resolved.

It has been said that in the 1920s, Rovers really belonged to the Keetley family. The four brothers made a total of 390 League appearances for Rovers and scored 233 League goals. Tom was a living legend during his stay at Belle Vue and, again, everyone was shocked when he did not sign before the start of the 1929/30 season. The reason was that Tom had established a business in Derby and wanted to live and train there. He would only join the team on match days. The Rovers board refused his request and, in July 1929, Notts County were only too pleased to have his signature.

On his debut for County in the Second Division, Tom soon proved that scoring goals in a higher division was just as easy, when he got a hat-trick. In one season, he hit 3 successive hat-tricks in away games. When County won the championship of the Third Division (South) in the 1932/33 season, he managed 15 goals from 20 games. In his 103 outings at Notts County, he hit 94 goals. For the 1933/34, Second Division campaign, he signed for Lincoln City, hitting 5 goals in 10 games. He then blew the whistle on his career. Over 330 League games, he had scored 284 goals. During the latter years of his life, he was at the Rose and Crown Hotel at Chellaston. He died at Chellaston, Derby, aged fifty-nine, during August 1958.

Brian Leslie Kelly
Full-back 1964-1968

Football League
Appearances: 130 (+1 as substitute)
Goals: 3

FA Cup
Appearances: 8
Goals: 1

FL Cup
Appearances: 10
Goals: 1

Total appearances: 149

Brian will always be remembered as a useful and important member of the 1965/66 Fourth Division championship-winning side. He was born in Ilkley on 22 May 1943, and as a teenager played football for Bradford Boys and Yorkshire Boys. He signed amateur forms for Bradford City AFC at fifteen and progressed through the Northern Intermediate League and Reserve sides to the first team, playing 83 League games and scoring 2 goals.

He was transferred to Rovers on Friday 22 January 1965 for the princely sum of £1,500. He was signed by player-manager Bill Leivers and made his debut the next day at full-back in the Fourth Division game at Notts County, which was lost 4-2. After this, Brian missed only one League game for the remainder of the season, the side finishing ninth in the League. At the beginning of the 1965/66 season, Brian got married. This was on the strict proviso that the wedding took place mid-week, so as not to interfere with the Saturday fixture. However, in the mid-week League Cup match with Burnley on 22 September, Brian sustained a leg injury. 'Bill Leivers was convinced I'd got myself injured deliberately,' recalled Brian, 'so as to avoid playing away at Newport on the Saturday. This was probably because he ended up

playing at right-back against Gil Reece, who ran rings round him that day! Prior to that, my wife and I were persuaded into inviting the whole team, plus the manager and his wife, to our wedding and a "right good do" it was.'

Following the Newport game, Rovers had a bleak spell. They struggled throughout October, collecting only 2 points until the 5-1 away win at Barnsley on 29 October. Brian believes this win was the beginning of the push towards promotion, when the team was unbeaten for 6 consecutive games. After losing the game at Barrow, the team picked up momentum and at the end of the season clinched the Fourth Division title.

The 1966/67 term began well, but Brian recalls that the crash in which skipper John Nicholson lost his life and Alick Jeffrey was seriously injured inevitably affected every member of the Belle Vue staff. Brian recalls that the team's performance did not pick up until they beat Swindon away on 1 October 1996. In the return match at Belle Vue, on 7 February 1967, Brian played with strapped-up fractured ribs and found himself up against Don Rogers – at that time the trickiest and fastest left winger in the division. Said Brian: 'Amazingly, I had a good game against him –

Brian Kelly is pictured on the right.

a headline in the local evening paper reading: 'Strapped up Kelly is superb.'

However, at the end of the season, Rovers were relegated and Keith Kettleborough was relieved of his managerial duties. Brian felt that the new manager, George Raynor, was a rather strange man with odd ideas: 'On one occasion, he visited our home to discuss terms regarding my new contract and spoke of his "new" ideas regarding training. For some obscure reason, he suddenly laid down on the lounge carpet, started to do press-ups and informed me he'd got a heart condition. Nevertheless, he appointed me club captain – that says it all! However, this was to be short-lived. Within a few weeks, I was replaced as

captain by Graham Shaw – who was supposed to bring experience to the side.'

Brian played 28 games during the 1967/68 season, and at the end of it was considered surplus to requirements, along with several other colleagues from the 1965/66 championship-winning side. His wages at Doncaster during 1965/66 were £18 per week (basic wage), £4 for a first-team appearance and a crowd bonus of £1 per thousand over 8,000. In 1966/67, his basic weekly wage was £23 10s, £3 for a first-team appearance and £1 per thousand between 8,000-12,000 crowd. He also got £4 per thousand over 12,000. In July 1968, he was transferred to York City (32 appearances, 1 as substitute).

Michael Peter Kitchen
Forward 1970-1977

Football League
Appearances: 221 (+7 as substitute)
Goals: 89

FA Cup
Appearances: 12
Goals: 6

FL Cup
Appearances: 16
Goals: 6

Total appearances: 256

'They don't come like that any more,' is how some people react when the name of Peter Kitchen is mentioned. His record of 27 goals, made during the 1976/77 season, has not been surpassed since by a Rovers player. Striker Peter 'Kitch' Kitchen remains the fourth highest League goalscorer in Rovers' history.

He was born on 16 February 1952 in Mexborough, South Yorkshire and attended Mexborough Grammar School. He played for Don & Dearne Boys and at national schools level, before joining the Rovers under Lawrie McMenemy in July 1970. During the 1970/71 season, Peter made steady progress in the juniors, before appearing in the reserves. He made his League debut in the Third Division away at Shrewsbury in front of a crowd of 5,184 on 27 November 1970 and scored. He also played a vital part in Rovers' third goal as they swept to a 3-1 victory. In the forward line with him on that day were Rabjohn, Watson, Regan and Irvine.

In his first season in the first team, he made 13 appearances (1 as substitute) and scored 6 goals. During the mid-1970s, he was partnered up front with Brendan O'Callaghan, whose aerial presence created numerous chances for him. Nobody who was around at the time will

ever forget the time when Peter nearly scored the winning goal for Rovers in the FA Cup tie against Liverpool at Anfield, on 5 January 1974. He had scored earlier in the game and there were only a few minutes to go as he nearly stole the show with a header that glanced off the bar with Clemence beaten. In 1974/75, Brendan and Peter scored 32 goals between them, Peter's share being 21. At the end of that season, he was voted Player of the Season by the supporters' club.

The following season, winger Ian Miller arrived at Belle Vue. With his electric pace, Miller provided chances galore for Peter and Brendan O'Callaghan. Together, they scored 22 apiece, with Miller adding 9 himself. Peter bettered his own total during 1976/77, and this was his last season at Belle Vue. In fact, he was on the transfer list for most of the season yet during that period he made 43 League appearances and scored 23 goals. In the *Doncaster Evening Post* of 2 May 1977, Rovers manager Stan Anderson stated: 'I am planning for next season without Peter. He wants to get away and we will have little choice but to sell him when his contract runs out at the end of the season.' Peter said: 'I feel I am at the crossroads of my career and want to go on to play

Peter Kitchen is second from the right.

in higher football. Apart from a few Third Division games in my early days at Belle Vue, I have played all my football in the Fourth Division and I want to prove that I am good enough to play elsewhere. I feel that if I don't make the break now, I will remain a Third and Fourth Division player all my life and that is not what I would want.'

Soon afterwards, Peter went for a four-day trial with Ipswich Town, under Bobby Robson. He had been watched on several occasions by Ipswich scout Ron Gray, and things looked good when the trial period was extended. But, eventually, Peter moved to Second Division Orient – the fee involved was believed to be around £45,000, which was well below the Rovers asking price of around £75,000. It was said that Orient saw Peter as the man to solve their goal drought, which had carried the side to within a hair's breadth of relegation to the Third Division. After the transfer was completed, Peter said 'I am really happy that I am at last moving into higher football. I have had my good times at Rovers,

now I must start again and prove myself with Orient. I know I will be under pressure to score goals, but that is the strong part of my game and I cannot wait for the season to start.'

Peter played a major role in Orient reaching the FA Cup semi-final in 1978. Later, he played for Fulham, Cardiff City, Hong Kong, Orient (again) and Chester City, before retiring in 1985. Before joining the Hong Kong club Happy Valley in July 1982, Peter was offered terms by Rovers manager Billy Bremner and three other English clubs. He was also offered a trial period with Dutch side Sparta Rotterdam, but plumped for Happy Valley, one of Hong Kong's two biggest clubs. Their offer was believed to have been financially superior to the ones Peter was offered to stay at home. Rovers' assistant manager Dave Bentley said: 'Peter has not contacted us with a final decision on our offer, but he did mention the last time we spoke to him that he had received a couple of offers from abroad.'

Joseph Daniel Laidlaw
Midfield 1976-1979

Football League
Appearances: 127 (+1 as substitute)
Goals: 27

FA Cup
Appearances: 5
Goals: 1

FL Cup
Appearances: 9
Goals: 0

Total appearances: 142

Midfielder Joe Laidlaw was born up in the north-east at Whickham in July 1950. He joined Middlesbrough as an apprentice professional and signed pro in August 1967. He made his first-team debut for the Boro later that season. He went on to make 104 League appearances, as well as 7 as substitute, and scored 20 goals, before joining Carlisle United during the close season of 1972. Whilst there he notched up 146 League appearances and 5 as substitute and bagged 44 goals. He came to Belle Vue in May 1976 and in the *Doncaster Evening Post* of 21 May 1976, under the heading 'Anderson gets Joe Laidlaw'. Rovers manager Stan Anderson said: 'We got him against some pretty stiff opposition from clubs much better placed than we are, clubs in higher divisions of the Football League. But he wanted to join a progressive club, he wants to be successful, and Doncaster is the place for that.'

It was also reported that the twenty-five-year-old, who was best known as a striker, had also been a midfielder – the position in which Stan Anderson was likely to play him. The departure of Les Chappell had left this spot a vacant one and the Rovers boss knew Joe's capabilities since he had been one of his men whilst Anderson was manager of Middlesbrough.

Joe went on to do sterling work and he became a favourite with the crowd. He marked his League debut for the Rovers with a brace of goals in a 2-2 draw at Southport in August 1976. He won many friends with his hard no-nonsense tackling in midfield, although this was not his only strength. He could pass the ball with some precision, and his powerful shooting, especially from long range, was always likely to cause problems to any defence. Joe was a specialist at penalty kicks. The secret of his success in this department lay in the fact that Joe was a 'blaster', and his spot-kicks were invariably aimed dead centre, with the sheer pace of the ball beating the goalkeeper. His 8 successful spot-kicks during a season remain a club record. He stayed until 1979, joining Portsmouth for a fee of £15,000 in June 1979, and then Hereford United, and finally Mansfield Town. He retired from the first-class game in 1983, with 118 goals in just over 500 League games.

John Christopher Lawlor

Inside forward 1950-1954

Football League
Appearances: 127
Goals: 47

FA Cup
Appearances: 8
Goals: 2

FL Cup
Appearances: -
Goals: -

Total appearances: 135

Known as Kit Lawlor, John was born in Dublin on 3 December 1922. Together with fellow Irishman Chris Giles, he joined Rovers under Peter Doherty in June 1950 from Drumcondra. This was just after Rovers had made a small tour of Ireland after winning promotion from the Third Division (North). But promotion had been achieved at great expense, and a number of players were released in the close season. This was the backdrop against which Kit made his first-team debut in the Second Division home game against Southampton on 30 August 1950. He replaced Tommy Martin, who had been injured in a previous game. The Southampton game ended in a 0-0 draw and was watched by 23,444. He played at inside right on that day, and his colleagues on the front line were Calverley, Doherty, Harrison and Tindill.

During his time with Rovers, he played in both inside forward positions. Kit scored his first Rovers goal in the away game at Hull City on 9 September. His first goal at home was netted in the thrilling 4-3 win against Manchester City in front of 32,937 spectators. Rovers had clawed their way back to win after being 3-0 down at half-time. At the end of his first season, Kit saw Rovers finish eleventh and he also won a cap whilst playing for the Republic of Ireland. From 33 League appearances, he had scored 10 goals.

However, during October 1951, Kit went home to Dublin and insisted that he was not coming back. Chris Giles also went home, but then both players returned in December, the whole incident being quickly forgotten. At the end of the 1951/52 season, both players disappeared once more. Giles never returned, but Kit came back during November and carried on where he had left off.

During December, Kit was transferred back to Ireland and in time made way for the young Alick Jeffrey to make his mark. A headline in the *Doncaster Gazette* of Thursday 16 December 1954 read: 'Kit Lawlor goes home: Coll is replacement.' Beneath this was the following information: 'Kit Lawlor, Doncaster Rovers' Eire international inside forward, was transferred to the Irish club, Ballymena United [last] Friday and the Rovers signed twenty-three-year-old Liam Coll, an outside right or inside forward, in exchange.' It was added that the move came as a surprise to most Doncaster fans, but Lawlor, described as a brilliant ball-player and a fine opportunist, had been anxious to return to his own country to his wife and children. Kit's last game for Rovers was in the Second Division away game at Leeds United on 13 November 1954. In total, Kit gained 3 full Irish caps.

Anthony Leighton
Striker 1959-1962

Football League
Appearances: 84
Goals: 44

FA Cup
Appearances: 2
Goals: 0

FL Cup
Appearances: 2
Goals: 1

Total appearances: 88

Striker Tony Leighton hit the back of the net with astounding regularity for nearly every team he represented. Starting at Rovers and carrying on with his subsequent clubs, he had a hit rate of a goal every other game. He was born in Leeds on 27 November 1939, and after enjoying success at schoolboy level, he signed for the Elland Road club, shortly after his seventeenth birthday. However, he never turned out in the Leeds United first-team colours, and instead signed for Rovers in June 1959.

He made his debut on 27 August 1959 in the Fourth Division home game against Millwall, which finished in a 0-0 draw. His first Rovers League goal was at home against Barrow on 8 September. From the end of that month, he was out of action until February, but then scored 3 goals in 3 games. By the end of the season, he had bagged 15 goals in 26 League games. He was also leading scorer in the reserves with 16 goals in 14 games, hitting 6 goals against Stockport Reserves at Belle Vue in January 1960. The 1960/61 season was his best for Rovers, recording 16 goals in 28 games.

In his last term at Belle Vue, he was once again Rovers' top marksman and following a clear-out at Belle Vue at the end of the 1961/62 season, arguably brought about by the abolition of the maximum wage in professional football, he was given a free transfer. Under the heading 'Rovers' retained list shock for seniors', the *Yorkshire Evening Post* of 2 May 1962 announced: 'There were shocks in the post this morning for several Doncaster Rovers senior professionals, who were informed that they had been given free transfers by the Belle Vue club. This list contains such well-known names as goalkeeper Willie Nimmo, centre forward Tony Leighton, wing-half or inside forward Jack Haigh, winger Bobby Lodge and full-back John Parry. Tom Garnett, general manager and secretary of Rovers, commented on the retained list. 'Our team manager, Oscar Hold, has assessed the playing staff and reported to the board of directors on whom he wants to keep and who should be given free transfers, and for whom replacements have to be found.'

Tony subsequently joined Barnsley in May 1962. Whilst at Barnsley, he also played well at cricket, appearing in the Doncaster & District Cricket League for local team Hatfield Town. At one point in a season, he had a batting average of 120, which attracted an offer from the Lancashire County Club. Playing football at Oakwell, he averaged better than a goal every two games before moving across West Yorkshire to Huddersfield Town in January 1965. Whilst with the Terriers, he continued his goal-scoring ways, bagging 40 goals in 90 League outings.

Leighton finally ended his professional career at Bradford City, having moved there in March 1968. He then held the position of player-manager at Bradford Park Avenue and fought hard, along with many others, to keep the ailing club alive. He was relieved of his duties in October 1973. Tony died aged just forty, from multiple sclerosis.

Stephen Haley Lister
Central defender 1979-1985

Football League
Appearances: 228 (+8 as substitute)
Goals: 30

FA Cup
Appearances: 16
Goals: 0

FL Cup
Appearances: 14
Goals: 1

Total appearances: 266

Steve was born in Doncaster on 18 November 1961. He signed as an apprentice in the summer of 1978, before accepting professional terms during May 1979, when Billy Bremner was the manager. Steve made his debut in the Fourth Division home game against Reading on 20 March 1979. In the team on that day were: Peacock, Lister, Flanagan, Hemsley, Bradley, Cannell, Lewis, French, Lewis, Bentley and Pugh. The match ended in a 2-2 draw, with 2,487 in attendance. Between that day and the end of the season, he recorded 9 League appearances.

He played his part in the team that finished third at the end of the 1980/81 season. During that period, Steve made 36 League outings (3 as substitute) and scored 3 goals. His first goal for the club was scored on 11 September 1979, in the home game versus Torquay United.

In subsequent seasons, he made regular appearances in the side playing alongside other former apprentices and youth-team members, including Ian and Glynn Snodin, Shaun Flanagan, Tommy Meagan and Glenn Humphries. They all experienced the joy of promotion and ignominy of relegation during Billy Bremner's reign between 1978 and 1985. Steve also shared with them the joy and despair of the cup games, winning at home against QPR in the FA Cup but then losing in the next round at Goodison to Everton.

Steve played his last game for Rovers on 11 May 1985 in the Third Division away game against Gillingham. He refused to sign a new contract during the early close season and moved along with Billy Russell to Scunthorpe during July 1985. Steve played for them on 176 occasions (6 as substitute) and scored 30 goals. He went on loan for a period to York City from March 1991.

Football League
Appearances: 84 (+1 as substitute)
Goals: 11

FA Cup
Appearances: 6
Goals: 2

FL Cup
Appearances: 2
Goals: 0

Total appearances: 93

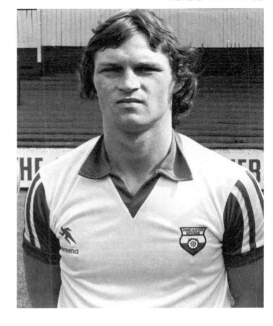

Early in December 1979, it was announced that Rovers were splashing out a club record fee for Barnsley midfield player Alan Little, in an attempt to step up their bid for promotion from the Fourth Division. Twenty-four-year-old Alan, the brother of former Aston Villa striker Brian Little, was to go into the first team in place of Dave Bentley, who had taken a new role as reserve- and youth-team coach.

Alan was born in Horden on 5 February 1955. During his career, he was a much-travelled player and spent time at three other clubs before arriving at Belle Vue, then under manager Billy Bremner, in December 1979. The previous clubs were Aston Villa (2 appearances, 1 as substitute), Southend (102 appearances, 1 as substitute, 12 goals) and Barnsley (91 appearances, 14 goals). Even though the fee was allegedly the largest Rovers had ever paid for a player, manager Billy Bremner stuck to his usual policy of refusing to divulge the amount, but it was believed to be about £30,000. Bremner also added: 'I believe [Alan] can be a big asset to the team. I've been watching him for some time and now the opportunity has arisen to sign him.'

Alan made his debut for Rovers in the Fourth Division home game against Darlington on 21 December 1979. He played in midfield alongside players including Flanagan, Lewis, Nimmo and Pugh. In his first season with the club, Alan made 22 appearances and scored 2 goals. At the end of the 1980/81 campaign, he won the Player of the Season award, having appeared in 37 League games and scored 7 goals. On 13 October 1982, it was revealed that Rovers were near to clinching a swap deal in which 'record signing Alan Little will join Torquay in exchange for defender Clive Wiggington, who had spent the end of the previous season on loan at Belle Vue.' Alan was widely regarded as one of the hardest tacklers in the game, but Bremner, without money to spend on transfers, had to trade players to make signings. However, in a parting shot, Bremner said 'Alan always gave 100 per cent effort.'

In October 1982, he was transferred to Torquay United (51 appearances and 4 goals) and then Halifax Town (68 appearances and 6 goals) and Hartlepool United (12 appearances and 1 goal).

Edward James McMorran

Forward 1952-1958

Football League
Appearances: 128
Goals: 32

FA Cup
Appearances: 13
Goals: 6

FL Cup
Appearances: 0
Goals: 0

Total appearances: 141

Eddie McMorran was a typical tough, bustling 1950s centre forward, playing his heart out and giving as good as he got without complaint. This type of player is always popular at Belle Vue and the fans took to him even though he didn't score many goals.

Eddie was a native of Northern Ireland, born in Larne on 2 September 1923. He was a schoolboy international and started work as a fireman on the Irish railways, until training as a blacksmith in a local paper mill. He joined Linfield as an amateur and, after a short period with Larne FC, he turned professional with Belfast Celtic. At this club, he won his first full cap for Northern Ireland, against England, and began to attract the attention of scouts from across the water. In August 1947, he moved to Manchester City. After eighteen months with them, making 33 outings and scoring 12 goals, he went to Leeds United. Whilst at Elland Road, he made 38 appearances and bagged 6 goals.

In a reputed £10,000 deal during July 1950, McMorran was transferred to Barnsley, where he won a second Northern Ireland cap. At Oakwell, he donned the first-team shirt 104 times and found the back of the net on 32 occasions.

Eddie came to Belle Vue in February 1953, in a deal which saw the Rovers pay a record fee of around £8,000, which allowed their South

Yorkshire rivals to recoup some of their previous outlay. He made his Rovers debut in the Second Division home game against Southampton. Rovers won the game 1-0 in front of a crowd of 16,787. Eddie soon settled in well with his Belle Vue team-mates and whilst he was enjoying life with Rovers on the field, away from it was a different story.

Within weeks of his marriage to wife Muriel, she contracted an illness which left her an invalid for the rest of her life. Putting this aside, Eddie continued to give 100 per cent to Rovers, and it was stated that it had always been a habit of the player to give his best before the biggest crowds.

Probably his best ever game for the Rovers was in the third round of the FA Cup against Sunderland at Roker Park, when he scored both of Rovers' goals in their 2-0 win before a crowd of 49,435. This was one of the shock wins of the round. By the time he left Belle Vue in November 1957, he had scored 32 goals in 128 League games.

His next club was Crewe Alexandra in the Northern Section. The fee was not stated, but it was understood that Crewe, who were at the foot of the table with only eight points from sixteen matches, had paid only a nominal fee for a player whom they hoped would provide experience in their attack. Eddie made 24 appearances with Crewe and scored 6 goals. He won his fifteenth and final international cap just months before announcing his retirement at thirty-five. Eddie moved back to Larne in 1981 and died there three years later.

Brian Makepeace
Full-back 1951-1961

Football League
Appearances: 353
Goals: 0

FA Cup
Appearances: 27
Goals: 0

FL Cup
Appearances: 0
Goals: 0

Total appearances: 380

Brian was a consistent and solid full-back, making 353 League appearances for Rovers over a ten-year period. He was born at Rossington on 6 October 1931 and worked at Rossington Colliery as a surface worker, repairing wagons before joining Rovers under Jackie Bestall on a part-time basis at seventeen. 'At first, I used to get about £3 a week and train at Belle Vue at nights,' said Brian, 'and it was not until I was twenty-six that I went full-time.' He had played for the Rossington Colliery side and started out as a centre half, but converted to right-back.

He made his Rovers debut in the Second Division home game against Blackburn Rovers on 17 February 1951. There was a crowd of 21,605, but unfortunately Rovers lost the game 4-2. His colleagues in the back line that day were Hardwick, Graham, Bycroft, Miller and Jones.

Although Brian made a large number of appearances, he never scored a goal for Rovers, although an own goal was credited to him. When pressed, Brian said that he would describe himself as a good, honest, hard-working and dedicated player. He was never sent off, but was booked on a number of occasions. 'I was always told,' said Brian, 'that if you kept your hands down and your mouth shut, you would be OK.'

He considered one of the most exciting games that he competed in to be the first round FA Cup tie away at Roker Park, Sunderland, on 9 January 1954. Rovers surprised everyone by beating the First

Division side 2-0. 'It was particularly satisfying,' said Brian, 'because their team included noted players such as Billy Elliott and Len Shackleton.' Much of Brian's football at Rovers was played in the Second Division and in front of crowds at Belle Vue averaging 22,799. Brian paid tribute to manager Peter Doherty, whom he considered to be a very intelligent, fair man who was not afraid to give a player a roasting when it was necessary. 'During the first half in a game at Southampton,' recalled Brian, 'I was playing badly and Peter Doherty told me so in no uncertain terms at half-time. I did much better in the second half and at the end of the game the manager made a point of congratulating me. But he wanted my full commitment for ninety minutes next time. He was a genuine man and as long as you gave 1000 per cent he was OK. I think the club went down hill after he left.'

Brian mentioned that during his time there was a good team spirit, and if he had to single out the best players he had lined up alongside he would choose Alick Jeffrey, Bill Paterson and Harry Gregg. He said that for part of his time as a player, he struggled with a stomach muscle problem. 'I think that I returned to play quicker than I ought to have done,' said

Brian, 'and that aggravated the problem, cutting my career short. That's one good thing about the substitute system today – a player can come off the field and not aggravate an injury. In my day, the only way players were going to get off the field after being injured was on a stretcher.'

The *Doncaster Chronicle* of 4 May 1961 reported that the drastic pruning of their senior professional playing staff by Doncaster Rovers had not come as a surprise, although the decision to give 50 per cent of the players a free transfer would no doubt have shocked some of the club's supporters. No more than twelve senior players had been offered terms for the following season. Rovers chairman, J.G. Garnham, made the comment: 'We have had to make these drastic cuts for the obvious reason

[that] we have been getting insufficient support in revenue.' The same newspaper said the following about Brian: 'Two of the players from whom Rovers have parted – Brian Makepeace and Ronnie Walker – are long-service men and have never been on the books of any other League club. Ironically, they both played in the final matches of the season, and played well too. In each case, the player has given the Rovers loyal service, and if the financial position had been better, no doubt the Rovers would have retained these two.'

For a time after leaving Belle Vue, Brian played at Scarborough, Boston and Worksop. He then worked for a considerable time at International Harvesters (which later became Case International) in Doncaster.

David Miller
Wing half 1947-1953

Football League
Appearances: 140
Goals: 3

FA Cup
Appearances: 7
Goals: 1

FL Cup
Appearances: 0
Goals: 0

Total appearances: 147

Dave Miller was born in Middlesbrough on 21 January 1921. He played at three clubs before joining Rovers under manager J.G. Bestall, but made few appearances for them. His former clubs were Middlesbrough in September 1938 (no appearances); Wolverhampton Wanderers in August 1945 (2 appearances) and Derby County in April 1947 (1 appearance).

The *Yorkshire Evening Post* of Thursday 15 January 1948 said that Dave had been a regular playing member in County's Central League side. Owing to the fact that the Rams had a particularly good back line, he had been unable to command a place in the first team. His only appearance with County was against Sunderland at Roker Park, when he led the attack at a time when Derby were experiencing considerable difficulty with the centre-forward position. It was also mentioned that Dave could also play at centre half and was regarded as a robust, aggressive and attacking wing-half and that his acquisition should do a great deal to strengthen a weakness in the Rovers side.

At nearly 6ft, Dave made his Rovers debut at West Ham on 24 January 1948, with 17,082 in attendance. Whilst Dave made his debut in this game, two well-known players made their last appearance in a Rovers shirt: Clarrie Jordan and Ernie Swallow. With Dave in the back line that day were: Hardwick, Swallow, Bycroft, Stirland and Tomlinson. He did not play in the next home game, but appeared in the following away game. After that, he was absent for the rest of the term through a recurring muscle injury.

At the end of the season, Rovers were relegated to the Third Division (North). Dave was still living in Wolverhampton at this time, and he regularly visited a specialist there who carried out an intensive programme of manipulative exercises on Dave's muscle injury. It was diagnosed as 'an adhesion of the muscles' and the treatment brought Dave back to full fitness. During the following season, Dave was part of the defence that conceded only 40 League goals. This was largely due to the defensive play by Dave, Syd Bycroft and Sid Goodfellow.

Dave competed for his place in the half-back line with Arnold Lowes. He also played in the game against Hull City on 2 October 1948 which saw the largest ever crowd at Belle Vue – 37,099.

When Dave eventually moved to Doncaster, he found lodgings at a Mrs Baker's in Rainton Road. Also there at the time were Bert Tindill, Sid Goodfellow and Georgio Antonio. In the 1949/50 campaign, with Peter Doherty installed as player-manager and Ray Harrison leading the attack, Rovers won the Third Division (North) championship. During this time, Dave made 12 appearances. Dave's reward for performing so well in the 1950/51 season (playing 38 League games) was that Peter Doherty made him captain of the side. Dave led by example, being a formidable, hard opponent in Rovers' middle line. It was also reported that he 'was one of the best constructive wing-halves the Rovers have ever had.' The crowds responded too – at one time during his sojourn at Belle Vue, the average gate was 22,799 per match.

Dave was transferred to Aldershot during March 1954 (11 appearances). Shortly before the transfer, the *Yorkshire Evening Post* of 19 February 1954 informed readers: 'He lost his place in Rovers' first team in February last year and has only played in an odd game since, although he has been leading the forward line with skill for most of the season, helping to put them on top of the Midland League.'

Football League
Appearances: 124
Goals: 14

FA Cup
Appearances: 4
Goals: 0

FL Cup
Appearances: 11
Goals: 0

Total appearances: 139

Rovers' Scottish ginger-haired winger Ian Miller once finished in the top three of a professional footballers' national sprint championship. No wonder then he regularly left defenders for dead, whilst providing strikers O'Callaghan and Kitchen with goal opportunities during some of the best years of football seen at Belle Vue.

Ian was born in Perth, Scotland in May 1955, but started in football as an apprentice at Bury in August 1973. He made his League debut for the Shakers later in the 1973/74 season. He played a further 8 League games for them before Nottingham Forest signed him during the summer of 1974. Curiously, he did not have a single League outing whilst at the City Ground. Within twelve months, he featured in a remarkable transfer, which saw Terry Curran move to Forest, with goalkeeper Dennis Peacock, Ian and a handsome cash adjustment in return. 'Windy', as he became known at Belle Vue, impressed from his first game, which was the Fourth Division game against Crewe on 30 August 1975.

During this year, Rovers recorded their highest number of goals scored for the past ten seasons. At the end of the 1975/76 season, he was voted the supporters' club Player of the Year. He won this award again during the following year. However, the 1977/78 season saw the break-up of the Miller-Kitchen-O'Callaghan trio. Ian joined Swindon Town (123 appearances, 4 as substitute and 9 goals) during July 1978 in another player/cash deal. His other clubs included Blackburn Rovers (252 appearances, 16 as substitute and 16 goals), Port Vale (14 games, 7 as substitute, 1 goal) and Scunthorpe United (8 appearances, 4 as substitute).

John Mooney

Winger 1953-1959

Football League
Appearances: 168
Goals: 33

FA Cup
Appearances: 14
Goals: 4

FL Cup
Appearances: 0
Goals: 0

Total appearances: 182

Johnny Mooney, the skilful and much-admired Rovers right-winger of the 1950s, was born in Fauldhouse, situated eighteen miles from Edinburgh, on 21 February 1926. Johnny, as he was popularly known, signed from Hamilton Academical during May 1953. The Accies were his only previous club, and he had joined them from junior football. At the time, several other clubs had been in the running for him, including Aldershot, the Irish club Distillery and Southport. During the previous season, Rovers had finished thirteenth in the Second Division and playing at this level convinced Mooney to head to Doncaster.

In the summer he arrived, Alf Calverley and Jack Hodgson retired and other signings made included Paddy Gavin and Reece Nicholson. Johnny's brother, Frankie, also played on the right wing, and for a time he was with Blackburn. On one occasion that the brothers came up against each other, the Lancashire side beat Rovers 7-2.

Johnny gave an impressive performance on his debut, with Rovers' reserves in the Midland League game against Mansfield at the outset of the 1953/54 season, and topped it by scoring two goals. Johnny made his debut at outside right in the Second Division away game against Bristol Rovers on 24 August 1953. Rovers won the game 1-0 through a goal by McMorran, with a massive crowd of 28,117 in attendance. With him on the forward line were Tindill, Lawlor, Harrison and McMorran. Jack Hodgson, Rovers' reserve-team manager, was impressed by Johnny's skill and he would have destined for more first-team appearances, but a number of pulled muscles restricted these for the remainder of the season, and he could manage just another 7 outings.

In the following season, he became more accustomed to the physical demands of Second Division English football, making 32 League appearances and scoring on 6 occasions. He also played in all 5 of the FA Cup games against First Division Aston Villa and scored in one of them, Rovers eventually emerging as winners. For one of the games, there were 57,800 spectators – this is the highest crowd that Rovers have ever played in front of.

Whilst at Belle Vue, Johnny could not fail to be impressed with his team-mates, who included Harry Gregg, Bill Paterson, Len Graham, Bert Tindill and the young promising star Alick Jeffrey. It was Bert Tindill and Johnny displaying their trickery on the flanks that provided the opportunities for strikers such as McMorran and, eventually, Alick Jeffrey. It was once said of Johnny that he was a great trier: 'he goes hard from start to finish.' One of his finest moments for Rovers was scoring a hat-trick in the Second Division home game against Swindon on 1 December 1956. Rovers won 4-0 in front of a 13,143 crowd, and the opposing side included noted players and personalities such as Johnny Haynes and Jimmy Hill.

In recalling his own best personal performance, Johnny mentioned the home game against Nottingham Forest in the third round of the FA Cup on 7 January 1956, when it was reported that he played a 'blinder'. In recalling goal-scoring memories, he mentioned that the majority of his strikes were hit with his right foot from close range, but a thirty-yard drive with his left peg in the home game against Notts County on 8 April 1955, with 12,223 watching, held one of the best memories for him. Some of the opposing defenders against whom he enjoyed testing his skills included George Hardwick, the Middlesbrough and England full-back, and the Blackburn full-back, Bill Eckersley.

Johnny's career with Rovers ended after the 1958/59 season, when manager Jack Crayston put him on the transfer list. Thereafter, John played for Southern Leaguers Boston United and Retford Town in the Midland League, before returning for a spell to Scotland. However, he came back to Doncaster and worked for a time as a technical assistant at Bridon, and also found time to coach and eventually manage the Frickley Colliery side. Johnny died in 2000.

Darren Mark Moore
Central defender 1995-1997

Football League
Appearances: 76
Goals: 7

FA Cup
Appearances: 0
Goals: 0

FL Cup
Appearances: 4
Goals: 0

Total appearances: 80

Darren was born on 22 April 1974. He signed for Torquay United during November 1992 and played 102 games, 1 as substitute, and scored 8 goals. He was transferred to Belle Vue during July 1995. The 6ft 2in defender made his debut in the Third Division game against Scarborough on 12 August 1995. He played 35 games in the 1995/96 season.

During June 1997, he was transferred to Bradford City, agreeing a three-year contract with the Valley Parade outfit. Initially, Rovers slapped a £750,000 fee on his head, but the final sum was decided by a tribunal. Player-manager Kerry Dixon said: 'Some people might think that figure is a little over the top for a Division Three player, but it is how highly we rate Darren. He is only a young man and we consider him to be the best centre half in the lower divisions. He is unbeatable in the air and he is very quick for such a big man. I

am sorry to see Darren go, but with all that is happening at the club at the moment, maybe the money we receive from him will eventually go towards saving the club.'

Over the previous two seasons, Darren had won the supporters' club Player of the Season award. Darren said he had mixed feelings about leaving the club. 'I am excited by the challenge offered by Bradford, but at the same time I am sorry to be leaving Doncaster because I have been happy here ... I always gave 100 per cent for Doncaster Rovers every time I went out and I think that the fans respected me for that ... Hopefully, the money the club will get for me will help it to survive.'

At Bradford he made 62 appearances, scoring 3 goals. In 1999, he was transferred to Portsmouth. He is a Jamaican international and now plays for West Bromwich Albion.

Steve Nicol

Full-back/Midfield 1998-1999

Football Conference
Appearances: 25
Goals: 0

FA Cup
Appearances: 5
Goals: 0

FA Trophy
Appearances: 1
Goals: 0

Total appearances: 31

Although Steve only made 31 appearances for Rovers (25 in the League, 5 in the FA Cup and 1 in the FA Trophy), he left such an impression on Rovers fans that it was deemed fit to include him in this book. He is arguably one of the best players to have turned out for the club since its fall from the Football League in 1998. No one during the dark days of the previous season would ever have guessed that in the following campaign in the Conference that a player of Steve's calibre would turn out in the club's colours. Rovers struggled for much of the first season in the Conference, but Steve helped to turn things round, providing the team with a much-needed anchor at the back. He also firmly held his ground in the midfield, especially when he was partnered with two other 'name' players, Dave Penney and John Sheridan.

Steve was born in Irvine on 11 December 1961. Initially, he played for Ayr United before moving to Liverpool (328 games, 15 as a substitute, and 36 goals), winning every domestic honour. He played there throughout most of the 1980s and during the early 1990s alongside many Anfield greats. These included Alan Hansen, Kenny Dalglish and Mark Lawrenson.

He was voted Footballer of the Year in 1989. Steve was also a Scottish international, turning out 21 times for the Under-21 side and on 27 occasions for the first team. From Liverpool he moved to Notts County, in January 1995 (32 games and 2 goals), Sheffield Wednesday, (41 games, 8 as substitute) and a loan period at West Bromwich Albion in 1997.

He came to Belle Vue in the club's first season in the Conference – 1998/99 – with Glynn and Ian Snodin at the helm, and made his debut on 12 September 1998 in the away game at Hayes. This was in front of 773 fans and Rovers lost 2-0. Rovers' defence and midfield at that time included Simon Shaw, Kevin McIntyre, Lee Warren, Dave Penney and Colin Sutherland. Steve played in both games against Rushden & Diamonds in the second round of the FA Cup, with Rovers eventually losing 4-2. Later in the season, in March 1999, Steve moved to the United States and eventually became coach of New England Revolution. He played his last match for Rovers in the home game against Stevenage on 26 March 1999. He is pictured in the Rovers programme for the second-leg final tie against Farnborough Town on 3 May 1999 with the following caption alongside: 'Steve Nicol receives his Player of the Month award for October from members of our Lincoln branch of the supporters club. Steve was a runaway leader in the overall table at the time of his departure for America in March.' In the programme for the home game against Stevenage, the manager at the time, Ian Snodin, had the following to say: 'During [Steve's] stay at Belle Vue, he has proved a marvellous acquisition, always giving nothing less than 100 per cent during both training and the 31 games he has played for us ... He has been a pleasure to work with and leaves with my very best wishes.

John Purcel Nicholson

Centre half 1965-1966

Football League
Appearances: 41
Goals: 0

FA Cup
Appearances: 2
Goals: 0

FL Cup
Appearances: 2
Goals: 0

Total appearances: 45

After one appearance for Liverpool and an illustrious career at Port Vale, playing 184 games, John Nicholson joined Rovers for £6,000 at the end of September 1965. 'Nicco', as he was known, was born on 2 September 1936 in Liverpool. He was discovered by Doncaster's 'man in the Midlands'. First of all, he found Graham Ricketts, followed by John Wylie and then John Nicholson. He had seen John Nicholson on many occasions during the previous three seasons and, following his reports, general manager Tom Garnett, player-manager Bill Leivers and chief scout Jack Bestall had seen him too.

It was reported that John, with the fantastic record of being a constant feature in Port Vale's team for four consecutive seasons, was never up for transfer. But after playing in nearly 200 games on the run, he was dropped because the club thought he might benefit from a break after such an amazing run. Where other players might have welcomed a rest, John became unsettled and the Rovers were quick to step in. The deal was clinched at a cost to Rovers of around £6,000. The Port Vale fans were not happy at all. An article in

a local newspaper said: 'Without exception they [Vale supporters] made gloomy prophesies and there were even a couple of threats to boycott the club [because of selling John]. Nicholson was a mighty popular player.'

John made his debut for Rovers at Newport County on 25 September 1965. Although Rovers suffered a heavy defeat in this game, John's influence in defence and as captain was to play a major part in the team winning the Fourth Division championship at the end of the season. Most fans will remember him reappearing from the dressing room not long after the whistle had blown on the away game at Bradford City, the last fixture of the of the 1965/66 season, and shouting 'We want to thank you all, you're great.' It had truly been a great season, Rovers were promoted and in time became Fourth Division champions.

John played 39 League games in his first season at Belle Vue. He either played at left-back or centre half, but mainly the latter one. Curiously, he never scored a goal for Rovers in the League or any of the cup competitions. There were great hopes from

the fans for the 1966/67 season and the team had a good start.

Unfortunately, however, John played his last game on Tuesday 30 August 1966, in the 5-2 League Cup first round victory replay at home against Bradford City. Early in the morning of 1 September, his car was involved in a collision with a lorry near Butterbusk Farm at Warmsworth, two miles west of Doncaster. As a result of the injuries he sustained, John died two days later. Team-mate Alick Jeffrey was with him and

lucky to escape with comparatively light injuries. John's death was mourned by everyone and the club immediately set up a memorial fund. On 31 October 1966, Bill Shankly kindly brought his Liverpool team for a game at Belle Vue against a Rovers Representative XI, which included George Best, in aid of the memorial fund. Over 14,000 attended the game, raising £2,730. Various other fundraising events took place, and John's widow finally received a cheque for around £4,000.

William Brown Nimmo

Goalkeeper 1957-1962

Football League
Appearances: 182
Goals: 0

FA Cup
Appearances: 11
Goals: 0

FL Cup
Appearances: 4
Goals: 0

Total appearances: 197

Willie, said to have been a hero of Kevin Keegan's (and who could have a better accolade than that?), was born in Forth on 11 January 1934. He played for Alloa Athletic before joining Leeds United during February 1956. At Elland Road, he only made 1 appearance before joining Rovers in March 1958. The 1957/58 season was a very difficult and significant one in Rovers' history, as it had seen the departure of arguably Rovers' most inspiring and successful manager, Peter Doherty, and the subsequent installation of the joint managership of Jack Hodgson and Syd Bycroft. All this was set against the backdrop of the team nose-diving to the Third Division. Other goalkeepers used during that season included Harry Gregg, before his departure to Manchester United, and David McIntosh. Willie made his debut in the Second Division home game against Lincoln City on

12 April 1958. Unfortunately, this was not a happy occasion, as the game was lost 3-1 in front of a crowd of 9,459. Amongst Willie's team-mates on that day were Charlie Williams, Tommy Cavanagh, Brian Makepeace, Ronnie Walker and Maurice White. In his second season with the club, under the new managership of Jack Crayston, the former Arsenal boss, Willie made 44 out of a possible 46 League appearances and played in all 3 FA Cup ties. However, Rovers' misfortune continued with a drop into the Fourth Division at the end of the season. During the 1959/60 season, Willie played in every League and cup game. In the 1960/61 period, he only missed 1 game and in the following season appeared in every League, FA Cup and League Cup game. He was eventually replaced between the sticks by Fred Potter. He was transferred to Mansfield Town in July 1962, but made no first-team appearances.

Brendan Richard O'Callaghan

Centre forward 1973-1978

Football League
Appearances: 184 (+3 as substitute)
Goals: 65

FA Cup
Appearances: 10
Goals: 2

FL Cup
Appearances: 15
Goals: 7

Total appearances: 212

It has been argued that Brendan O'Callaghan was one of the most useful target-men and headers of the ball to have ever played for the club. He not only created many chances, but put them away too. Brendan was born in Bradford on 23 July 1955 and as a junior played at centre half for Bradford Boys, Yorkshire Boys and then the Great Britain Catholic Schools XI. He also excelled in athletics, becoming the Yorkshire Schools long jump champion. Later, he switched positions to centre forward and made his debut in that position for the Rovers Reserves during the 1972/73 season. This was all while he was still at school.

Brendan signed as a full-time professional for Rovers in July 1973. At just under eighteen and standing at 6ft 2in tall, he made his debut on 1 September 1973 at Bradford City. Rovers' team on that day included: Woods, Elwiss, Kitchen, Higgins and Irvine. In his first season, Brendan notched up 35 appearances (3 as substitute) and scored 10 goals.

By the mid-1970s, Brendan, along with his strike partner Peter Kitchen and winger Ian Miller, were terrorising Fourth Division defences. One of O'Callaghan's many goals for the club included a remarkable effort on 7 February 1976 at Huddersfield Town. Before scoring, Brendan had left the field to receive treatment. When the referee waved him back on with play still in motion, the strapping young striker ran, unmarked, half the length

of the field to score, much to the dismay and protests of the home defenders. Fans will also recall his memorable strike in the FA Cup tie away at Liverpool on 5 January 1974, where Rovers almost snatched surprise victory. The team went 2-1 in front after eighteen minutes, thanks to Brendan. Clever work by Peter Woods led to a cross and the Rovers striker was on hand to volley the ball past Liverpool goalkeeper Clemence and into the net.

Peter Kitchen's transfer in 1977 saw the break-up of a remarkable partnership and, in March 1978, Brendan moved to Stoke City, Rovers receiving £40,000 for him. The *Doncaster Evening Post* of 2 March 1978 recounted some of the background details surrounding the transfer. 'Stoke's new boss, Alan Durban, and his assistant, Howard Kendall, were at Rovers' home match with Grimsby Town last night, and after the game they had talks with O'Callaghan and Rovers' boss Stan Anderson. Durban has for some time been interested in signing the transfer-listed striker, and he made an unsuccessful offer, believed to be around £30,000, earlier this season, when he was managing Shrewsbury Town.'

Brendan stayed at Stoke until 1985 and switched to centre half towards the end of his time there. From the Victoria Ground, he moved to Oldham Athletic in February 1985, and his career came to an end shortly afterwards, having played only 10 games.

Brendan Thomas Christopher Ormsby

Central defender 1990-1992

Football League
Appearances: 78
Goals: 7

FA Cup
Appearances: 4
Goals: 0

FL Cup
Appearances: 3
Goals: 0

Total appearances: 85

Brendan was born in Birmingham on 1 October 1960. He was an England Schoolboy international and captain of the England Youth side. He was an apprentice with Aston Villa, before signing for them during October 1978. In time, he made 115 appearances (2 as substitute) and scored 4 goals. He played in the side that won the European Cup in 1982, although he missed out on the final victory over Bayern Munich. From there, he moved to Leeds United during February 1986 (46 appearances, 5 goals).

He scored on his debut for Leeds and captained the side on the tremendous FA Cup run when they reached the semi-final. Then it was on loan to Shrewsbury Town in January 1990 for a single appearance. He arrived at Belle Vue in July 1990 under Billy Bremner, who had signed him previously whilst manager at Leeds. He was to be immediately installed as club captain. A delighted Billy Bremner told the *Doncaster Star* on Friday 20 July 1990: 'I am very pleased he has agreed to sign. Apart from being a good player, Brendan is one of the best talkers on the pitch I've come across, and his ability to communicate and organise will be a tremendous asset. He has played in Europe and at international level as a youngster and it hasn't been an easy decision for him to drop down to the Fourth Division – but our supporters deserve the best.'

On arriving at Belle Vue, Brendan said: 'I haven't come here to sit around on my backside and waste away two years ... I wouldn't have come to Doncaster if I didn't believe they were ambitious to win promotion ... Doncaster made me a good offer, but obviously the opportunity to team up with my old manager Billy Bremner again was a big factor in my signing.' On being made Rovers captain he added: 'It's something I'm used to, but I feel it is a great honour to captain any side.'

Brendan made his debut in the Fourth Division away game against Carlisle United on 25 August 1990. Rovers won the game with 4,218 in attendance. In the back line with him were Crichton, Rankine, Brevett, Holmes and Douglas. In his first season, he made 43 outings and scored 4 goals, the team finishing eleventh. He was transferred to Scarborough in August 1992 (15 outings, 1 as substitute and scored 1 goal). For a time he was at Wigan Athletic (2 appearances) as a non-contract player, and has also been assistant manager at Waterford in Ireland and Farsley Celtic. Since leaving football, he has worked as a postman and for Leeds United's Football in the Community scheme.

William Alexander Kennedy Paterson

Centre half 1950-1954

Football League
Appearances: 113
Goals: 0

FA Cup
Appearances: 7
Goals: 0

FL Cup
Appearances: 0
Goals: 0

Total appearances: 120

Bill Paterson was born in Kinlochleven on 25 February 1930. According to the *Yorkshire Evening Post* of 15 October 1954, he never played serious football until he left school. His enthusiasm was so great, however, that he travelled ninety miles at weekends to play for Inverness Thistle in the Northern Scotland League. While in the Army and stationed at Newark, he guested for Midland League club Ransome & Marles. The *Yorkshire Evening Post* stated that Bill cost the Rovers only the £10 signing on fee, for he was discovered when playing in Army football – it was in a final and he was so outstanding that the Rovers lost no time in securing his services when his Army service ended.

He joined Rovers from Ransome & Marles in March 1950 and for a spell understudied veteran Syd Bycroft. He stood just over 6ft, and weighed 12st 4lb. His debut was in the Second Division away game at Chesterfield on 7 April 1951. With him in the back line on that day were Hardwick, Graham, Bycroft, Miller and Makepeace. Rovers won the game 3-1, with 13,833 in attendance. Bill was a Scottish B international and gained his first cap in March 1954 against England B at Roker Park. He had also the distinction of captaining the Scottish team – a great honour at only twenty-two years of age. At the time, Peter Doherty commented: 'I am delighted at the news [of him captaining the side] for no one has deserved the honour more. I know he will uphold the tradition of the club.'

It was reported that the player was in consistently good form during the 1953/54 season, but he reached peak form in the following campaign. When it became known that the Scottish selectors had twice sent representatives to watch him, it was generally realised that he had an excellent chance of gaining international honours for his country.

The *Yorkshire Evening Post* of 15 October 1954 also announced: 'The threat which Doncaster Rovers made some time ago, that they may have to part with some of their best players unless the gates at Belle Vue improved, was carried into effect today by the announcement that they had very reluctantly transferred their Scottish B international centre half, Bill Paterson, to Newcastle United.' After the negotiations had been completed, the Rovers chairman, H.A. Butler, said that Rovers had not wanted to part with Paterson, but they did not want to stand in the player's way. Butler added that he felt Bill would have a better chance of international honours with Newcastle. Then there was the burning question of gates at Belle Vue to consider – the club simply could not continue to pay its way on its present attendance. The fee received for Paterson would be a big help in their financial struggle. At Newcastle United, Bill played just 22 games and scored 1 goal between 1954 and 1957. He then joined Rangers in July 1958.

Dennis Peacock

Goalkeeper 1975-1980, 1982-1986

Football League
Appearances: 329
Goals: 0

FA Cup
Appearances: 14
Goals: 0

FL Cup
Appearances: 26
Goals: 0

Total appearances: 369

Late in July 1975, it was revealed that 6ft 2in goalkeeper Dennis Peacock was joining Rovers from Nottingham Forest on a month's loan. With Graham Brown still in America, playing summer football for Portland, Oregon, Dennis was certain to play in the pre-season friendlies for Rovers. Billy Millar, the amateur goalkeeper with the reserves in the season just past, had signed semi-professional forms for Alfreton, and would not be available to play for Rovers in the ensuing year. Rovers' third line of defence was young apprentice Mickey Wroe, yet manager Stan Anderson had made it clear that he wanted Wroe to get more experience at junior level before being pitched into League football.

Dennis, born in Lincoln on 19 April 1953, had been with Forest since joining as an apprentice, and was Forest's first choice after Jim Barron's departure for Swindon. But manager Brian Clough gave John Middleton a chance in goal and Middleton was preferred to Peacock at Forest. He made his debut in the Fourth Division home game against Cambridge United on 16 August 1975. On 28 August, the headlines on the front page of the *Doncaster Evening Post* announced: 'Rovers sell Curran, buy two players – and pocket £40,000.' It was revealed that Terry Curran, Rovers' winger, who twice asked for a move because he wanted a higher class of football, had joined Second Division Nottingham Forest for a fee 'in excess of £70,000'.

Rovers' boss wasted no time in spending some of the money. He gave Forest £30,000 back for goalkeeper Dennis Peacock and Ian Miller. Anderson added: 'On the face of it, it is a good deal for us.' He had replaced Curran, solved the problem of having only one experienced goalkeeper – and the club still had £40,000 left.

In the home game against Hartlepool on Tuesday 11 March 1980, Dennis received a Mecca long-service award to mark his 200th League appearance for the club. Only a day later came the announcement that he had linked up with ex-Rovers boss Stan Anderson once more, joining First Division Bolton Wanderers for £70,000. Rovers manager Billy Bremner, who rated Dennis as one of the top goalkeepers in the lower divisions, said that the sale was forced on the club by its financial position. He also added that he thought Bolton were getting Dennis very cheaply. The sale of Dennis would put Rovers 'in the black' on transfer deals. Willie Boyd was to replace Dennis between the sticks.

After making only 16 appearances with Bolton, Dennis returned to Doncaster on a free transfer in August 1982 and played a further 130 times for Rovers. For a period, he had a short spell on loan at Burnley, making 8 appearances for the Turf Moor side.

David Mark Penney
Midfield 1998-

Football League
Appearances: 83 (+11 as substitute)
Goals: 14

FA Cup
Appearances: 5 (+3 as substitute)
Goals: 0

FL Cup
Appearances: 5
Goals: 0

Total appearances: 107

Dave was born in Wakefield on 17 August 1964. On leaving school, he became a bricklayer and played for the Pontefract Colliery side. He signed for Derby County during September 1985, making 6 appearances and 13 as substitute. From there, he moved to Oxford United for a fee of £175,000 in June 1989 (76 appearances, 34 as substitute and 15 goals). He went on loan to Swansea City (12 outings and 3 goals) in March 1991, then signed for them during March 1994, playing on 112 occasions (7 as substitute) and scoring 20 goals. A further move followed, to Cardiff City in July 1997 (33 appearances, 2 as substitute and scored 5 goals).

He came to Belle Vue under the Snodin brothers for Rovers' first season in the Conference during the summer of 1998. He made his debut in the Nationwide Conference away game at Kingstonian on 29 August 1998. Resilient, reliable and with a 'takes no prisoners' attitude when he tackles, Dave is a player with a keen eye for goal who uses the ball intelligently in mid-field. He also has great leadership qualities, inspiring both young and old alike. He was captain of the side that beat Farnborough Town to win the Endsleigh Challenge Trophy.

Following the departure of the Snodin Brothers from Belle Vue towards the end of the 1999/2000 season, Dave became caretaker-manager along with Mark Atkins. The two experienced players helped guide the club to safety during the remainder of the season. At the start of 2000/01 season, Dave became reserve-team manager – the team won promotion at the first attempt. In time, Dave replaced Alan Lewer as assistant to manager Steve Wignall. When Steve Wignall left Belle Vue in January 2002, Dave became caretaker-manager, with the experienced youth-team coach Mickey Walker as his assistant. Dave took over the reins two months later.

Daral James Pugh

Winger 1978-1982

Football League
Appearances: 136 (+18 as substitute)
Goals: 15

FA Cup
Appearances: 9
Goals: 1

FL Cup
Appearances: 12
Goals: 1

Total appearances: 175

Daral was born in Neath on 5 June 1961. He joined Rovers as an apprentice in August 1977 and signed pro during December 1978. He made his debut as a substitute under manager Billy Bremner in the Fourth Division home game against Hereford United on 30 January 1979. A further substitute appearance was recorded before Daral made his first full outing on 10 February 1979 in the home game against Northampton Town. Amongst the forwards on that day were Mickey French and Jack Lewis.

In Daral's first season, he made 16 outings, 5 as substitute, and scored 1 goal. The goal came on 11 February 1979 in the 4-2 away victory at Crewe. At the end of the 1978/79 season, Rovers finished in twenty-second position, only scoring 50 goals and conceding 71.

In the 1979/80 season, he turned out in 37 games, scoring twice. This went some way towards helping the team to finish in twelfth place – a big improvement on the previous term. Then, in the promotion-winning side of 1980/81 – Rovers finishing in third place – he made 39 appearances, 3 as substitute and

found the net on 3 occasions. He was one of the main supply lines to the goalscorers, Nimmo and Warboys. In that year, Rovers scored 58 goals and conceded 48. Daral also played twice for the Welsh Under-21 side.

He was transferred to Huddersfield Town in September 1982 in a deal that involved Terry Austin moving to Belle Vue. Daral played his last match for Rovers on 25 September 1982, taking part in the 7-5 home victory over Reading. He received praise from Rovers' manager for the way he contributed to his farewell appearance: 'A lot of players on their way to a new club wouldn't have taken any chance ... but Daral fought for every ball and was a credit to his profession. He adopted a super attitude and everyone here wishes him well.'

Whilst at Huddersfield, Daral made 52 appearances, 33 as substitute, and scored 7 goals. A move to Rotherham United followed in July 1985 (106 appearances, 6 as substitute and 5 goals). He went on loan to Cambridge United (6 appearances, 1 goal) in December 1987 and then joined Torquay United during August 1988 (29 appearances, 3 as substitute).

Christopher Rabjohn
Midfield 1967-1973

Football League
Appearances: 137 (+16 as substitute)
Goals: 8

FA Cup
Appearances: 10
Goals: 1

FL Cup
Appearances: 5
Goals: 0

Total appearances: 168

Chris played his part in the Rovers Championship side of 1968/69, and he said that he rated the season as satisfying as any he had experienced during his career. 'Some players,' he quite rightly said, 'go all their lives without winning anything.' He was part of the 'Big Deal' in February 1968, which involved Harold Wilcockson, Colin Clish and himself moving to Belle Vue, under George Raynor, in exchange for cash, Dennis Leigh and Graham Watson. This made a reported nine players transferred from Millmoor in manager Tommy Docherty's short reign there.

Chris was born in Sheffield on 10 March 1945, and in his younger days played for Sheffield Boys, Sheffield Boys' Clubs and, to top them all, the England Boys' Clubs side. He was with Rotherham United Juniors before signing pro for them in July 1963. Whilst at Millmoor, he played 76 times, twice as substitute and scored 5 goals. It was once said that 'his silky skills had attracted the attention of First Division clubs.'

He made his first-team debut for Rovers as a right half in the Fourth Division away game at Bradford Park Avenue on 17 February 1968. Whilst at Belle Vue, he played as a defender,

midfield man and attacker, proving himself a really useful utility player. He once listed fishing, golfing and gardening as his main hobbies outside soccer. For the remainder of his first season with Rovers, he missed only 3 games, making a total of 15 appearances. During his second season, 1968/69, Chris played 28 times (1 as substitute) and scored 3 goals, the team eventually winning the Fourth Division championship and promotion.

In December 1968, Lawrie McMenemy was appointed manager, and he asked the players for consistency. Chris played no mean part in the team that responded by only losing 2 out of 28 League games, setting a new club record of 20 consecutive games without defeat. 'By doing this,' said McMenemy, 'they displayed the consistency which I had asked for ...' During that campaign, in finishing top the team scored 65 goals and conceded 38. In his last season for Rovers, 1972/73 – at this point managed by Maurice Setters – Chris played 36 times and scored 1 goal. He was released in the summer, along with his former Rotherham team-mate, Harold Wilcockson. Glen Johnson, Brian Joy, Brian Usher and Steve Briggs were also released.

Simon Mark Rankine
Right-back/Midfield 1987-1992

Football League
Appearances: 160 (+4 as substitute)
Goals: 20

FA Cup
Appearances: 8
Goals: 2

FL Cup
Appearances: 8 (+1 as substitute)
Goals: 1

Total appearances: 181

Mark started out in Rovers' junior squad and was very skilful and highly rated even at that stage. He was a consistent player who was always likely to pop up with a goal, but he played his games with Rovers at a time when financial problems were spiralling out of control. Amongst his many other achievements, Mark will always be remembered by Rovers fans for the splendid goal he scored in the FA Youth Cup semi-final game at White Hart Lane against Tottenham Hotspur in 1988. He also captained the team in the final.

Mark (nicknamed 'Ranks') was born in Doncaster on 30 September 1969 and was previously a Manchester United Schoolboy. He signed pro for Rovers during June 1988. Standing 5ft 9in tall, he made his first-team debut in the Third Division home game against Grimsby Town on 15 August 1987 whilst still an apprentice. Lining up alongside him on that day were Rhodes, Stead, R. Robinson, Humphries, Flynn, Cusack, Russell, Chamberlain, Deane, Burke and Kinsella. During his first season, he made 14 appearances (4 as substitute) and scored 2

goals. The first one was scored in the away game against Gillingham on 27 February 1988. During the following term, he played in all 46 League games and found the net on 11 occasions. He once mentioned that his favourite player was Bryan Robson.

In January 1992, it was said that Mark had been training with Wolves and was set to sign for them for £70,000. Rovers had been forced to accept a knockdown fee for the midfield ace because of the club's financial plight. Mark said: 'It's a pity I'm leaving Doncaster with the club in its present state, but I feel I'm going at the right time to benefit my career and the move is also helping Rovers as well. I've gained valuable experience here which I am sure will stand me in good stead in the future.' At the same time as Mark's departure, Rovers were set to launch a series of fund-raising activities in a bid to stave off a winding-up petition served on the club by the Inland Revenue. At Molineux, he played 112 games (20 as substitute) and scored 1 goal. During September 1996, he was transferred to Preston North End for £100,000.

Neil David Redfearn

Football League
Appearances: 46
Goals: 14

FA Cup
Appearances: 3
Goals: 1

FL Cup
Appearances: 2
Goals: 0

Total appearances: 51

Whilst not playing a great many games at Belle Vue, midfielder Neil once won the Rovers Player of the Year by quite a great margin. Neil was born in Dewsbury, West Yorkshire on 20 June 1965, and started his playing career as an apprentice with Nottingham Forest. During August 1982, he was signed on a free transfer by Bolton Wanderers, for whom he played 35 times and scored 1 goal. He was signed by Lincoln City in March 1984 (96 appearances, 4 as substitute, and 13 goals) before moving to Belle Vue, under Dave Cusack, for a fee of £17,000 during August 1986. The fee was fixed at a transfer tribunal, after both clubs had failed to agree between themselves.

During the 1985/86 season, Rovers had finished in eleventh position in the Third Division. Amongst the players who had moved out that summer were Colin Douglas, John Buckley and Brian Flynn. Neil was one of the replacements brought in, the others included Colin Russell and Gary Clayton. Neil's debut was in a Third Division away match at Mansfield Town on 23 August 1986, with a crowd of 3,969 in attendance. Neil's main attributes were being able to pass the ball accu-

rately, tackle aggressively and shoot on sight. All of these things contributed to making him quickly appreciated by the Belle Vue faithful.

During his time with the club he formed useful partnerships, first with Jim Dobbin, until the latter's transfer, and then with Colin Miller. It was quite remarkable that in his only season with Rovers he played in every League, FA Cup and League Cup game. All this, however, was against a backdrop of the Popular stand being closed by safety experts, and financial hardship the club's overdraft reaching over £276,000. It was also estimated that the club was losing around £5,000 a week. No wonder, then, that Neil was transferred to Crystal Palace in July 1987, the cash from the sale swelling the Belle Vue coffers to the tune of £100,000.

Redfearn played 57 games for Palace and scored 10 goals. In subsequent years, Neil played for Watford (22 games, 2 as substitute, 3 goals), Oldham Athletic (56 games, 6 as substitute, 16 goals), Barnsley (289 games, 3 as substitute, 72 goals), Charlton Athletic (29 games, 1 as substitute, 3 goals), Bradford City (14 games, 3 as substitute, 1 goal) and Wigan Athletic (18 games, 1 as substitute, 6 goals).

Graham Anthony Ricketts

Wing half 1964-1968

Football League
Appearances: 143 (+8 as substitute)
Goals: 15

FA Cup
Appearances: 11
Goals: 2

FL Cup
Appearances: 12 (+1 as substitute)
Goals: 0

Total appearances: 175

After an impressive appearance record at both Bristol Rovers (32 appearances) and Stockport County (119 appearances and 6 goals) in the early part of his career, Graham joined Rovers during July 1964. Speaking with a country accent, Graham allegedly took the nickname of 'Dan' after the Dan Archer character in BBC Radio series *The Archers*. At the end of the previous season, Rovers had finished fourteenth in the Fourth Division and there was a massive clearout of players in the close season.

When Graham signed for Rovers, the *Doncaster Evening Post* of 8 July 1963 commented: 'Team-building Doncaster Rovers plunged into the transfer market again today and snapped up two more players to bring the total of close-season signings to six. The new men are Stockport County's twenty-four-year-old left half Graham Ricketts and twenty-two-year-old centre forward John Henderson. Both deals have been in the balance for some time and Rovers have paid something in the region of £3,000 for the pair ... Ricketts, who first attracted the Rovers' attention when he played a blinder against them early last season said: "I am very happy about the move. [My wife and I] have had a look at a club house and are well satisfied."'

During the summer of 1964, Graham was retained by Stockport and the Cheshire club had turned down the Rovers' original bid a couple of months earlier. But the player later refused Stockport's terms and said that he would not play for them again. During the previous three seasons at Stockport, Graham

was ever present in the Stockport side.

Graham was born in Oxford on 30 July 1939 and joined Bristol Rovers as a junior. He also played for the England Youth side. He made his Rovers debut in the Fourth Division away game against Bradford Park Avenue on 22 August 1964. The line-up on that day was: Potter, McMinn, Watton, Ripley, Marsden, Ricketts, Barlow, Jeffrey, Tait, Broadbent and Grainger. In his first season playing at left half he made 42 appearances out of a possible 46 and scored 4 goals. The first of these was in the 2-0 home win against Torquay United on 5 September 1964. He also played in all the FA Cup and League Cup games that season.

In the 1965/66 campaign, Graham eventually formed a unique partnership at the back with Nicholson, Wylie, Kelly and Watton. During this period in particular, Graham was a very intelligent player, sound in defence, and a good tackler. He was not afraid to go upfield and linked usefully with his forwards, particularly Jeffrey and Sheffield. He was well respected by all those around him and his part in Rovers winning promotion and the Fourth Division championship cannot be underestimated.

By the end of the 1965/66 season, he had played in all 46 fixtures and every FA Cup and League Cup game. In the FA Cup replay game away at Wigan he had worn the number ten shirt. He also scored 6 League goals. During March 1968, he was transferred to Peterborough United for £2,500, making 46 appearances, 3 as substitute, and scored 1 goal.

Stuart John Robertson
Centre half 1966-1972

Football League
Appearances: 224 (+3 as substitute)
Goals: 8

FA Cup
Appearances: 16
Goals: 1

FL Cup
Appearances: 9
Goals: 2

Total appearances: 252

Stuart Robertson stepped into the heart of the Rovers' defence after the tragic, untimely death of skipper John Nicholson. Two years later he was to become club captain himself and develop into one of the finest players the club has seen. His name is remembered with affection.

Stuart was born in Nottingham on 16 December 1946, and when he left school played as an amateur for Nottingham Forest, who were in the First Division. Stuart was in Forest's youth side that won two tournaments in Amsterdam and he also toured the South of France. At the same time, he was studying to be a surveyor. Eventually, however, he was forced to make a decision that was to affect his life for at least the next fifteen or twenty years. He had to decide whether to be a footballer or take a job as a surveyor. After much thought, he chose soccer and signed full-time for Forest.

However, he found it difficult to gain a first-team place at centre half, having to compete with the veteran Bob McKinley – a fixture in the Forest defence. So he had a trial with Rovers, resulting in him signing for the club in July 1966. At this point, the club and probably Stuart himself may have envisaged that he would spend a period in the reserves and then progress into the first team, which had, after all, just won the Fourth Division championship. However, Nicholson's death, early in September 1966, accelerated matters and nearly a month later Stuart made his debut in front of a crowd of 7,940 in the Third Division away game at Swindon on 1 October 1966. In the back line with him on that day were Kelly, Watton, Wylie and Ricketts. The match was won 1-0. For Stuart, his first season with Rovers was a baptism of fire, the club dropping back into the Fourth Division after conceding 117 League goals.

As Stuart progressed as a player, and a number of talented players were brought to the club, success and stability were achieved when, at the end of the following season, they finished in a mid-table position. Success was achieved again when Rovers won the Fourth Division championship at the end of the 1968/69 campaign. In contrast to Stuart's first season in the Rovers defence, the team only conceded 38 goals in this championship year. For good measure, he scored a goal in the final game at Grimsby. Unfortunately, the club was not able to build on this success and after the departure of a number of key plays and only two seasons in the Third Division, Rovers fell through the trapdoor once more into the Fourth Division.

During the 1971/1972 season, Stuart resigned as captain and in the close season signed for Northampton Town. Whilst with the Cobblers, he turned out in their colours 254 times and scored 27 goals. He subsequently became manager of a sports complex in the Northampton area.

Football League
Appearances: 111 (+8 as substitute)
Goals: 3

FA Cup
Appearances: 4
Goals: 0

FL Cup
Appearances: 12 (+2 as substitute)
Goals: 0

Total appearances: 137

Robinson started out with Rotherham United Juniors and signed for the club during January 1973, yet only made 4 appearances for the Millers. He arrived at Belle Vue, under Stan Anderson, on a month's loan during the summer of 1975 after the Millers gave him a free transfer. At the end of the 1974/75 season, Rovers finished in seventeenth place. Fred played in several pre-season friendlies before he signed in September 1975.

The *Doncaster Evening Post* of Wednesday 3 September 1975 reported: 'Martin Alesinoye and Fred Robinson today signed professional contracts with Doncaster Rovers. Both players came to Belle Vue on a month's trial and both have impressed enough to be offered terms by Rovers ... Robinson, formerly with Rotherham United, made his first appearance for Rovers when he came on as substitute against Crewe, but has been playing well with the reserves. The signing of the two players increases Rovers' senior playing strength to 18 and, for the time being, ends manager Stan

Anderson's quest for new talent at Belle Vue. At the end of last season he said he was looking for two or three players to strengthen his squad.'

Fred made his first full appearance in the away match at Bournemouth on 6 September 1975. In his first season at Belle Vue, Fred notched up 26 appearances, 5 as substitute, and scored 1 goal, the team ending the season in tenth position. Whilst at Belle Vue, Fred played all his games in the Fourth Division and for much of this period his name regularly appeared on the team sheet. He was a consistent, reliable and popular full-back, playing in defence alongside Owen, Steve Wignall and Taylor.

During the latter part of his time with Rovers, Fred underwent two cartilage operations and, along with nine other players, was released by the club at the end of the 1978/79 season. He joined Huddersfield Town in August 1979, making 72 appearances for them and scoring 2 goals.

Leslie Robinson

Right-back/Midfield 1987-1990

Football League
Appearances: 82
Goals: 12

FA Cup
Appearances: 5
Goals: 0

FL Cup
Appearances: 4
Goals: 0

Total appearances: 91

Les was born in Shirebrook on 1 March 1967 and spent some time with Chesterfield Juniors before joining Mansfield Town in October 1984, making 11 appearances (4 as substitute). From there, he was transferred to Stockport County (67 appearances and 3 goals) in November 1986.

Les came to Rovers as a highly-rated midfield player, in March 1988, for around £20,000. He was Dave Mackay's first cash signing after taking charge at Belle Vue. In signing Les, Dave had beaten the transfer deadline, and commented: 'This is only the start ... We shall be rebuilding the club at the end of the season and we need to bring in at least another three or four players. But I am delighted to make the breakthrough because he is a player I've been after for some time. He caught my eye when I watched him and although he is relatively inexperienced, he plays like a man already.'

Les made his debut in the Third Division away game against Port Vale on 2 April 1988.

He scored his first Rovers goal in the away game at Brentford on 30 April 1988. He signed as a midfield player, but under Billy Bremner he switched to play a right-back role and started to attract attention from other clubs. He commented: 'I wasn't too sure about playing there at first, but the way things turned out the gaffer's done me a right good favour and now I feel very comfortable in the position.'

He was transferred to Oxford United during March 1990 for a fee reported to be worth £200,000. Les said that the Oxford manager had made him an offer that he could not refuse: 'I want to prove myself at a higher level and even if Doncaster had made me a fantastic offer to stay, it would have made no difference.'

Before he left, he was leading the supporters' club Player of the Season award. He said 'The fans have been great to me at Belle Vue and I've enjoyed my time here'. At Oxford, he made a staggering 289 appearances, as well as 5 as substitute, and scored 3 goals.

William McKnight Russell

Right-back 1979-1985

Football League
Appearances: 241 (+3 as substitute)
Goals: 15

FA Cup
Appearances: 16
Goals: 0

FL Cup
Appearances: 17
Goals: 0

Total appearances: 277

Billy was noted for his long throws whilst at Belle Vue and was able to operate as a left-back or play in midfield if asked to do so. He was born in Glasgow on 14 September 1959 and played for the Scottish national side as a schoolboy and youth international. He signed for Everton in July 1977 though he made no first-team appearances for them. He did play for Everton in one of the FA Youth Cup finals, though.

From Goodison, he joined Celtic and came to Doncaster in July 1979 under manager Billy Bremner. During the previous season, Rovers had finished twenty-second in the Fourth Division with 71 goals against and just 50 for. During that summer, after successfully seeking re-election, Billy Bremner strengthened the team for his first full season in charge at Belle Vue. Along with Billy came the return of Alan Warboys, Ian Nimmo, Hugh Dowd and John Dowie. So, there was a mixture of new defenders and attackers – much needed when looking over the previous season's statistics.

In the 1979/80 season, Rovers were going into their centenary year. So, there was an added incentive for the team to play well and have something to show at the end of it. Billy made his first-team debut in the Fourth Division in the home game against Northampton Town on 18 August 1979. By the end of the season, he had made 41 appearances, with 1 as substitute, and the team finished in twelfth position. This was a much more respectable situation than the previous year, with 63 goals against and 62 for. The crowd average also increased.

Over the next three seasons, Billy saw Rovers yo-yo from the Third to the Fourth Divisions, yet he almost made the number two shirt his own, playing in every League game in the 1980/81 season. He also scored his first goal in that period – in the 3-2 home victory against York on 20 February 1981. Whilst at Belle Vue, he was described as a speedy and quick-tackling defender who liked to have a go at goal. From Rovers, he signed for Scunthorpe United in August 1985, playing 113 games (4 as substitute) and scoring 7 goals. His last League club was Rotherham United, for whom he made 103 appearances (2 as substitute) and scored 2 goals.

John David Schofield
Midfield 1994-1997

Football League
Appearances: 107 (+3 as substitute)
Goals: 12

FA Cup
Appearances: 2
Goals: 0

FL Cup
Appearances: 4
Goals: 0

Total appearances: 116

John, nicknamed 'Schoff', was born in Barnsley on 16 May 1965. After a spell with Gainsborough Trinity, he began his League career at Lincoln, signing for them in November 1988. In time, he made 221 appearances for them, 10 as substitute, and scored 11 goals. He once said that his best moment in football, apart from captaining both Lincoln and Doncaster, was leading Lincoln out at Goodison Park in the second round of the Coca-Cola Cup. He arrived at Belle Vue under Sammy Chung in November 1994.

Standing at 5ft 11in and weighing 11st 8lb, he made his debut in the Division Three home game against Hartlepool United on 19 November 1994. Before the game, Rovers were third in Division Three. His colleagues on that day included Hackett, Brabin, Wilcox and Parrish. John once stated that amongst the players he admired were David Batty, Paul Ince and Bryan Robson. He listed his honours in the game as being Player of the Year at Lincoln City, and captain of both Lincoln City and Rovers.

During his first season at Belle Vue, he made 25 appearances and scored 1 goal, Rovers finishing ninth. John became one of the most popular players in recent times with the fans. His leadership skills and organisa-tional abilities were a joy to watch, but it was inevitable with the terrible events unfolding at the club during the late 1990s that he would soon leave. The team finished nine-teenth during the 1996/97 season, and fans were sorry to see the following headline in the *Doncaster Star* of 4 August 1997: 'Schofield leaves for Mansfield. Skipper goes in £10,000 deal.' The newspaper explained that he was the latest big-name player to leave Belle Vue during the close season when he joined Mansfield Town over the previous weekend. 'John was one of the biggest earners at the club and he was out of contract at the end of the season,' general manager Mark Weaver is alleged to have said. 'There was no way we would have been able to offer him a new deal on the sort of money he was on, so in all prob-ability we would have got nothing for him. Having said that, we didn't want to lose John, and Ken Richardson tried hard to keep him at the club, but he wanted to leave. Mansfield approached us last week and, as is club policy, we told Schofield of their interest. It was up to him whether or not he wanted to speak to them.'

John subsequently made 81 appearances with Mansfield (5 as substitute) and then went to Hull City, making 13 outings (12 as substitute) before returning to Lincoln.

Laurence Joseph Sheffield

Centre forward 1965-1967, 1969-1970

Football League
Appearances: 71 (+2 as substitute)
Goals: 41

FA Cup
Appearances: 5
Goals: 1

FL Cup
Appearances: 7
Goals: 6

Total appearances: 85

Laurie Sheffield insists he never tires or gets annoyed with people talking to him about football, especially about the time when he played in Rovers' successful 1965/66 Fourth Division championship side, when attendance often reached 14,000 and over. 'A footballer is a working-class hero, an icon rarely forgotten. And it's nice to be remembered,' said Laurie. 'People introduce themselves and ask if they can talk to me. I usually say "certainly". Occasionally fans go on a bit, but I don't mind. Most of them once paid my wages, so I feel it's my duty to talk to them. They frequently tell me how I was part of their Friday night entertainment: starting with a few pints in the Park Hotel near the ground, progressing to watch me and Alick Jeffrey score a couple of winning goals, moving back to the Park after the game for a few more pints, and then [going on] to a night club, getting home at about 3 a.m. I have never found fans' behaviour towards me intrusive or a nuisance.'

Centre forward Laurie Sheffield first signed for Rovers in the summer of 1965, and before long he teamed up with Alick Jeffrey to form one of the most potent strike forces in Rovers'

history. This was following a successful time at Newport County, where he'd been since 1962, making 91 appearances and scoring 46 goals. In actual fact, Laurie broke the post-war scoring record at County during the 1964/65 season, with 27 goals in just 38 matches.

Laurie was born in Swansea on 27 April 1939. His position from a young age was centre forward, and he played for the Welsh Schoolboys' side during the 1953/54 season. He signed for Second Division side Bristol Rovers in the summer of 1956, but during 1958, after limited success, joined Southern League side Barry Town on loan. National Service intervened shortly after, and Laurie served two years with the Royal Welsh Fusiliers.

Once this was completed, he returned to Bristol Rovers, but not long afterwards signed for Newport County for a modest £1,000. He found a regular first-team place and was a favourite with the Welsh side's supporters. He came to Belle Vue for £8,000 and Alfie Hale, who was part of the deal. In signing Laurie, Rovers fought off competition from Bolton and Norwich.

Although only relatively small for a striker, it has often been said that Sheffield had the

Laurie Sheffield (second from right) wins a header.

ability to 'leap like a salmon' and he led the forward line with strength and courage.

He made his debut in the Fourth Division home game on 21 August 1965 against Lincoln City. Rovers won the game 4-1 and Laurie bagged two goals. In the 1965/66 season, when Rovers won the Fourth Division championship, the partnership between Alick Jeffrey and himself notched up a total of 50 League goals, with Laurie's share being 28.

Crises hit the club in the following season, with the untimely death of John Nicholson and the long lay-off of Alick Jeffrey, both players having been involved in a car crash. So it came as a surprise to everyone when the club sold Laurie Sheffield to Norwich City, even though they gained a handsome profit. The local press was full of letters from disconcerted fans who couldn't understand the deal. To make matters worse, Rovers crashed 4-1 in their next game at Bournemouth. To

aggravate matters, Laurie scored a hat-trick in his first game with the Canaries and thereafter hit the back of the net quite frequently. However, he started the following season back in South Yorkshire, at Rotherham United.

In subsequent years, he joined Oldham Athletic and Luton Town before rejoining Rovers in October 1969, but only made 13 appearances (with 2 as substitute) and 6 goals over the 1969/70 season. He ended his career at Peterborough United, having signed for them in August. For a time after hanging up his boots, he worked with car dealers Hayseldens, then United Builders Merchants, and later Allied Dunbar, along with ex-Leeds player Mick Bates, before becoming a self-employed financial adviser. He admits that he's always been quite disciplined, something he inherited from his parents, and that he has used his positive disciplined thinking which he once had as a player, in another profession.

Glynn Snodin

Left midfield 1976-1985

Football League
Appearances: 288 (+21 as substitute)
Goals: 59

Football Conference
Appearances: 1 (as substitute)
Goals: 0

FA Cup
Appearances: 15 (+1 as substitute)
Goals: 1

FL Cup
Appearances: 12 (+2 as substitute)
Goals: 1

Total appearances: 340

Glynn Snodin was one of two famous brothers whose names will always recall fond memories amongst Rovers fans for their time at Belle Vue as players and then as part of the first Conference management team.

Glynn (nicknamed 'Snod') 'of the sparkling left foot' was born in Thrybergh, Rotherham on 14 February 1960 and came to Belle Vue straight from school when Stan Anderson was at the helm. Standing 5ft 6in tall, he made his debut as a substitute on 2 April 1977 in the Fourth Division away game at Bradford City, attended by 6,882. His first full start came on 12 April 1977 in the 3-0 home win against Halifax Town. He was most comfortable on the left flank, adopting an attacking left-back or left-wing role, and possessed a powerful shot, frequently letting fly when the goal was in sight. He often took free kicks, his powerful, seemingly unstoppable drives being made to swerve in any direction. Billy Bremner once said of him: 'Glynn is a bit special; he has the ability to make scoring goals from long range look easy.'

Glynn topped the scoring for two seasons whilst he was at Belle Vue. He once admitted that the best goal he scored was in an away game at Darlington. During 1986, Bobby Robson called him into his squad of forty for the World Cup, although he was not amongst the final twenty-two. Between 1976 and 1985, he made 288 appearances (21 as substitute) and scored 61 goals. He said that the biggest influences on his career were his wife, parents and Johnny Quigley. His favourite player was Terry McDermott.

Glynn moved to Sheffield Wednesday in June 1985 for £115,000, and said: 'I was always a Wednesday supporter as a youngster and a move to Hillsborough is ideal for me.' Nottingham Forest boss Brian Clough had also shown an interest in him. Whilst at Hillsborough, Glynn appeared 51 times (8 as substitute) and bagged 1 goal. From there it was to Leeds United, making 83 outings (11 as substitute) and scoring 10 goals. Thereafter, he went to Oldham (8 appearances and 1 goal), Rotherham (3 appearances) and Barnsley (18 outings and 7 as substitute).

In 1998 he was offered an assistant manager's position at Barnsley, but chose instead to become director of coaching under his brother, Ian, as the two brothers took control in Rovers' first season in the Conference. Glynn managed to play some games even at the age of thirty-nine. Both brothers were sacked towards the end of the 1999/2000 season. Glynn is currently employed at Charlton Athletic.

Ian Snodin
Midfield/Right-back 1979-1985, 1998-2000

Football League
Appearances: 181 (+7 as substitute)
Goals: 27

Football Conference
Appearances: 11 (+2 as substitute)
Goals: 0

FA Cup
Appearances: 11 (+1 as substitute)
Goals: 1

FL Cup
Appearances: 9
Goals: 1

Total appearances: 222

There is no doubt that Ian Snodin is ranked amongst the great Belle Vue heroes. He made his first-team debut at seventeen, captained the side two years later, played as an international whilst at the club and later returned as manager – a truly remarkable record. He was born in Rotherham on 15 August 1963. He made his debut on 29 March 1980 as a substitute in the Fourth Division home game against Bournemouth. He made his full debut in the home game on 5 April 1980 against Walsall. It has been submitted that Ian is the most gifted player to have pulled on a Rovers shirt during the last twenty-five years.

On 16 March 1982, Ian reached another milestone in his career by captaining the side in a home game against Carlisle United. He was eighteen and, at the time, the youngest skipper in the Football League. In this first stint at Belle Vue, Ian played 181 games (21 as substitute) and scored 25 goals.

After a dazzling career at Rovers, Leeds United snapped him up for £200,000 in a club record deal during May 1985. After signing Ian said: 'It was a difficult decision. I've always said I wanted to play in the First Division, but West Brom wanted me to sign a four-year contract and I wasn't sure I'd settle in the Midlands. Leeds is only up the road. It will be a wrench leaving Belle Vue, and especially the manager, because he's been like a father figure to me and I can't pay enough respect to him.'

Billy Bremner said: 'I always knew the day would come when he would have to go, but I feel a mixture of sadness and happiness now it's arrived. Players like Ian don't come around too often. I think he has the ability to become a great player for his country and possibly a world-class star. As far as I'm concerned, Leeds have got a bargain and I think there will be a lot of managers kicking themselves next season when they see what they have missed.'

Ian had been the subject of constant transfer speculation during the previous season. Several top managers, including Nottingham Forest boss Brian Clough, Southampton's Lawrie McMenemy and Arsenal's Don Howe, had watched him more than once. Rovers chairman Ian Jones said that Ian was one of the most gifted players to emerge from Belle Vue. He had always been reluctant to sell Ian, but the board decided they could not stand in his way. The cash was also badly needed to wipe out the club's overdraft, which stood at almost £170,000.

At Elland Road, Ian became captain for a period, made 51 appearances and scored 6 goals. During January 1987, he was transferred to Everton for £840,000. At Goodison, he made 142 outings (6 as substitute) and scored 3 goals. During his first season there, he won a League title medal. In October 1994, he went on loan to Sunderland, playing for them 6 times. He was transferred to Oldham Athletic in January 1995 (55 games, 2 as substitute) and Scarborough in August 1997 (33 games, 2 as substitute) before becoming manager at Belle Vue for the club's first season in the Conference.

During the 1998/99 season, Ian played a handful of games himself as the team struggled to survive, yet they won the MacMillan Trophy in front of a capacity crowd of 7,300. No one was more disappointed that things didn't work out for Rovers during his spell in charge at Belle Vue than Ian. None of the previous managers, not even Billy Bremner, cared more passionately for the club than Ian. Commenting on his enforced departure, Ian said: 'I know that we were only seven points off the relegation zone, but I was confident that we would pull clear in the last month of the season. I don't think we have been given the time to turn things around considering the state of affairs when we took over. Rovers were just like a pub team at the time, but Glynn and I have brought professionalism back to the club and I think that we were on the right track. It is a very sad day for the pair of us because we are both fans at heart. No one has worked harder than Glynn and me to bring success to the club. I have had just one day off in the last eighteen months.'

Football League
Appearances: 85
Goals: 0

FA Cup
Appearances: 4
Goals: 0

FL Cup
Appearances: 2
Goals: 0

Total appearances: 91

Barry hails from Scawthorpe near Doncaster and was born on 9 September 1938. He began playing football while a pupil of Highfields Junior School. After moving up to the Highfields Senior School, he played for the intermediate (Under-13) team for one season and then in his second year with the school played for both the intermediates and seniors.

Barry was originally a centre forward, but moved to centre half while at Highfields. According to the *Yorkshire Evening Post* of 20 January 1960, the ex-Doncaster Technical High schoolboy's rise to honours started in 1953. Then, Barry, already captain of the Doncaster Boys' team, was watched by England's schoolboy selectors. Within weeks, Barry, along with Alick Jeffrey, was chosen for the match against Wales and given the additional honour of skippering the side. He allegedly became the fourth Doncaster schoolboy within six years to play for England and he led the side out at Wembley.

More honours came his way and in November 1954, again with Alick Jeffrey, he was chosen for the FA Youth (amateur) XI at St James' Park, Newcastle. He joined the Rovers' groundstaff during 1954, and was also honoured that year by the Sheffield and Hallamshire FA.

The 6ft Barry made his Rovers debut at left half in the Third Division home game against Middlesbrough on 3 May 1956, the last game of the 1955/56 season. With him in defence on that day were Gregg, Makepeace, Graham, Gavin and Williams. Rovers ended the season in seventeenth place.

In the following season, he made only 2 appearances, but a blow to his progress came with his call-up papers in August 1957. Within a month he was in Germany, but soon became a great success with the BAOR team. Just when he was ready for a full Army honour, he damaged a knee on one of his weekend at home games with the Rovers at Stockport. On 5 January 1959, a *Yorkshire Evening Post* headline ran 'Third of Belle Vue Players Injured. Not enough for practice game.' Beneath, it was stated: 'Barry Staton is a certain non-starter. The former youth international skipper, who should have returned to his Army unit in Germany yesterday, has been examined by the club's doctor, and is to see a specialist later this week. Barry is really disconsolate, especially about the goal he gave away at Stockport [3 January], but he should remember his brilliant display before his injury.'

Barry did not make another appearance during the remainder of the season. In subsequent months, he made several transfer requests and did not get a run of games in the first team until the 1960/61 season, appearing 26 times. In the following one, he appeared 39 times.

Barry, a contemporary of Alick Jeffrey, showed great promise as a youngster, but due to the interruptions of National Service, injuries and the team nose-diving after the departure of Peter Doherty, he was never able to properly display his unquestionable ability at Belle Vue. At the end of the 1961/62 season, when Rovers finished in twenty-first position, he moved to Norwich City (23 appearances, 1 goal).

John Charles Stiles

Midfield 1989-1992

Football League
Appearances: 88 (+1 as substitute)
Goals: 2

FA Cup
Appearances: 3
Goals: 0

FL Cup
Appearances: 4
Goals: 0

Total appearances: 96

John is the son of England 1966 World Cup hero Nobby Stiles and nephew of John Giles. He was born in Manchester on 6 May 1964, beginning his career with Shamrock Rovers. He also played in Vancouver, Canada before joining Leeds United in 1984. He played 49 times for Leeds and joined Rovers from there in August 1989 for a fee of £40,000, playing in midfield.

He made his debut at Exeter on 19 August 1989. Amongst his colleagues on that day were McGinley, Turnbull, Rankine and G. Jones. He was consistent during his first season, turning out 42 times and scoring 2 goals. He also played in 1 FA Cup game and 2 League Cup games, although the team could only finish in twentieth position. John's consistent appearances continued in the following season with 37 outings and the team finished eleventh.

In his time at Rovers, he was a supply line for strikers such as Noteman, Muir and D.

Jones. But with the departure of his mentor, Billy Bremner, early in November 1991, and an unsettling financial crisis unfolding off the field, it came as no surprise to read the news in the *Doncaster Star* of 27 March 1992. It was reported that Rovers boss Steve Beaglehole was left to survey the remnants of his squad following three more departures from Belle Vue before the transfer deadline. 'Goalkeeper Mark Samways and midfield schemer John Stiles both moved out on loan and Billy Whitehurst joined Crewe on a free transfer ... Samways and Stiles have joined clubs at the other end of the table for specially-agreed two-month loan spells.'

John Stiles went to Rochdale and it brought the total of departures from Belle Vue to seven over the previous couple of months. Manager Beaglehole said: 'None of the moves have brought any money into the club, but unfortunately they had to be done to cut the wage bill.' At the time, Rovers had received another PFA loan to meet players' wages, and Beaglehole added: 'It is a sad state of affairs, but these deals had to be done so that we don't have to keep looking elsewhere for someone to bail us out.' After playing at Rochdale (2 games, 2 as substitute), John became a financial consultant and played on a non-contract basis for a while.

John Cecil Stirland

Wing half 1939-1949

Football League
Appearances: 68
Goals: 0

FA Cup
Appearances: 6
Goals: 0

FL Cup
Appearances: 0
Goals: 0

Total appearances: 74

'Cec' was once described as 'a wholehearted player, he is useful in attack as well as defence.' He served the club consistently over a ten-year period. Cec was born in Adwick-le-Street, near Doncaster, on 15 July 1921. He joined Rovers under Fred Emery, as an amateur in May 1938, before signing professional forms just before his seventeenth birthday. Standing 6ft tall and weighing around 11st 7lb, he made his debut in the first game of the East Midlands War League. This was a home game against Sheffield Wednesday on 21 October 1939.

Due to the outbreak of the war, the Third Division (North) was suspended, football being played on a regional basis. Rovers played a total of 20 games in this League between 21 October 1939 and 1 June 1940. Cec played in 13 of these games and made 1 appearance in a League Cup game.

During the war, Cec was employed as a grinder in David Brown's engineering firm at Huddersfield. Nevertheless, he continued to play football when circumstances would allow. In fact, at one point he played for Bradford Park Avenue under former Rovers player-manager Fred Emery. But a glance at the Rovers teams that played throughout the war shows that he appeared for the club quite regularly during this period.

When the Third Division (North) was restored in August 1946, Cec became a regular in the Rovers side, appearing 38 times in the 1946/47 campaign when Rovers won promotion to the Second Division, conceding only 38 goals and scoring 113. But, unfortunately, they were relegated in the following season, with 65 goals against and 39 for. Yet the crowd average for that year was 22,261.

In his last full season, Rovers finished third, and in the following one won promotion once more. But Cec did not see this, as he signed for New Brighton during January 1950. He stayed with the Rakers for eighteen months and played 51 games for them. He then moved to Scunthorpe during August 1951 and made 17 appearances for the Iron. After retiring from football, he followed the path of many other ex-footballers and went into the licensed trade, before retiring from the business in 1985.

Wing half 1950-1956

Football League
Appearances: 113
Goals: 0

FA Cup
Appearances: 7
Goals: 0

FL Cup
Appearances: 0
Goals: 0

Total appearances: 120

Jackie, whose terrier-like tackling and close proximity tactics in dealing with opposing inside men were legendary, was born in Rossington, near Doncaster, on 15 March 1929. He came to Belle Vue in October 1949, with Peter Doherty at the helm and the club on the verge of experiencing its halcyon years. Yet, Jackie had to wait in the wings for a while before making his debut at right half in the Second Division away game at Chesterfield on 7 April 1951 in front of 13,832. For that match, he took over from Walter Jones, who had been a regular for much of the campaign. The game was won 4-1, although it was the only one that Jackie played in during the season. Thereafter, he appears to have switched to left half for a period, sharing the position for the most part with either Dave Miller or Tom Brown. He then reverted to right half for a spell. Jackie began to play on a regular basis during the 1953/54 campaign (37 League games plus 3 in the FA Cup). At the end of the season, Rovers finished twelfth with an average home crowd of 16, 919. He played in the left-half position in the memorable 2-0 win at Sunderland in the first round of the FA Cup on 9 January 1954. In the back line with him on that day were Makepeace, Graham, Brown and Paterson.

He made the most appearances in the club's colours during the 1955/56 period, making 39 in the League and 4 in the cup. He is one of only a few Rovers players who can claim to have played all their games with the club in the Second Division. Unfortunately, a bad knee injury sustained on an FA tour of South Africa eventually cut short his career at the age of twenty-seven. The *Doncaster Gazette* of 28 March 1957 reported the following: 'His selection for the FA tour of South Africa was reward for his vastly improved form during last season, and his progress had obviously been noted in the right places. South Africa's hard grounds caused Teasdale's knee trouble which even a double operation has failed to put right. The player's entry into hospital for a third time this week raises doubts about his future playing career, and although hope has not been completely abandoned, it would seem that his chances of playing League football again are now remote.'

Football League
Appearances: 401
Goals: 124

FA Cup
Appearances: 28
Goals: 9

FL Cup
Appearances: 0
Goals: 0

Total appearances: 429

Over a twelve-year period, Herbert Tindill became a permanent fixture in the Rovers attack, notching up 401 League appearances. He is one of only three Rovers players to have played this number of games. A native of Hemsworth, he was born on 31 December 1926, the son of a local publican. Cliff Jordan – brother of former Rovers favourite, Clarrie – first spotted Bert, and he was invited to Belle Vue for a trial. This was during 1943, and Bert made such a profound impression that he was signed.

On being conscripted into the Armed Forces in late 1945, Bert was based in the West Country, where he made guest appearances for non-League Yeovil Town. He made his Rovers debut on 31 Aug 1946 in the Third Division (North) home game against Rochdale. He was described as a useful finisher, with 122 goals under his belt. He moved to Bristol City in February 1958, following Rovers manager Peter Doherty, who had left Belle Vue a little earlier. He made 56 appearances there and scored 29 goals. Bert then went on to play for Barnsley.

It has been claimed that in a home game against Notts County that Bert scored what was considered to be one of Belle Vue's finest goals ever, a superb cross shot from twenty-five yards.

During the weeks immediately after Peter Doherty's departure from Belle Vue and his installation as manager at Bristol City, it was reported that there were numerous transfer requests made by Rovers players. However, the most startling news came on Monday 3 February 1958, with the transfer of Bert to Bristol City. The *Doncaster Gazette* of 6 February 1958 said that there were two surprising features about the transfer: 'Firstly Tindill had indicated only a few days earlier, when he had turned down the chance of joining Blackburn Rovers, that he did not wish to travel far from Doncaster. The second point is that Mr Doherty is to be congratulated on persuading the Rovers to part with such an accomplished and experienced forward, especially to a club fighting an anti-relegation battle against the Rovers. The departure of Tindill severs a long association between club and player and the Rovers have lost an extremely valuable forward, who was quite capable of slotting into any front line position at a moment's notice.'

Once his playing days were over, Bert followed his father into the licensed trade, where he stayed for seven years. Afterwards, he spent time in the motor body repair business, before he bought a partnership in a similar set-up in the area. Bert Tindill collapsed and died at his home on 10 July 1973, at the relatively early age of forty-six.

Paul Raymond Todd

Inside forward 1946-1950

Football League
Appearances: 160
Goals: 49

FA Cup
Appearances: 12
Goals: 8

FL Cup
Appearances: 0
Goals: 0

Total appearances: 172

Paul Todd joined the Rovers in September 1945 after being spotted playing in an RAF side during the Second World War. He was born in Middlesbrough on 8 May 1920 and on leaving school took a job as a telephone switchboard operator, but later worked in a gents' outfitters. Whilst at school, he had represented his home town's representative side and played cricket for them too.

Whilst playing for Stockton in the Northern League, he was invited for trials by Wolves and Leicester City. When war broke out in 1939, he joined the RAF and was stationed in Singapore and Ceylon. Whilst serving with the RAF in the Doncaster area, he was invited to guest for Rovers in the wartime League. Thereafter, when he was demobbed, he signed for Rovers in September 1945.

His Rovers debut came on 31 August 1946, in the Third Division (North) 2-1 home win against Rochdale. In the forward line with him on that day were Tindill, Thompson, Jordan and Maddison. He scored his first Rovers goal in the 5-0 home win against Accrington Stanley, on 28 September 1946.

Paul was captain of Rovers' side for a period and played a major part in the Third Division

(North) championship team of 1946/47. During the 1946/47 season, Paul played 40 League games and scored 23 goals. The team itself scored 113 goals and only conceded 38, the average crowd attendance being 15,339. Paul also played in all 4 FA Cup games in that season. He was described as a cultured player and a dangerous man in front of goal. He scored 40 goals in 160 League appearances. He is clearly one of Rovers' greats, and played at a time when the team could play some exceptional football.

Paul played his last game for Rovers on 3 May 1950 in the Third Division (North) home match against Tranmere Rovers. He was transferred to Blackburn Rovers in July 1950 for £10,000. This was greeted with dismay by the Rovers fans, being seen as a mere cash-raising exercise. For Blackburn, Paul made 46 outings and scored 13 goals. His only other club was Hull City (27 appearances, 3 goals). He was an all-round sportsman and won trophies at soccer, rugby and boxing, winning the novices' light-heavyweight championship. He was the club's guest at the Division Three home game with Hull City on 8 March 1997. He died in 2000.

Lee Mark Turnbull
Striker 1987-1991, 1993-1994

Football League
Appearances: 118 (+16 as substitute)
Goals: 22

FA Cup
Appearances: 7 (+1 as substitute)
Goals: 0

FL Cup
Appearances: 3 (+1 as substitute)
Goals: 2

Total appearances: 146

Lee was born in Stockton on 27 September 1967. After joining the youth team at Middlesbrough, he moved to Aston Villa in August 1987, but made no appearances for them. He joined Rovers under Dave Cusack in November 1987 for £17,500.

He made his debut in the Third Division away game at Brighton & Hove Albion on 4 November 1987. He scored his first Rovers goal in the home game against Fulham on 9 January 1988. Lee's hat-trick in the 6-0 away win at Hartlepool on 30 September 1989 was one of only five scored by Rovers players against that team during the 1980s. He scored another hat-trick in the home game against Aldershot on 1 December 1990.

In a player profile in the team magazine, he said that his favourite player was Andy Gray and his biggest disappointment was being relegated with Middlesbrough and Doncaster.

Lee completed a £35,000 move to Chesterfield in February 1991 and then admitted that, in some respects, he was sad to be leaving. 'For most of the three years I've been here, the club has been through a bad time. So I'm sad in a way to be leaving just when they have a chance of going up. But I'm looking forward to joining Chesterfield. Their offer came out of the blue and it's a fresh challenge for me.' Rovers were doubling their

money for him after having signed him for £17,000. He had been on the transfer list since the previous summer, after failing to agree a fresh contract with the club and had been playing on a week-to-week basis all season. The arrangement meant he could have left at any time, with his fee being decided by a tribunal, but Rovers and the Blues agreed the price.

Turnbull had been keen to move at the end of the previous season, despite turning down an offer to join Peterborough. But he had said that he would be happy to stay if an improved contract with Doncaster could be agreed. He said: 'I asked to come off the list a few weeks ago, but the club wasn't in a position to offer me a new deal, so I felt the writing was on the wall and it was time to leave. But I'm parting on good terms. I think that the gaffer and Steve Beaglehole are a great team and they have certainly turned the club around.'

At Chesterfield, he made 80 appearances (7 as substitute) and netted 26 times. He returned to Belle Vue in October 1993 until a move followed to Wycombe Wanderers in January 1994 (8 appearances, 3 as substitute, 1 goal). Later came moves to Scunthorpe United in March 1995 (37 outings, 10 as substitute and 7 goals) and Darlington in July 1997.

Brian Usher

Outside right 1968-1973

Football League
Appearances: 164 (+6 as substitute)
Goals: 6

FA Cup
Appearances: 6
Goals: 0

FL Cup
Appearances: 7
Goals: 0

Total appearances: 183

It has been said that Brian Usher was a fine example of a winger being prepared to test his speed against an opponent. It was also added that there had been none better than him during the fifty years prior to him coming to Belle Vue under George Raynor in June 1968. He was born in Durham on 11 March 1944. As a youngster he played for Lambton and Hetton Boys and progressed to Young England and the England Under-23 international side.

Usher joined Sunderland after deciding to take up football as profession and, after a spell with Roker Park Juniors, signed for the club in March 1961. He made 61 appearances and scored 5 goals before his transfer to Sheffield Wednesday in June 1965. It has been said that Brian had some happy memories with both Sunderland and Sheffield Wednesday. He missed only one game during the season, as Sunderland carried all before them and won promotion to the First Division.

While with Wednesday, he played in the first four rounds of the club's run to Wembley in 1966. At Hillsborough, he appeared 55 times (1 as substitute) and scored 2 goals. During June 1968, he came to Belle Vue in a cash-and-player deal also involving Alan

Warboys, who made the journey to Sheffield Wednesday.

Brian made his debut in the Fourth Division home game against Bradford City on 10 August 1968. Rovers drew the game 1-1 with an attendance of 10,130. With him on the forward line were Gilfillan, Jeffrey, Webber and Rabjohn. During his first season at Belle Vue, he made 26 appearances (1 as substitute) and netted twice. He quickly became a hero of the Belle Vue faithful, winning a Fourth Division championship medal with Rovers during the 1968/69 season when the crowd average was 10,212.

During that period he made 26 appearances (1 as substitute) and scored 2 goals. He also played his part in helping the team to score 65 goals. He made 43 outings in his second season and became the scourge of the Third Division defenders for a couple of seasons at least. He saw Rovers fall from grace once more into the Fourth Division at the end of the 1970/71 campaign and crowd figures eventually plummet to an average of 2,258. He was released at the end of the 1972/73 season along with Glen Johnson, Harold Wilcockson, Brian Joy and Chris Rabjohn and Steve Briggs.

Steve Uzelac
Defender 1971-1977

Football League
Appearances: 182 (3 as substitute)
Goals: 9

FA Cup
Appearances: 11
Goals: 3

FL Cup
Appearances: 11
Goals: 0

Total appearances: 207

Steve was born in Doncaster on 12 March 1953 and worked his way through Rovers Juniors alongside Stan Brookes and Mike Elwiss. He made his debut as a central defender at Newport County on 16 October 1971. His colleagues on that day included experienced professionals such as Branfoot, Wilcockson and Robertson. He was then chosen to play in 31 games over the remainder of the season, the team finishing in twelfth position, conceding 63 goals and scoring 56.

Over the 185 games he subsequently played for Rovers, he earned a reputation as a tough, no-nonsense defender. It is often mentioned amongst Rovers fans that he scored only 9 goals despite his massive appearance record. The first goal he scored for Rovers was in the 3-1 defeat away at Peterborough on 14 October 1972. There was also one quite spectacular long-range strike against Brentford on 15 September 1975 – the ball was hit with such power that it wedged itself within the stanchion of the goal.

All of Uzelac's games for Rovers were played in the Fourth Division. The highest position he saw them reach was eighth. Yet he was a consistent and useful member of the teams of the 1970s, which saw a number of comings and goings on the managerial, as well as the playing side. He played in both FA Cup games against Liverpool during January 1974. In the FA Cup away game versus Bury, he scored two goals. However, this was to no avail, as Rovers went down 4-2.

Steve went on loan to Mansfield Town (for 2 games) in February 1976, before finally waving goodbye to Belle Vue in May 1977, when he joined Preston North End (9 games). His final football years were spent at Stockport County (31 games and 2 goals), after he joined them in March 1980.

Alan Warboys

Centre forward/Central defender 1966-1968, 1979-1982

Football League
Appearances: 128 (+1 as substitute)
Goals: 32

FA Cup
Appearances: 10 (+1 as substitute)
Goals: 3

FL Cup
Appearances: 9
Goals: 1

Total appearances: 149

Alan, standing 6ft 1in tall, a big, raw honest centre-forward, had two periods with Rovers, playing over 125 games in total for the club. Later, he was to mention that the biggest influence on his career was Frank Marshall (an ex-Rovers trainer). Nicknamed 'Warby', Alan was also a much-travelled player, playing for six other clubs in the intervening years.

He was born in Goldthorpe on 18 April 1949 and worked for three weeks as a miner at the local colliery. He played centre half for his school teams, but a Don & Dearne representative team picked him at centre forward, and he scored 10 goals in his first 3 games for them, including six on his debut against Denby Dale. 'At the time I first joined Doncaster,' began Alan, 'I was a big lad with no skills but I worked hard, training on my own and kicking a ball against a wall. But I was still a borderline case before Rovers took me on as an apprentice, and that was still the case when I signed full professional forms in April 1967. The three weeks I spent down Goldthorpe Colliery made me all the more determined to make it in football, and people like Oscar Hold, Frank Marshall, Bill Leivers, Jackie Bestall and George Raynor helped me.'

Alan made his first-team debut on 15 April 1967 in the Third Division away game at Leyton Orient, where Rovers crashed 4-1. He scored his first League goal in the home game against Scunthorpe on 5 May 1967. The 1967/68 campaign began with him leading the attack, and he ended it with only Alick Jeffrey ahead of him in the goal-scoring for that season. In 39 appearances, Alan found the net 12 times, before signing for Sheffield Wednesday in June 1968. There he made 66 appearances, 5 as substitute, and scored 13 goals. Whilst he was at Wednesday, it was said by the *Sheffield Star* sports correspondent that he was not the most skilful or gifted of players in the game at that time, but his honesty and joy transmitted itself to the Kop. Hillsborough admired him for these qualities, and the name of Alan Warboys has always been respected.

A move to Cardiff City occurred in December 1970 (where he had 56 outings, plus 4 as substitute, and scored 27 goals). A return to Yorkshire followed in September 1972, when he signed for Sheffield United (7 appearances, no goals).

Following his transfer to Bristol Rovers during March 1973, he formed a unique strike partnership with Bruce Bannister. Warboys

once said that his own magic moment in football was winning promotion with Bristol Rovers. Alan made 141 appearances (3 as substitute) and scored 53 goals. His next move was to Fulham in February 1977, turning out 19 times for the London club and finding the back of the net twice. Whilst he was at Craven Cottage, his colleagues included George Best, Bobby Moore, Rodney Marsh and Peter Storey. He then went to Hull City in September 1977 (44 appearances, with 5 as substitute, and scored 9 goals).

Alan found his way back to Belle Vue in July 1979, playing for a period as a central defender, and he found success in this position. He was voted Player of the Season for 1979/80. Rovers' ex-manager, Billy Bremner, said the following about Alan: 'Alan Warboys is the best professional I have worked with and I can't pay him a bigger tribute than that. I knew when I brought him back to Doncaster Rovers that he was

popular with the fans and he is equally popular with the players ... He has always battled to improve his own game and he has done the same in matches. I have been in the dressing room when Alan has come in at the final whistle, covered in perspiration, and has had to sit near the door to get his breath because he's put so much into his performance. You can't ask for more than that ... Most people don't know that he actually took a cut in money when he re-signed after his first two years back at Belle Vue because of his love for the club.'

Warboys retired after struggling with a back injury suffered in an FA Cup tie against Cambridge on 2 January 1982. Rovers had never beaten Cambridge in ten previous encounters, but Alan scored the winning goal to put the Belle Vue club into the fourth round for the first time in twenty-six years. It was a fitting end to a distinguished career. Alan subsequently went into the licensed trade.

Graham Sydney Watson

Midfield 1966-1968, 1969-1972

Football League
Appearances: 152 (+5 as substitute)
Goals: 33

FA Cup
Appearances: 9
Goals: 2

FL Cup
Appearances: 8
Goals: 0

Total appearances: 174

Graham (known more popularly as 'Willie') Watson, was born in Doncaster on 3 August 1949. He joined Rovers as an apprentice and signed pro during the autumn of 1966. He made his debut in the Third Division away game at Swindon Town on 1 October 1966. On that day, he lined up alongside experienced professionals such as Alan Finney, Laurie Sheffield, Tony Coleman and Bobby Gilfillan. In a fixture three days earlier, the team had been hammered 6-1 away at Oxford, but in the Swindon game they managed a 1-0 victory.

By playing for Rovers at this time, he'd really been thrown in at the deep end as the results were erratic to say the least. However, during this period he made 21 appearances, 1 as substitute, and scored 3 goals. He scored his first goal on 15 November 1966, in the home game against Swansea Town. He made 2 appearances in the FA Cup games against Halifax and played in 2 of the League Cup matches, scoring when Rovers met Swindon at home.

Disappointingly, in the 1966/67 season, Willie saw Rovers relegated back to the Fourth Division. They had finished twenty-third, with a mere 32 points, 117 goals against and only 58 for. Yet it is interesting to note that, whilst Willie was part of a relegation side, a small consolation was that he had been playing at home, at least, in front of an average crowd of 7,908.

At the start of the 1967/68 term back in the Fourth Division and under new manager George Raynor, Rovers lost their first 2 games and didn't record a win until the sixth game, away at York

City. Willie only missed 1 League game between August and February, when he was transferred along with colleague Dennis Leigh to Rotherham United during a player exchange and cash deal. Defending the move, Rovers chairman Frank Wilson told the *Doncaster Evening Post* of Thursday 8 February 1968: 'The two youngsters have not been sold for money. The cash we shall receive will only just about cover the signing-on fees to which the three Rotherham players are entitled ... Selling these boys was the last thing we wanted to do. But they were the only bargaining power we had to get the players with whom to re-orientate the club ... I have told both Watson and Leigh that we are extremely loath to part with them. They are great lads with great potential ... Any straight fee we would have got for the two at this stage would not have got us the players we needed.'

At Millmoor, Willie played 13 games and scored 1 goal. He then returned to Belle Vue during January 1969 and initially had a better time in than his previous spell at Belle Vue. Between January and May, he appeared 18 times, once as substitute, and scored 8 goals, and was part of the team that lifted the Fourth Division championship at the end of 1968/69.

He was transferred to Cambridge United in September 1972, where he made 206 appearances, 3 as substitute, and scored 24 goals. From there he moved to Lincoln City in September 1978 (43 outings and 2 goals), and back to Cambridge United in March 1980 (1 appearance as substitute).

James Watton
Left-back 1964-1968

Football League
Appearances: 121 (+3 as substitute)
Goals: 0

FA Cup
Appearances: 6
Goals: 0

FL Cup
Appearances: 13
Goals: 0

Total appearances: 143

Jimmy will always be remembered for the part he played as a solid, hard-tackling defender in the mid-1960s promotion push. He was born in Wolverhampton on 1 November 1936, and after a period with De Graafschap (Netherlands), he joined Port Vale in September 1962. Whilst there, he made 5 appearances. He arrived at Belle Vue during July 1964 with Bill Leivers at the helm. The latter, having just replaced Oscar Hold, was looking for a promotion push in the coming season. At the end of the previous campaign the team had finished fourteenth in the Fourth Division, and Leivers was obviously keen to return the club to the glory years of the 1940s and 1950s. During the 1963/64 period, the left-back position had been shared by Meadows, Myers and Conwell, and Jimmy made his debut in the Fourth Division away game at Bradford Park Avenue on 22 August 1964. With him on the back line that day were Potter, McMinn, Ripley, Marsden and Ricketts.

In his first season with Rovers, Jimmy played in all 46 League games, the team eventually finishing in ninth position. He also appeared in the 4 FA Cup matches and the 3 appearances in the League Cup. In fact, until the game against Newport County on 25 September 1965, the *Doncaster Gazette* of 30 September 1965 reported that he had made 63 consecutive appearances for the club. During the 1965/66 season when Rovers became Fourth Division champions, Jimmy was an important member of the side that conceded 54 goals, the fewest for a number of years. He was ever present in the 1966/67 season, making 39 League appearances, plus 2 in the FA Cup and 6 in the Football League Cup. He made his last appearance for Rovers in the away game at Darlington on 4 November 1967. He played for no other League club after leaving Belle Vue.

Richard White

Centre half 1962-1964

Football League
Appearances: 83
Goals: 0

FA Cup
Appearances: 7
Goals: 0

FL Cup
Appearances: 2
Goals: 0

Total appearances: 92

Dick was born in Scunthorpe on 18 August 1931. After a spell with Scunthorpe SC, he played 133 games for Scunthorpe United and scored 7 goals. From there it was a move to Liverpool in November 1955, where he played 203 games. Standing 5ft 11in tall and weighing 12st 1lb, he was transferred to Belle Vue under manager Oscar Hold in July 1962, for a reported £4,000.

In the previous season, Rovers finished twenty-first in the League, conceded 82 goals and scored 60. So it was perhaps obvious that the board should seek a reliable anchor-man in defence. Dick made his debut in the Fourth Division home game against Brentford on 18 August 1962. Rovers lost the game 2-0 with 8,247 in attendance. The back line on that day was Potter, Wales, Cornwell, Raine and Ripley. This defence only contained one player – full-back Tony Wales – who had appeared in the last game of the previous term.

In time, Dick became team captain and during his first season he made 40 appearances. The team finished in sixteenth position, which was an improvement on the previous year. They conceded 78 goals and scored 64, but attendances increased. At the end of the following campaign, the team finished in fourteenth place, conceding 75

goals, but scoring 70. Dick appeared in 43 of the 46 League games. He also played in 4 FA Cup games and 1 League Cup game.

Whilst Dick must have been reasonably pleased with what had been achieved over the previous two years, he was looking to the future. On 9 April 1964, the *Doncaster Gazette* announced that the Rovers skipper had been released to take up the position of player-manager with Southern League club Kettering Town. A small fee was involved. He was due to leave Belle Vue on the completion of Rovers' League fixtures. His two-year contract was due to expire in June 1964. Rovers chairman, Jack Garnham, said: 'White has stated that his reason for wanting to leave is the likelihood of his being unable to continue much longer as a player owing to an arthritic condition in his knee.' It was with 'great reluctance' that the board acceded to his request.

It is tempting to suggest that Dick's time at Belle Vue as centre half and captain was very useful indeed, steering the team to finish seven places higher than when he first joined the club. It may also be argued that he pointed them in the right direction to finish ninth in the following season and champions the one after. Later, being a keen golfer, he became president of Scunthorpe Golf Club.

Steve Wignall
Centre half 1972-1978

Football League
Appearances: 127 (+3 as substitute)
Goals: 1

FA Cup
Appearances: 6 (+1 as substitute)
Goals: 0

FL Cup
Appearances: 4 (+1 as substitute)
Goals: 0

Total appearances: 142

Steve (christened Steve not Steven) Wignall signed schoolboy forms for Liverpool at fourteen, after showing early promise at both rugby and soccer. He also played basketball in the Cheshire League. He came to Doncaster, aged seventeen, on a three-month trial from Liverpool FC. He used to stay in the Woodborough Hotel, near Belle Vue on Friday nights and play in Rovers' Youth team on Saturday. He would then travel back to Liverpool by train on Saturday evenings. He played with the likes of Willie Straw, Stephen Reed and Stan Brookes. Sometimes Mike Elwiss and Steve Uzelac would play, even though they had just progressed into the first team. Maurice Setters was the manager at this time, and he put together a very young side and, in Steve's opinion today: 'was not given enough time to develop the players and take the team forward.'

Wignall made his Rovers debut on 11 November 1972 in the Fourth Division home game against Crewe Alexandra. One of his greatest memories from his playing days between 1972 and 1977 was the FA Cup games against Liverpool in 1974. 'I had only left Liverpool some eighteen months earlier,' recalled Steve, 'and here I was lining up at Anfield against my old club, which I had also supported as a youngster. We played out of our skins in our very unusual "African violet" kit against the big names of Keegan, Hughes and Clemence etc. What a day for me, as an eighteen-year-old. We could have won the game in the last minute when Kitch (Peter Kitchen) hit the bar. A 2-2 draw was a great result for the club. I came out of the players' entrance after the game and was engulfed by about twenty cheering members of my family and friends from Merseyside, who would normally have supported the Reds! I'm sure I did not succeed in speaking to them all as the whole occasion was quite overwhelming for me at such a tender age. Due to the power cuts in the 1970s, the replay was staged on a Tuesday afternoon, 8 January 1974, in front of 22,499. Liverpool made no mistake this time, winning 2-0, but we didn't let ourselves down and fortunately I was voted Man of the Match. Great memories.'

Steve considered the worst memory of his playing days at Belle Vue to be the sacking of Maurice Setters: 'He was my first manager, signing me as a full-time professional at seventeen. He gave me a chance and I went on to make over 700 appearances in League and cup competitions. I feel I owe him a lot.'

Steve was transferred to Colchester in September 1977, making 279 appearances, 2 as substitute, and scoring 22 goals. He then joined Brentford in August 1984, appearing 67 times for them and netting twice. His final League club was Aldershot, for whom he signed in

September 1986, playing for them 158 times, coming on as substitute 3 times and scoring 4 times. He stayed with Aldershot after they lost their Football League place and for a time managed the newly-formed Aldershot Town. He became manager of Colchester in January 1995 and non-League Conference side Stevenage Borough in March 2000. However, he soon left as he took the vacant Rovers managerial position in May 2000, with Alan Lewer as his assistant.

'When I took the job,' reflected Steve, 'I knew there was a lot of work ahead. What I did not know was the next eighteen months were going to be the hardest of my managerial career, due to exceptional circumstances off the field and upsets in my personal life. It was particularly hard going, as not long after I had taken the job, a minority of the crowd decided to abuse me, the chairman, John Ryan, and some of the players. This was something I was not used to. I had always received great support, especially early on, at all my previous

clubs where I had been very successful.'

At the end of Steve's first season in charge, the team finished in an average position in the League. At the start of the 2001/02 season, Alan Lewer left and Dave Penney became Steve's assistant. There were new signings and a new kit, and everyone was enthusiastic. 'Our pre-season went well,' began Steve, 'Dave Penney and myself were quite pleased and thought we had put together a squad capable of challenging for the Conference championship. Unfortunately, disaster struck almost immediately when two players suffered broken feet. From then on it was just a catalogue of injuries. Despite this, the squad performed well, and after 24 games we had only lost 4. One of these was away from home. We had drawn too many games, but I felt we would get stronger as more players returned to fitness and other clubs started to feel the pinch. Unfortunately, my contract was terminated in January 2002. I hope Doncaster Rovers return to the Football League soon. The real supporters deserve it.'

Harold Wilcockson

Full-back 1968-1969, 1971-1973

Football League
Appearances: 111
Goals: 4

FA Cup
Appearances: 6
Goals: 0

FL Cup
Appearances: 5
Goals: 0

Total appearances: 122

Harold was described as a full-back who loved to go forward, but for someone as accomplished as he was, it may be surprising to learn that Harold made no impression on the soccer world at all in his younger days. He was born on 23 July 1943 and started his career at Rotherham United, playing 109 games for them and scoring 2 goals. He once mentioned that his best games with the Millers were those against Manchester United, Coventry and Sheffield Wednesday.

He came to Belle Vue in February 1968 as part of a player-exchange deal. Looking at the reasons behind the deal from the Rotherham angle, it has been said that 'The Millers were at the foot of the Second Division ... mercurial manager Tommy Doherty was brought in to plot their escape from the jaws of relegation and to plan for the First Division' – hence the clear-out of older players.

Harold made his Rovers debut in the Fourth Division home game against Brentford on 10 February 1968, and following the upheaval of the 'two out, three in' deal, there were a number of changes in the line-up on that day. Sports writer Joe Slater commented in the *Doncaster Evening Post* of Friday 9 February: 'Doncaster Rovers parade all three of their new signings against Brentford at Belle Vue tomorrow. The former Rotherham men form the backbone of the defence. Harold Wilcockson is at right-back, Colin Clish at left-back, while Chris Rabjohn lines up at right half.' In total, Slater predicted, there would be nine changes – five positional – from the previous week's team.

Harold played in 18 of the remaining 19 games of the season and also managed 2 goals. At the end of the season, back in the Fourth Division, the team finished tenth with 56 goals against and 66 for. This, of course, was a big improvement on the previous season's tally in the Third Division where the team had conceded 117 and scored 58. So the introduction of the former Rotherham men could be seen to have steadied the ship.

In the following season, Harold was a useful member of the team that won promotion under manager Lawrie McMenemy. He made 36 appearances at right-back in the team that finished at the top of the table, conceding 38 goals and scoring 65. In the following season, he played in every League game (21) until he moved to Sheffield Wednesday in December 1969. This was in another player-exchange deal where Archie Irvine and Ian Branfoot came to Doncaster in exchange for Harold. Whilst at Hillsborough, Harold played in 40 games and scored 1 goal.

He returned to Belle Vue in May 1971, making 35 outings in his first season back, but only made 1 the following year, when he left Belle Vue. He had a number of sporting interests and was also a useful performer at golf, tennis and cricket. In fact, during the summer months, his name appeared as regularly among the week's top cricket scorers as it did on the scoreboard during the football season.

Russ Wilcox

Central defender 1980-1981, 1993-1996

Football League
Appearances: 82
Goals: 6

FA Cup
Appearances: 3
Goals: 0

FL Cup
Appearances: 5
Goals: 2

Total appearances: 90

Curiously, former Rovers favourite Russ Wilcox made his League debut for the club as a youngster in the last match of the 1980/81 campaign, but did not play his next League game until the start of the 1993/94 season. Russ was born in Hemsworth, South Yorkshire, on 25 March 1964. He showed promise as a youth player, and made his debut under manager Billy Bremner on 6 May 1981 in the Fourth Division away game at Mansfield, which finished goalless. Another Rovers favourite, Glenn Humphries, also pulled a Rovers shirt on for the first time in this match.

Unable to improve on this solitary appearance, Russ moved to Cambridge without playing a game, then signed for non-League side Frickley Athletic. There he won a number of caps at semi-professional level for England. He became a player who was attracting attention, indicated by the fee of £15,000 paid for him by Northampton Town in June 1986. His sound defending helped the Cobblers to win the Fourth Division championship at the end of the 1986/87 season. He turned out for them 137 times, before Hull City paid £120,000 for him in August 1990.

Wilcox had all the characteristics that make a good central defender – he was aggressive, confident and dominant in the air. He roared with the Tigers first team on 92 occasions (plus 8 as substitute) until Rovers persuaded him to return to Belle Vue for a club record-equalling fee in July 1993. There was some controversy over this, as the *Doncaster Star* explained on 11 August 1993. 'Doncaster Rovers have been ordered to pay a club record £60,000 transfer fee for defensive kingpin Russ Wilcox – but Hull

City say it is not enough. City chairman Martin Fish was fuming after the tribunal in London yesterday and plans to protest to the Football League. Hull valued Wilcox at between £150,000 and £200,000 and Fish said: "I'm disgusted with the tribunal." Russ looked set to sign for First Division Peterbrough a year ago, but the Posh pulled out when the tribunal fixed the fee then at £120,000.'

Hull wanted to know why their former captain and Player of the Year's price had halved in a year when he was a first-team regular the previous season and had been offered a new, improved contract. Rovers boss, Steve Beaglehole commented: 'We are just delighted to get him. We were aware of the fee quoted to Peterborough last year, but the new owners [at Belle Vue] were prepared to make the signing unconditional, and I think that speaks volumes for their ambitions and commitment to the club.' Rovers were ordered to pay 25 per cent of any future fee for the player, whose price equalled the club record paid to Stirling Albion for John Philliben in March 1984.

As Rovers captain, Russ was immensely popular on the terraces. He was also a player that a manager could rely upon and trust, on and off the field. Perhaps seeing the light as he watched events at Belle Vue off the field, Russ made his exit to Preston North End in September 1995. At the end of his first season at Deepdale, he won a Division Three championship medal and managed 62 outings, before Scunthorpe signed him for £15,000 in Septem-ber 1997, where he ended his playing career after 30 appearances.

Charlie Williams
Centre half 1949-1959

Football League
Appearances: 157
Goals: 1

FA Cup
Appearances: 14
Goals: 0

FL Cup
Appearances: 0
Goals: 0

Total appearances: 171

Charlie Williams is arguably one of the best-known former Rovers players, having found fame and fortune after his playing days were over. In his abrasive comedy act, he turned the hard, macho man's game attitude and racially-prejudiced atmosphere of the 1950s on its head and made thousands laugh.

Charlie was born in Barnsley on 23 December 1928 and, on leaving school, worked at Upton Colliery. Whilst playing for the colliery's football side, he attracted the attention of the Rovers scouts, and signed for the club under Jackie Bestall in October 1948.

Charlie made his Rovers' debut in the Third Division (North) home game against Tranmere on 3 May 1950. Amongst his colleagues in the back line on that day were Hardwick, Hainsworth, Lowes, Bycroft and L. Graham. Playing at centre half, Charlie always said that he was 'never a fancy player but could stop the buggers that were.'

After his debut, he did not make another appearance until the 1954/55 season. He was competing against the likes of Bill Paterson, Dave Miller and Syd Bycroft for the number five shirt, but whilst Charlie played infrequently for the first team in his early years at Belle Vue, he was a regular in the reserves. It has been claimed that 'Charlie was something of a novelty in the Football League at this time,' as there were very few black players around and he never reacted to the occasional racist abuse hurled at him. He was frequently referred to in the press as 'the coloured player.'

In the 1954/55 season, after Paterson had left for Newcastle, there was competition for the centre-half position, Charlie taking it for the last 19 games. In the following term, 1955/56, he made the position his own, appearing in every League and FA Cup game. The team finished in seventeenth position, with an average home gate of 12,420. He also scored the only goal of his Rovers career. This was in the Second Division away game at Barnsley on 24 March 1956. The match ended in a 2-2 draw and was watched by 9,892.

In the next term, he made 40 outings and the team finished in fourteenth position. The following year was a different story, when manager Peter Doherty unexpectedly departed and the team was relegated from the Second Division. During his last season at Belle Vue, 1958/59, Charlie lost his centre-half position, first to Barry Staton and then to Billy Mordue.

Once Charlie's footballing days were over, he concentrated on a career in entertainment singing in local clubs, but eventually turned to comedy. He appeared regularly on *The Comedians* and later was host on the *Golden Shot* television programme.

Defender 1964-1968

Football League
Appearances: 123 (+1 as substitute)
Goals: 2

FA Cup
Appearances: 8
Goals: 0

FL Cup
Appearances: 13
Goals: 0

Total appearances: 145

John Wylie was born on 25 September 1936, and during his school days played for Newcastle Boys. He started his football career by joining the groundstaff at Huddersfield Town, turning professional at seventeen. Later, in May 1957, and after National Service, he signed for Preston North End, staying there for 6 seasons, making 91 appearances and scoring 2 goals. By November 1962, he had signed for Stockport County, where he made 68 League appearances and netted twice.

Wylie came to Belle Vue in August 1964. In the previous season, Rovers had finished fourteenth, and they were hoping for better things, if not promotion, during the 1964/65 campaign. Two other defenders also arrived that summer – Jim Watton and Graham Ricketts, both of whom in time would help to form a unique unit with John in defence.

John made his debut in the Fourth Division game against Aldershot on 29 August 1964, in front of 6,449. The back line on that day was Potter, Raine, Watton, Wylie, Ripley and Ricketts. This was to be the nucleus of the defence that would lift the Fourth Division championship during the following season.

John didn't play in the first 2 League games of the 1964/65 term, but held the number four spot in every one thereafter. He played at right half in all the FA and League Cup games during that season. He also managed to find the net on 1 occasion. This was in the 4-4 draw away at Crewe on 16 April 1965. At the end of the season, Rovers took ninth place in the League and things were looking up. The average crowd attendance during the previous season was 6,360, whereas in the 1964/65 campaign it was 8,557. Also, the defence had not leaked as many goals – 62, as compared with 75 in the previous season. In addition, the team had scored more goals.

Consequently, everyone was looking forward to a further improvement during the 1965/66 campaign. Quite remarkably, John played in every League, FA Cup and League Cup game in the season. He also managed 1 more goal. For much of the time the back line remained the same – Kelly, Watton, Wylie, Nicholson and Ricketts. The defence conceded just 54 goals and this obviously contributed to the team winning the Fourth Division championship and gaining promotion.

John stayed for a couple more seasons, making 29 appearances (and 1 as substitute) in 1966/67 and 4 in the 1967/68 campaign. His tenacity in midfield and the part he played in the 1965/66 promotion side mean he will always be held in affection in the hearts of the Belle Vue faithful.

Railway Memories 1

YORK TO SCARBOROUGH, WHITBY & RYEDALE

il the 1960s, the legendary Scarborough Flyer provided a direct and fast summer service between the Yorkshire coast and London. ing one of the seemingly endless glorious 1950s summers(at least that's how we remember them!) B16/3 4-6-0 No.61472 storms past Works signal box on its way out of Scarborough with the King's Cross-bound express. The B16 will work the train only as far as ᴋ where, after attaching the Whitby portion, it will be taken forward to London by a Pacific, calling only at Grantham.
Hoole/Neville Stead collection

BELLCODE BOOKS
21 DALE AVENUE
TODMORDEN
WEST YORKSHIRE OL14 6BA
email: bellcode4books@yahoo.co.uk

Copyright © 2008 Bellcode Books
ISBN 9781871233 19 3

Edited by Steve Chapman

Printed in the UK by The Amadeus Press, Cleckheaton, West Yorkshire.

ABOVE: Whitby-based BR Standard Class 4 2-6-4T No. 80117 calls at Robin Hood's Bay in 1957 with a service from Middlesbro' to Scarborough. *TG Hepburn/Neville Stead collection*

FRONT COVER: Excursion traffic to Scarborough peaked in the late 1930s before being stopped in its tracks by the second world w In this splendid August 1938 scene, the dark utilitarian form of LNER J39 0-6-0 No. 1537 contrasts with the elegance of ex-North E ern Railway C7 Atlantic No. 706 and D49/2 4-4-0 No. 258 *The Cattistock* as they wait in Scarborough's Gas Works Up carriage sidi with the stock for returning trains. *The Pendragon collection/Colour-Rail NE132.*

BACK COVER TOP: The early 21st century brought a remarkable opportunity to relive the glorious era of the Scarborough Flyer w Hertfordshire Railtours ran a monthly King's Cross-Scarborough special. V2 2-6-2 No. 60800 *Green Arrow* thunders past the tra verse signal box and gated level crossing at Weaverthorpe with the London-bound Flyer on Thursday 29th May 2003. At York, the handed its train over to electric loco No. 90017. *Stephen Chapman*

BACK COVER BOTTOM: A Leeds to Scarborough Metro-Cammell DMU stands under the York & North Midland Railway trains roof at Malton in 1980. Wagons can be seen lining the coal drops in the goods yard beyond the station. Both goods yard and the tra shed roof are now just memories. *Stephen Chapman*

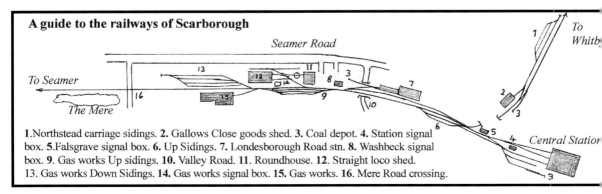

A guide to the railways of Scarborough

1.Northstead carriage sidings. **2.** Gallows Close goods shed. **3.** Coal depot. **4.** Station signal box. **5.**Falsgrave signal box. **6.** Up Sidings. **7.** Londesborough Road stn. **8.** Washbeck signal box. **9.** Gas works Up sidings. **10.** Valley Road. **11.** Roundhouse. **12.** Straight loco shed. **13.** Gas works Down Sidings. **14.** Gas works signal box. **15.** Gas works. **16.** Mere Road crossing.

INTRODUCTION

Railway Memories No.18 we covered the railways leading to
[W]hitby from the north. It was a huge success so now, sooner
[th]an intended, Railway Memories No.19 covers those lines to
[W]hitby from the south, including the North Yorkshire Moors
[lin]e, still operated by steam to this day and famed for its role in
[th]e ITV 1960s period drama *Heartbeat*.

[T]he railways of Scarborough and Whitby will always be asso-
[cia]ted with childhood trips to the seaside. With packed summer
[ho]liday trains racing along the plain out of York, winding their
[wa]y cautiously through the delightful Derwent Valley around
[Ki]rkham Abbey, slogging up from Pickering to Goathland - an
[ex]perience still to be savoured - and making the breathtaking
[rol]ler coaster journey atop 500ft cliffs between Whitby and
[Sc]arborough, lamentably no longer available to us.

[T]o the people who live in this rural part of Yorkshire, the rail-
[wa]y has been a lifeline to the outside world and even after a
[sta]tion's passenger service had been withdrawn, it often
[rem]ained central to the local community by still handling goods,
[pa]rcels and the occasional special train allowing local people to
[es]cape their quiet solitude and experience the crowds and big
[sh]ops of the city.

[I]n Railway Memories No.19 we recall the days when the line
[fr]om York to Scarborough was swamped with summer excur-
[sio]ns from usually industrial connurbations far away, as local
[sta]tions and branch lines continued their daily business of
[ser]ving the rural community amidst the mad holiday rush.

[T]he scale of the railway at Scarborough was immense for a
[tow]n of its size - and it was nearly all to cater for the seaside
[ho]liday trade which lasted for only about 10 weeks of the year.

Scarborough Central once had as many platforms as King's
Cross and still an extra station was needed to deal with the
overflow - and there were five groups of carriage sidings
plus a big eight-road engine shed.

The Esk Valley line from Whitby to Battersby, Picton and
Middlesbrough is fully detailed in Railway Memories No.18
as are the lines north of Whitby.

On 7th September 1964 British Railways began using the
24-hour clock in its working timetables so we use am and
pm up to that date and thereafter the 24-hour clock except
where direct comparisons are made between times of
different eras.

Contents

**A typical late 1940s Malton to Whitby stopping train near
Goathland Summit hauled by LNER G5 0-4-4T No. 7275 of
Malton shed.**
Ernest Sanderson/Stephen Chapman archive

SETTING THE SCENE

The railways linking Scarborough and Whitby with York and the major trunk routes to the rest of the country weave their way through a landscape that is rural, varied and scenic. In the 40 miles from North Yorkshire's rugged coastline to the arable plain that is the Vale of York, it comprises the remote and heathered heights of the North Yorkshire Moors soaring to over 1000ft above sea level in the north, and the agricultural chalk uplands of the Yorkshire Wolds, more modest in height, in the south, while the broad Vale of Pickering forms a natural thoroughfare between the two. The Howardian hills set up a barrier between the vales of Pickering and York that is breached by the narrow and winding valley of the River Derwent.

At the start of the railway age there was virtually no inland industry to attract the railway entrepreneurs. There was, however, an emerging need to connect both Whitby and Scarborough with industrial and population centres further afield by more efficient means than horse-drawn carts and coaches on meandering dirt roads.

Whitby was one of the most important seaports and shipbuilding centres in the North East at the time. It was a major centre for the whaling industry as well as fishing and the trade in minerals and general cargo. Transport to the developing industrial centres of the North East was often by sea but Whitby's ability to reach the similarly growing West Riding to the south was inhibited by the barrier of the North Yorkshire Moors. Crossing this vast obstacle involved a trek over hostile terrain along treacherous roads and often in appalling weather. No wonder local businessmen quickly latched onto the new transport innovation that was the railway as a means of breaking through to the south. They backed the Whitby & Pickering Railway - the first line to be built in the area covered by this book. Built under the guidance of George Stephenson, it was an economy version worked by horses and followed the River Esk inland for 6.25 miles to Grosmont where it turned southwards towards Goathland and Pickering. The section to Grosmont was opened in June 1835. The rest took another 11 months to complete and the whole line was opened on 26th May 1836. To reach 350ft-high Goathland, it required an incline up from Beckhole with an average gradient of 1 in 15. Too steep for the horses, carriages complete with passengers, were hauled up the bank at the end of a rope which was powered by the weight of a descending rail-mounted water tank which was emptied at the bottom to be hauled up again by the weight of descending coaches. This method was later replaced by a steam winding engine. From Goathland, the line descended steadily through Newtondale, to Levisham and finally Pickering, 24 miles from Whitby. Here, goods and passengers could be transferred to carts and carriages for the journey over a less inhospitable landscape to York and beyond. Trains may have been no more than a coach and horses on rails but even so, the W&P had transformed communications between Whitby and the south.

Significant quantities of ironstone were found around Grosmont, reputedly during construction of the W&P, and the new railway benefitted considerably by transporting the ore to Whitby for shipping to Tyneside. During the 19th century there were short-lived ironworks at both Grosmont and Beckhole. The Bagnall Brothers works at Grosmont, in production by 1864, had three towering furnaces working by 18?? a tramway over the main line bringing the ore down from mines beneath Grosmont village. However, it had closed 1891, unable to compete with bigger plants on Teesside. The Beckhole ironworks belonging to the Whitby Iron Co. was even less fortunate. Fed with ironstone by a 3ft gauge horse worked line from hillside mines, it had no sooner begun production in 1860 when one of the furnaces cracked spilling molten iron. Then one of the mine roofs collapsed burying much of the equipment and so the works had closed with little more than a year, taking with it the company's aspirations of turning tranquil Beckhole into an industrial complex.

Like Whitby, Scarborough, 22 miles to the south, was a significant fishing and seaport. It had been so since medieval times and Queen Elizabeth 1 invested considerably in expanding the harbour. It was also a long-established spa, water with health-giving properties being discovered there in 162?. Bathing had been popular since at least the 18th century and by 1820 Scarborough's population had reached 8000.

As the Railway Mania - the mad rush for building railways to just about every town and village in the country - gathered pace, Scarborough was keenly eyed by George Hudson, the Railway King - not least with a view to potential business of taking the fashionable classes to benefit from the waters and the sea air. As a result, his York & North Midland Railway opened the line from York to Malton and Scarborough on ? July 1845. Its builders met with few obstacles, the first miles eastwards from York and 21 miles onwards from Malton being over mainly level ground. Only the Howardian Hills stood in their way and a tunnel was considered. Instead though, they chose to follow the meandering River Derwent the resulting succession of sharp curves restricting train speeds to this day. The tunnel may have cut the journey time but it would have denied passengers the marvellous views this highly picturesque valley and the ancient ruins Kirkham Abbey, which the speed restrictions at least give them time to enjoy.

Also on 7th July 1845, the Y&NM opened a 6.75-mile branch from Rillington, just east of Malton, to Pickering. There it met the Whitby & Pickering which the Y&NM took over at around the same time, converting the horse-drawn sections to locomotive operation by 1847 and creating through route from Whitby to York and beyond. Hudson saw Whitby as having great potential as a resort and he set about developing the West Cliff area with large houses and the Royal Hotel. Alas, when Hudson became disgraced and bankrupt, his half-finished scheme was abandoned and the property sold off. In a 1920s paper for the London & North

e York-Scarborough line follows a fairly straight and level route except through the Howardian hills where it has to follow the andering valley of the River Derwent. B1 4-6-0 No. 61155 from Sheffield(Darnall) shed negotiates the curve into Kirkham Abbey with 'ork-bound train of empty coaches on 29th July 1961. *PB Booth/Neville Stead collection*

stern Railway, C. B. Fawcett, B. Litt., Reader in Geography Leeds University, wrote: "The Whitby & Pickering line s constructed as a light line for horse traction when Whitby s of much more importance as a seaport than it is now. The all population of the areas it connects, and its sharp curves d gradients, make it of little value." He described the Malton Driffield in much the same tone.

n 5th October 1846, Seamer, two miles out of Scarborough, came a junction when the Y&NMR opened its line to Filey, tage in the construction of the line to Hull which was mpleted throughout on 20th October 1847. The Railway ania was at its height but it was to be another six years fore any further lines were added when the York, Newcastle Berwick Railway opened its Thirsk & Malton line on 19th ay 1853. The 23-mile single track left the YN&B's York- rlington main line at Pilmoor, 16 miles north of York, and de its way through Coxwold, Ampleforth, Gilling and ngsby to reach Malton. Exactly three months later the dependent Malton & Driffield Railway completed its -mile single track branch into Malton from the Wolds. It s intended that the T&M would enter Malton directly from north but in the event it was joined to the M&D by a iffield-facing junction at Scarborough Road in Norton -called because the junction was immediately below the alton- Scarborough road) thus forming a direct route from iffield to the North East. Although rural and local in ture, these two branch lines became increasingly

useful during the 20th century for mineral and excursion traffic. Within months of these two lines opening, the original companies, the Y&NMR among them, were amalgamated to form the mighty North Eastern Railway, the dominant railway company throughout the North East and north and east Yorkshire until 1923 when it became a constituent of the London & North Eastern Railway.

So far as railway building was concerned, the bubble had burst, the unbridled optimism of the 1840s had given way to economically hard times and no major construction took place in this part of the country for almost two decades.

During this time, however, the NER did build one short but highly significant stretch of new line - from Grosmont to Fen Bog(near Ellerbeck two miles south of Goathland) which it opened on 1st July 1865. With a ruling gradient of 1 in 49 from Grosmont, it replaced the Beckhole incline and allowed locomotives to work throughout. As the original line was retained for goods traffic(and a summer passenger service from 1908 to 1914) as far as the incline foot at Beckhole, this created a new junction at Grosmont, called Deviation Junc- tion. To permit locomotive work, the low, narrow 119-yard tunnel between Grosmont station and Deviation junction, was replaced by a full-size double track bore. The original tunnel has been retained to this day for use as a footpath, originally to provide access to railwayman's cottages and now to the North Yorkshire Moors Railway's locomotive depot. Along with the deviation, a Scarborough-facing spur

Scarborough Road Junction, Norton, where the Thirsk & Malton line joined the Malton & Driffield Railway. Viewed from the T&M line from Gilling, B16/3 4-6-0 No. 61461 is on the rear of a train from Scarborough to the north which has just been led up the bank from Malton station by one of the local pilot engines on 29th July 1961. The B16 will then head its train forwards along the Gilling line. The signal box is not in use, having long since been replaced by a taller version hidden by the bus on the bridge. *PB Booth/N Stead c...*

was laid at Rillington so that a service could run between Scarborough and Whitby. It apparently saw few trains and is believed to have been taken out of use after only a year.

Also in 1865, the NER completed the final stage of the North Yorkshire & Cleveland Railway from Picton(see Railway Memories No.18), on the Northallerton-Stockton line, to a junction with the Whitby & Pickering at Grosmont, turning Grosmont into a 'V'-shaped junction station with two platforms on the Pickering side and one single track platform on the NY&C side.

New schemes resumed in the 1870s when between 9th October 1871 and 1st April 1875 the NER opened, in three stages, a branch from the Thirsk & Malton line to Pickering, serving the market towns of Helmsley and Kirbymoorside on the way. From the junction at Gilling the two single line branches ran parallel for two miles, giving the impression of a double track.

The following decade saw three new lines added in as many years but they would be the last, completing the main line network in this part of Yorkshire.

First on the scene, opening on 1st May 1882, was the NER's 16.75-mile single track from Pickering to Seamer via Thornton Dale(reputed to be the prettiest village in Yorkshire.) It

also served the Forge Valley beauty spots and was oft... known as the Forge Valley line. It was another very ru... branch but in years to come would handle considerable to... nages of mineral traffic. As with the branch from Gilling... entered Pickering from the Malton end.

In December 1883, the Whitby, Redcar & Middlesbro... Union Railway, which followed a precarious route along ... clifftops from Loftus to Bog Hall Junction in Whitby, wh... it joined the Whitby & Pickering line into Whitby Town s... tion, was finally completed. The NER had taken over ... scheme after a protracted and much troubled construction ... devilled by a lack of funds and cheapskate workmanship ... feated the original independent company(see Railw... Memories No.18.)

The final piece in the jig-saw came on 16th July 1885 wh... the independent Scarborough & Whitby Railway was co... pleted. This single line serving eight intermediate stations ... cluding Robin Hood's Bay, also clung to clifftops up to 50... high and was beset with severe gradients - as steep as 1 in ... between Fyling Hall and Ravenscar(631ft above sea lev... These and coastal conditions of sea spray and damp mists ... to slippery rails which could bring trains slithering to a sta... still.

he S&W was originally intended to be a totally isolated e running 21 miles from Gallows Close in Scarborough to south bank of the River Esk near Whitby Abbey. In the ent, a bold move was made to connect it to existing NER es at each end, involving major and expensive structures. the Whitby end, the 120ft-deep Esk Valley was bridged the dramatic 915ft-long 13-arch Larpool Viaduct to join Whitby-Loftus line at Prospect Hill, just south of West ff station. The junction faced Loftus, allowing trains from arborough to run directly to West Cliff and Teesside but ant them having to reverse in order to reach Whitby Town. the Scarborough end, a 260-yard tunnel was built by the t and cover' method to a York-facing junction at Fals-ve, right on the Scarborough station approaches. Clearly other route into Scarborough was available but the fact t the junction faced away from the station resulted in itby trains, after crossing the station approach lines, hav-g to reverse at Londesborough Road(the engine running nd the train as propelling out of Central station was not mitted) before proceeding through the tunnel and on to itby. This already protracted business could result in itby trains suffering considerable delay at busy times, es-cially if there was already a train standing on the Londes-rough Road through line. The S&W was operated from the rt by the NER which took it over completely in 1898.

he railway network was now at its peak but the next 30

years would see the mass of working people acquire the t.. and money to partake of a new phenomenon - the summer holiday with Scarborough growing into one of the most pop-ular resorts anywhere - not just with Yorkshire families but with holidaymakers from as far afield as London, the Mid-lands and Glasgow. Saturday became the day when holidays traditionally began and ended, leading to a mass movement of people to and from Scarborough and resorts all over the country on that one day of the week for about 10 weeks of the year. By the early 20th century so many extra trains had to be run that serious congestion was being experienced both at Scarborough and along the line from York. The NER tackled this in 1908 by opening a new excursion station at Londes-borough Road, just short of Falsgrave Junction. New carriage sidings and locomotive servicing facilities were provided at Northstead, on the Whitby line between Gallows Close and Scalby, the arrangement allowing incoming excursion trains to disgorge their passengers at Londesborough Road and then run empty straight to the sidings without impeding other services using Central station. Similarly, returning trains could run straight from the sidings to Londesborough Road where their passengers would already be marshalled into queues in a large circulating area ready to board with mini-mal delay. The NER extended Central station in 1904 by adapting the original goods shed on its south flank(though the platforms were too short for excursion trains,) goods traffic

arborough's Londesborough Road excursion station was opened by the North Eastern Railway in 1908 to help accommodate the r increasing number of excursion trains arriving at the resort. The roof, large circulating area and one of Scarborough's impressive nal gantries are evident as Fairburn 2-6-4T No. 42084 gathers pace with a local to Hull c.1957. *Ernest Sanderson*

switched to expanded facilities at Gallows Close ... goods shed was completed in 1902.

...rst world war behind them, people began flock-... ...orough in even greater numbers and by the late 1920s matters were becoming critical again, prompting the LNER to take somewhat drastic action. As an economy measure, but also to increase train speeds and capacity on the York-Scarborough line, it closed every intermediate station except Malton and Seamer. The passenger receipts from these stations were not enough to justify a regular stopping service and they closed in September 1930 but the platforms were retained for use by occasional excursions and parcels traffic for three decades afterwards. Platform 1 at Scarborough Central was also extended and an inset bay platform provided specifically for Whitby trains in time for the summer 1934 timetable. They still had to reverse but they could now be propelled in and out of the station and no longer did they have to cross all the approach lines.

Not being an industrial area there were very few industrial lines or light railways. One notable line was the 3ft gauge Ampleforth College tramway which climbed steeply for two miles from Gilling station to the school. Laid around 1895, its main purpose was to carry coal from the main line to the school's own gasworks as well as general goods. It also served a brickworks. For a time, it even carried passengers in a converted wagon. The 'trains' were normally hauled by a four-legged one horsepower locomotive with another added for the final pull to the gasworks. In later years the college had a small petrol or diesel loco for the job. The tramway is thought to have fallen out of use in the 1920s when the school converted to electric lighting and the gasworks closed.

One pure industrial line of 23.5 inches gauge connected t... Pickering sand quarry with the Malton-Whitby line at Ne... Bridge, a mile north of Pickering station. Between arou... 1870 and 1948 a narrow gauge tramway carried whinstone... Goathland station from quarries high up on the moors. Ori... inally it ran about two and half miles from a ridge away to t... north east but around 1911 it was cut back to new workin... nearer Goathland. It is believed that loaded tubs descended... Goathland by gravity and the empties were hauled back... horses while from about 1936 an old motor car with flang... wheels was used. The line descended to the top of the cutti... on the east side of the station by way of a reversal and t... stone was tipped through two chutes, one with a 40ft dr... into the main line wagons below and the other, behind t... water tower, via a crushing and cleaning plant. South... Grosmont, a horse-worked narrow gauge tramway ran dow... from Schofield's whinstone mines on the east slope of t... valley, underneath the 1865 deviation to a loading point... the Beckhole branch about 300 yards south of Esk Vall... Cottages. Between 1866 and 1886 ironstone mines on t... west side fed into a half-mile siding leading off the Beckho... branch. Scarborough came to have five cliff railways... which three remain in 2008 plus the North Bay Railway, t... miniature pleasure line opened in 1931 using a pair... Hudswell Clarke steam-outline diesel locos which are ve... fair representations of LNER A1(later A3) Pacifics, and st... going strong in 2008.

In 1902 work began on building the Lastingham & Roseda... Light Railway from the Gilling-Pickering line at Sinningt... to Rosedale Abbey but little progress had been made when... ground to a halt, never to be completed.

Passengers await a Whitby train on platform 1A alongside Falsgrave signal box on 24th July 1954 as nearly new BR Standard Class 2-6-0 No. 77013 emerges from Gallows Close tunnel with the stock of an excursion train that will start its journey from Londesborou... Road. Platform 1A was last used in 1964. *Ken Hoole/Neville Stead collection*

r most of the year, passenger services to Scarborough and
nitby were of a local nature and often lightly used but for
ew weeks in the summer it was a very different matter and
summer timetable was geared to accommodate the in-
se holiday traffic.

lthough merely a secondary line in terms of the national
l network(for maintenance purposes it was catagory B1
ed on line speed and the number of trains whereas main
es were catagory A,) the passenger service on the York-
arborough line was, and still is, the most important in this
a and for decades most trains have run as express passen-
. A small number of through Whitby trains increased the
ffic level between York and Rillington while the number of
ssenger trains between Seamer and Scarborough was con-
erably swelled by Hull and Pickering services.

hroughout the 1950s and into the early 1960s, the line's
mier train was, of course, the legendary Scarborough
er, a through summer service train from London which in
first post-war season, 1950, ran northbound on summer
days, Saturdays and Sundays and southbound on Satur-
ys, Sundays and Mondays until 10th September. It left
ngs Cross at 11.5am(11.45 on Sundays) and Scarborough
1.30am(10.40 on Sundays.) After that, the Sunday north-
und and Monday southbound workings were dropped and
1957, the northbound train ran until 7th September on Sat-
days and on Fridays from 26th July until 23rd August. It
t Kings Cross at 11.28am, arriving Scarborough at 4.14pm
both days. The southbound Flyer ran on Saturdays
oughout the summer timetable and on Sundays from 14th
y. It left Scarborough at 10.42am(10.35 on Sundays) and
ched Kings Cross at 3.28pm(3.40pm on Sundays.) Its only
ermediate stops were at York and Grantham(plus Malton
the Sunday trains) and it conveyed a through carriage
m Whitby which left at 9.33am on Saturdays(9.30am on
ndays) and was attached at York. The northbound through
riage was taken forward by the 3.40pm York-Whitby.

ntil the early 1980s, the year-round core weekday service
s predominantly composed of trains running between
eds or York and Scarborough with extras laid on during
summer holiday season. The summer 1950 weekday
etable, still under the influence of post-war austerity,
wed 10 trains to Scarborough and nine from Scarbor-
gh(plus the Flyer,) the first of the day being the 4.30am
m York and the last the 8.30pm from York(10pm on Fri-
ys.) The service included an 8.55am from Normanton and
5pm return, and an 8.45am from Bradford Forster Square
l 8pm return - the day's last train from Scarborough to-
rds York. The 8.5am Scarborough to Leeds and 5.30pm
urn conveyed a buffet car, while the 10.20am to Leeds and
5pm from Leeds included through carriages to and from
ngs Cross. No other mid-week extra trains ran during the
mmer holiday season.

y summer 1955, a number of peak summer weekday trains
re running in addition to the core service of 10 trains from
rk and 11 from Scarborough with four summer 'dated'

trains from Scarborough and five from York plus an 8.18pm
unadvertised relief to run from Scarborough when required.
The Bradford and Normanton trains were still running while
the dated trains included the 8.17am from Sheffield Victoria
and 5.25pm Scarborough to Swindon, both running from
16th July to 3rd September.

With diesel multiple units having replaced steam on many
services, the summer 1960 core weekday service consisted
of 12 trains from the York direction(10 of them originating at
Leeds) and 14 towards York(10 bound for Leeds.) Six additional trains ran each way during the summer peak, including
the 8.17am from Sheffield Victoria and 5.30pm to Swindon.
The Normanton and Bradford Forster Square trains still ran
but the train from Bradford ran only from 18th July until 12th
August.

Back in summer 1950, the York-Malton-Rillington section
saw the addition of three through Whitby to York trains on
weekdays and two from York, mainly Whitby-Malton trains
extended on certain days: they were the 7.2am Mondays and
Saturdays from Whitby, the 9.25am Mondays, Fridays and
Saturdays from Whitby, and the 10.30am Mondays and Saturdays which conveyed through carriages for the Scarbor-
ough Flyer to Kings Cross; and the 10.30am Mondays and
Saturdays from York, plus the 3.25pm Mondays, Fridays and
Saturdays from York which on Fridays and Saturdays conveyed through carriages off the Scarborough Flyer from
Kings Cross. The 7.2am from Whitby was booked to call at
closed Rillington station as required to set down railway staff.
By summer 1960, four trains were running from York to
Whitby and five from Whitby. In addition, were the summer
Fridays 9.11am from Whitby(9.33 on Saturdays) and the
3.35pm summer Fridays and Saturdays from York convey-
ing the Flyer through carriages.

During the 1950s the Hull line boasted a fairly intensive
service and in summer 1950 added another 10 trains each
way between Seamer and Scarborough. Only one was limited
to the peak holiday season, the 9.50am from York and 6pm
return which was routed via Market Weighton and ran from
10th July to 15th September. The service remained broadly
similar in summer 1957 but the York train reached Scarborough as empty stock for stabling as by then it only carried
passengers as far as Filey. By summer 1960, the Hull line
service, now almost entirely DMU, brought 11 trains each
way to the Seamer-Scarborough section plus the empty stock
off the seasonal York service.

The York-Scarborough line was not one of the many listed
for closure in the 1960s by the infamous Dr. Beeching, nor
was its counterpart from Hull, though the Hull line was to
endure closure threats later on. The late 1960s nevertheless
saw a much simpler service pattern and the May 1968 to May
1969 timetable showed nine year-round York-Scarborough
trains each way(seven from Leeds and six to Leeds.) The
Normanton and Swindon trains had been axed but a train still
ran from Bradford Exchange and return in the summer peak
and the 08.05 DMU from Scarborough continued through to

A 1950s Scarborough to Leeds service gets away from Seamer headed by D49/2 4-4-0 No. 62745 *The Hurworth*. The D49/2s were a va ant of the class with Lentz rotary cam poppet valve gear. *Ken Hoole/Neville Stead collection*

Manchester Exchange. Five holiday season trains ran to Scarborough in summer 1968 and eight towards York. The seasonal trains now included one out and back service each from Sheffield Midland and Wakefield Kirkgate. The number of weekday Hull line trains had been reduced to seven into Scarborough and six out but there were three more inwards and four outwards in the summer season. There were no York-Whitby trains, the Whitby line having closed in March 1965. The first train from York was still at 04.25, officially classed as a mail train and allowed 10 minutes at Malton compared with five in 1960, until being withdrawn in May 1980.

The York line service remained broadly similar until 4th January 1982 when it underwent a major transformation with the introduction of six loco-hauled Trans-Pennine services to Liverpool Lime Street and five from Liverpool - mainly York-Liverpool services extended to/from Scarborough in place of worn out local DMUs now considered to be in an unacceptable internal condition. At the same time DMUs on some remaining York/Leeds service were also replaced by loco-hauled trains.

By the May 1983-May 1984 timetable the number of Trans-Pennine services had increased to eight from Scarborough and seven to Scarborough and included trains to/from North Wales as well as Liverpool. There was also a loco-hauled 09.25 from Bradford Interchange plus a summer season train each from Wakefield Westgate and Sheffield.

The Hull service, having survived several closure threats, still added 10 year-round trains each way between Seamer and Scarborough plus a seasonal 21.05 from Scarborough

and two seasonal trains from Hull.

The loco-hauled era lasted only until 1987 when York-b Class 150/2 Sprinter multiple units began to take o TransPennine services(the hyphen having since been moved from the branding.) The first ones in service work the 07.03 Liverpool-Scarborough and 09.53 Scarborou Liverpool on 13th March 1987. From then on the new Spri ers gradually took over all Scarborough services followed 1989 by the more comfortable Class 156 Super Sprinters a at the start of the 1990s by the more superior air-condition 90mph Class 158s on what had by then become a two-hou Scarborough-Liverpool service. The alternate trains w also mainly Scarborough-Liverpool or Manchester Victo but ran via Bradford and Halifax. The 158s were replaced 2006/7 by new Siemens Class 185s on what by then was hourly Scarborough-Liverpool service. Regular loco-hau trains disappeared in the early 1990s upon withdrawal of peak summer Wakefield train. In summer 2007 the Yo Scarborough line carried 17 trains from York and 16 fro Scarborough plus just one holiday season extra from Yor all of them operated by Transpennine Express. The norm York-Scarborough journey time, with stops at Malton a Seamer, was 52 minutes, seven minutes faster than in su mer 1957. The fastest train in 2007, a summer Saturday se ice from London St. Pancras took 42 minutes non-stop fro York compared with the Scarborough Flyer's 51 minutes 1957.The Hull service still contributed another nine each w between Seamer and Scarborough.

Over the years, the weekday Malton-Whitby service co

ed of five or six trains each way with extras in the peak
[ho]liday season and in those days, Whitby had through serv-
[ice]s to/from London. In summer 1950, trains left Malton at
[9.3]0am, 11.10am, 2.20pm, 4pm and 6pm. The 11.10 started
[fro]m York on Mondays, and the 4pm from York on Mondays,
[Frid]ays and Saturdays until 9th September when it conveyed
[thro]ugh carriages from Kings Cross. Trains left Whitby Town
[at 7].2, 9.25, 10.30 and 11.40am, and 3.20 and 6.50pm. The
[7.42] continued through to York on Mondays and the 9.25 on
[Mo]ndays, Fridays and Saturdays. The 10.30 could be re-
[gar]ded as Whitby's premier train, being the through carriages
[to K]ings Cross running on Mondays and Saturdays only. Be-
[sid]es these, two trains ran each way between Whitby and
[Go]athland, leaving Whitby Town at 7.38am and 12.35pm,
[and] Goathland at 8.15am and 1.20pm. Between Grosmont
[and] Whitby the number of trains was almost doubled by the
[add]ition of the Battersby line service which at that time was
[ma]de up mainly of trains running between Whitby and Stock-
[ton] via Stokesley and Picton.

[D]uring the 1950s the Malton-Whitby service grew to six
[trai]ns each way in high summer while through carriages at-
[tach]ed to the Scarborough Flyer at York maintained a Whitby-
[Kin]gs Cross service in the summer peak. In 1957, for example,
[the]y came from London on Fridays(26th July to 23rd August)
[and] Saturdays(until 7th September), and returned south on Sat-
[urd]ays and Sundays. On Saturdays they were conveyed by the
[9.3]3am(9.30 on Sundays) from Whitby which was extended to
[Yor]k. Northbound, they were attached to the 4.15pm from
[Ma]lton which started back at York at 3.40pm.

Diesel multiple units were introduced in 1959 and as a result more trains ran through between Whitby and York but
parcels traffic and heavy summer loadings meant that some
still had to be loco-hauled. One example was the 10.28am
DMU from York which was specified in the working
timetable to be 'worked by steam' on weekdays from 4th July
to 26th August besides being steam on Saturdays throughout
the summer service when it started from Leeds. The 4.8pm
from Malton and 9.11am from Whitby(9.33 on Saturdays)
were also loco-hauled as they conveyed the Kings Cross
through carriages to and from York on the relevant days.
Other trains still loco-hauled were the 5.20am from Malton,
and the 8.55(Saturday) and 2pm(Saturday,) 6.5pm and 7.3pm
peak summer Whitby to York trains. Another summer peak
working was the 5am York Clifton to Whitby empty stock.

Battersby line trains joining and leaving the Whitby & Pickering line at Grosmont had run between Whitby and Middlesbrough since closure of the Battersby-Picton line to
passenger traffic in June 1954 and were increased to the lux-
urious level of nine trains into Whitby and 10 to Middlesbrough, plus extras in the summer peak, after being taken
over by DMUs in May 1958.

The passenger service between Scarborough and Whitby
consisted mainly of trains running between Scarborough and
Middlesbrough via the spectacular coastal route from Whitby
to Loftus and Brotton where they turned inland. Their journey involved three reversals, two to serve Guisbrough station as well as the reversal at Scarborough. They originally
ran to and from Saltburn but a switch to Middlesbrough in

The 1980s saw most services on the Scarborough-York line loco-hauled again for the first time since the late 1950s. A Brush Type 2(Class
[3]4) diesel waits beneath Malton's trainshed with the Scarborough to Bradford Interchange service on 3rd September 1983.
[Step]hen Chapman

1933 coupled with more attractive fares and day tickets brought a massive increase in passengers - at least in the summer. In Whitby they used West Cliff station with only the handful of Scarborough-Whitby trains reversing there and making their way to/from the more central Whitby Town. The summer 1946 timetable shows connections for Town maintained entirely by Middlesbrough and Scarborough-Whitby Town services but during the 1950s, additional shuttle trains ran between the two stations taking six minutes. In summer 1955 they consisted of seven each way, eight on Saturdays. Two-coach winter service Middlesbrough-Scarborough trains were permitted to serve both Whitby Town and West Cliff by propelling between the two - giving some trains no less than five reversals during their journey.

The 1950s saw the summer weekday Scarborough-Whitby service shrink from eight trains each way plus three extras in high summer during 1950 to around six each way plus four peak summer extras in 1957. Of these, three trains each way ran purely between Whitby Town and Scarborough. Trains running north of Whitby included a morning service from Darlington to Scarborough and an evening return, 8am from Darlington and 7.13pm return from Scarborough in summer 1955. Most of the summer dated trains north of Whitby ran to and from Stockton or West Hartlepool. The first train of the day in summer 1955 was the 6.10am Middlesbrough to Scarborough which the working timetable showed as booked to call at Scarborough Londesborough Road on school days to set down school children only. The last southbound train was the 4.20pm from Middlesbrough(6.19 from West Cliff) or

until 3rd September the 7.30pm from Whitby Town.

The first northbound train was the 8.12am Scarborough Middlesbrough and the last train the 8.15pm Scarborough Whitby Town. The Saturday Darlington-Scarborough a peak summer Saturday 8am Middlesbrough-Scarborou were the fastest trains over the whole route covering the miles from Middlesbrough in 2 hours 18 minutes. If t sounds slow by today's standards, most other trains took a thing up to three hours. In summer 2007 the fastest Sc borough to Middlesbrough time was one hour 54 minu with good connections at York and Darlington but the m usual time was around 2 hours 10 minutes.

The Scarborough-Whitby service was radically altered May 1958 when diesel multiple units replaced steam pov on all regular services and the line north of Whitby to Lof was closed completely. The summer 1960 working timetal shows that the midweek service had been increased to n trains each way between Scarborough and Whitby. Most s ran through to and from Middlesbrough and even Darling but now they reversed at West Cliff and ran via Whitby To and the Esk Valley line through Grosmont and Battersl All ran for the currency of the whole timetable but t 5.50pm Scarborough-Middlesbrough was extended to W Hartlepool from 4th July to 26th August.

The DMUs were initially popular with passengers. Ap from being clean and modern, they afforded superb views the dramatic coastal scenery that the Scarborough-Whit line had to offer. The ease with which they could rever direction compared with loco-hauled trains helped to sligh

The gradient post declares that Middlesbrough-based Ivatt Class 4 2-6-0 No. 43072 has just clawed its way up the 1 in 39 from Fyl Hall and is passing Ravenscar Summit with a Middlesbrough-Scarborough service on 23rd July 1957. *Ken Hoole/ Neville Stead coll*

rborough-Whitby services underwent a major transformation when diesel multiple units replaced steam in May 1958. e, a Derby Works 3-car unit is leaving Robin Hood's Bay for Whitby. Camping coaches that provided holiday accommodation at a number of stations along the line are visible just beyond the platforms. *Neville Stead collection*

uce journey times. Overall times from Middlesbrough to rborough were around two and a quarter and two and half rs even with four reversals but the Saturdays Only 0am West Hartlepool-Scarborough which did not call at st Cliff, reversing instead at Propsect Hill, covered the 5 miles in 2 hours 7 minutes. In the main, Scarborough-itby journey times were only marginally reduced but the 1pm Scarborough-Darlington completed the journey to ddlesbrough in 2hrs 8 minutes, 20 minutes faster than its 0 equivalent in 1957.

he DMUs also enabled the re-introduction of a circular nic tour first run by the LNER in the 1930s using the totype Armstrong Whitworth diesel railcar *Tyneside turer*. The 1960 working timetable showed the weekday dvertised special running from 4th July to 26th August. DMU left Scarborough at 11.20am and ran to Rillington ction where it reversed to travel via Pickering and the rth Yorkshire Moors to Whitby, arriving there at 2.31pm. ft at 4.46pm, returning via the coast to reach Scarborough .41pm.

he 1960s were notorious for the Beeching Axe and no re so than in this part of the world for had it been fully lemented, the Beeching plan would have wiped Whitby the railway network altogether. As it was, both its rail s to the south would be cut. Vigorous opposition to the itby closures was swept aside by BR and the government, fact that all lines were vital lifelines for remote rural

communities where roads were often narrow, winding, steep and circuitous or that Whitby was almost wholly dependent on them for its holiday trade, cut no ice with the authorities. The minister of transport did finally refuse closure of the Whitby-Battersby-Middlesbrough route but was unswayed so far as the Malton and Scarborough lines were concerned and their passenger services were both withdrawn with effect from 8th March 1965.

The Whitby-Middlesbrough service has faced several closure threats since it escaped the Beeching axe but has nevertheless survived albeit with stringent economies. In May 1991 it was slashed from seven to just four trains each way on weekdays in a bid to cut costs. The story of this service is told in Railway Memories No.18.

The passenger services along the branch lines feeding into Malton and Pickering were strictly local in character. Unless they were out just for the ride no-one would, for example, contemplate travelling throughout from York to Pickering via Coxwold and Gilling. The end to end journey took about an hour and three quarters compared with around an hour and 10 minutes via Malton. They did, however, provide a useful link from the north and as will be seen, the Pilmoor-Malton section came into its own on summer Saturdays. Back in 1910, the service consisted of trains between Malton and Pilmoor (two from Malton leaving at 6.40am and 12.10pm,) Malton and Gilling to connect with Pickering-York trains(trains leaving Malton at 10.10am and 3.20 and 5.46pm,) Pickering and

With the East Coast main line just under five miles behind it, D49/1 4-4-0 No. 62730 *Berkshire* heads the 10.23am Saturdays Only Y... to Pickering near Husthwaite Gate on a blustery 31st January 1953, the last day of services. York-based D49s were staple power for Ryedale local passenger service. Designed by Sir Nigel Gresley and introduced in 1927, the 3-cylinder D49/1s had Walschaerts valve g... and piston valves. *Neville Stead collection*

York via Gilling and Coxwold(York-bound trains leaving Pickering at 7.25 and 10.5am and 5.40pm,) Pickering and Pilmoor(the one train from Pickering leaving at 3.15pm,) plus a Saturday evening Pickering to Helmsley train at 8.20pm. By 1923 the Malton-Pilmoor trains had been withdrawn to leave only the shuttle service of three Malton-Gilling trains each way to connect with Pickering-York/Pilmoor services.

As the 1920s passed, more convenient buses took away most of what passengers the railway had. Towards the end of the decade, the LNER introduced Sentinel steam railcars on most routes in the area but with little economic effect and the last Malton-Gilling passenger trains ran on 30th December 1930. The second world war saw the remaining service stripped bare and in summer 1946, after the war had ended, it amounted to just the 4.30pm Pickering to York and 6.45pm return, plus a 6.45am Pickering to Alne on the East Coast main line(where it connected with a stopping train to York) and 9am return. By summer 1950, the service had been restored to the 7.25 and 10.30am and 6pm York to Pickering, and the 7.10 and 10.15am and 5.40pm Pickering to York trains - very similar to 1910. Nevertheless, this service was itself withdrawn in 1953 with the last trains running on 31st January - the very night of the devasting East Coast floods. From then on the Gilling branches were left to a sleepy existence disturbed only by occasional goods trains - except on summer Saturdays when they enabled heavy trains hauled by

big locomotives, including V2 2-6-2s and even the c... Pacific, carrying holidaymakers between the north and Sc... borough to avoid York. These trains travelled via Gilling a... Malton where they had to reverse at Scarborough Road Ju... tion and Malton station. Rather than the engine running rou... its train twice, one of Malton's pilot engines would attach... the rear and draw the train between Scarborough Road a... the station. They generally called at Malton station to... down only on the way to Scarborough and to pick up pass... gers only on the way from Scarborough. Two trains ran e... way in summer 1950, adding to the local service still extan... the time. They were the 11.5am Newcastle-Scarborou... which ran from 17th June to 2nd September and reach... Malton at 1.51pm, the 9.15am Glasgow to Scarborough wh... ran until 26th August and reached Malton at 4.7pm,... 10.35am Scarborough to Glasgow and 10.55am Scarborou... to Newcastle, both of which ran from 17th June to 2nd S... tember. During the course of the decade, the number of tra... increased until by summer 1960 there were a total of ei... summer Saturday trains during July and August. They w... the 10.45am Newcastle-Scarborough, the 8.5 and 9.27... Glasgow-Scarborough, the 7.50am Filey Holiday Ca... Edinburgh, the 8.40 and 10.25am Scarborough-Glasgow, a... the 9.8 and 10.50am Scarborough-Newcastle. The 1950s pub... timetables curiously showed these trains as routed "... Gilling" even though Gilling station was closed and they did... call there other than occasionally for the engine to ta...

ter. For a few years after the opening of Butlin's holiday
~~mp~~ at Filey in 1947, some trains between the north and the
~~np~~ took the Scarborough Road-Driffield route. Summer
~~urday~~ trains last used the Pilmoor-Malton line in summer
~~52~~ after which they had to reverse at York. Other ~~excur-~~
~~ns~~ running from time to time included those calling at
~~al~~ stations bringing ramblers to the area and offering local
~~ple~~ the chance to visit York and Leeds. Between 1959 and
~~53~~ an annual excursion organized by Helmsley porter ~~sig-~~
~~man~~ Desond Lee who later founded the Ryedale travel
~~ncy,~~ took local people for day trips to far away ~~destina-~~
~~ns.~~ The start and end of ~~scool~~ terms saw special trains to
~~1~~ from Gilling for boys attending Ampleforth College,
~~ain~~ worked by big engines.
~~he~~ Pickering-Seamer passenger service was another to
~~ickly~~ suffer from bus ~~competiton.~~ It consisted of five ~~Scar-~~
~~rough-Pickering~~ trains each way in 1910 and again ~~Sen-~~
~~el~~ steam railcars were tried in the 1930s. In summer 1946
~~ins~~ left Pickering for Scarborough at 7 and 9.43am and
~~.5~~ and 5.10pm, the 19.5-mile journey taking 49 minutes.
~~ey~~ left Scarborough for Pickering at 11am and 2.50 and
~~0pm.~~ Four years later, with effect from 5th June 1950, the
~~vice~~ was withdrawn and the line was closed completely
~~tween~~ Seamer and Thornton Dale. Had either it or the
~~lling~~ line entered Pickering from the opposite direction it
~~y~~ well have survived into the 1960s because it would have
~~vided~~ a direct route for the summer Saturday trains ~~with-~~
~~t~~ them having to reverse at Malton.
~~The~~ three daily passenger trains between Malton and
~~iffield,~~ known locally as "The Dodger," also succumbed
~~th~~ effect from 5th June 1950 after which the Driffield line
~~came~~ goods only. At that time, trains left Malton for
~~iffield~~ at 7am(to Bridlington,) 11am and 5.55pm.

Even the York-Scarborough line led a relatively quiet existence during the week, especially in the winter, but on summer Saturdays it once carried a continuous procession of
trains from and to most parts of the nation. The 20th century
saw more and more working people with the time and money
for a summer holiday which traditionally began and ended
on a Saturday and with Scarborough one of Britain's most
popular seaside resorts, it would, on that one day of the week
during a few weeks of the year, see thousands of holidaymakers descend on it to begin their holidays as thousands
went home at the end of their holidays. This called for intensive train services using all available resources, not least locomotives, rolling stock and crews. Holiday traffic reached
its peak in summer 1939, immediately before the outbreak
of war when such frivolities had to be suspended. It recov-
ered slowly after the war, spurred on by the opening of Butlin's Filey holiday camp complete with its own station in
1947, and again became heavy during the 1950s and early
1960s. The peak summer 1957 timetable shows a dozen
timetabled Saturday trains each way between York and Scarborough besides the normal service outlined earlier. They included two through trains from London King's Cross, one of
them the Scarborough Flyer, and trains from Derby, Leicester, Manchester Victoria and King's Norton(Birmingham)
with corresponding return workings plus trains from
Grantham and Hitchin. As well as these were the Glasgow
and Newcastle trains travelling via Gilling and Malton. Another nine trains came off the Bridlington line at Seamer:
from Sheffield Midland, Chesterfield Midland, Leicester
Central, Stalybridge, Sowerby bridge, Basford North, Liverpool Exchange and Manchester London Road plus the 8.8am
Filey Holiday Camp to Edinburgh. Most of these and their
corresponding return workings used Londesborough Road

**mid-1950s summer Saturday or bank holiday excursion from the Midlands passes Londesborough Road while approaching
~~arborough~~ Central behind grimy Hughes-Fowler 'Crab' 2-6-0 No. 42754 of Saltley shed(Birmingham.)** *Ken Hoole/Neville Stead colln.*

station. Empty stock movements also ran between Filey Holiday Camp and the various carriage sidings at Scarborough which also had to accommodate untimetabled relief trains and private charters.

Summer Saturdays on the Malton-Whitby line were mainly a case of trains being extended to and from York or Leeds. In summer 1957 four trains ran through to York and three from York plus one each way between Leeds and Whitby. Extra trains were laid on between Scarborough and Whitby on summer Saturdays, there being three extra Scarborough-Middlesbrough trains each way in summer 1957. Add all these together, from the York line, the Hull line, the Whitby line and various empty stock workings and a picture begins to emerge of just how hectic things were at Scarborough on summer Saturdays.

Almost all these extra trains faded away during the 1960s, killed off by increasing car use, overseas package holidays and BR economies including a cull of the coaching stock fleet and the abandonment of facilities for handling such traffic. Decline was at least slow and the summer 1968 timetable still showed 10 advertised Saturday extras from York to Scarborough and eight the other way. The most interesting trains were the 08.30 and 09.25 from Manchester Victoria, and the 13.35 return, the 10.20 from Edinburgh and 10.30 return, the

11.30 from King's Cross and 10.55 return(the Flyer in all b name,) the 13.55 to Bristol, and the10.43 Newcastle-File Holiday Camp and 10.10 return. Among the 10 summe Saturday trains still reaching Scarborough from the Hull lin were the 07.35 and 09.20 from Sheffield Midland, the 08.1 from Leicester London Road, and the 05.55 from Bristol. Th seven trains leaving Scarborough to travel via the Hull lin included the 10.00 to Plymouth, the 10.25 to Leicester Londo Road, and the 12.30 and13.30 to Sheffield Midland. Emp stock movements still ran between Scarborough and Fil Holiday Camp.

Summer 1992 still saw half a dozen extra summer Satu day trains each way on the York line. They consisted of tw Derby-Scarborough trains leaving York at 08.01 and 08.1 the 08.00 Glasgow Central to Scarborough and 13.15 retu High Speed Train, two extra York-Scarborough trains and th 12.00 York-Hull via Scarborough. From Scarborough wer the 09.49 DMU to Skegness, 10.13 to Swansea, and tw additional trains to York. Additional trains on summer Sunday in 1992 still included a return Wakefield-Scarborough as we as trains from Bradford, Halifax and Chesterfield.

The second half of the 1990s and the privatisation of B saw summer Saturday extras all but disappear and in 200 just one long-distance summer Saturday train remained: th

The 1980s were the last decade for true summer Saturday, Sunday and bank holiday excursions to Scarborough, and even then the weren't much compared with the 1950s. With regular services being loco-hauled as well, there were plenty of locos in evidence o Sunday 25th July 1982 as English Electric Type 4(Class 40) No. 40131 awaits departure from platform 1 with the 18.58 to Wakefiel A Type 3(Class 37) prepares to take a private charter back to Doncaster while other locomotives wait in the sidings for their turns duty. The fine signal gantry has since been swept away as has most of the railway on the right. A 285ft-long seat fixed to the retainir wall on the left has room for around 200 bottoms and is claimed to be the longest platform seat in the world. *Stephen Chapman*

One of the last remaining true summer Saturday extras from Scarborough in the 1990s was the 10.13 to Swansea, seen being hauled at Kirkham Abbey by Brush Type 4 No. 47839 on 25th July 1992. By then such trains were branded InterCity Holidaymaker expresses. The crossing gates were still lit by oil lamps embossed with 'LNER' at the time of this photo but they have since been replaced by battery lamps. *Stephen Chapman*

20 from London St. Pancras and 17.03 return bringing a Midland Main Line Class 222 'Meridian' set to relieve the monotony of TransPennine Express Class 185 units. But other traditional through services from places such as Glasgow and Newcastle were no more.

The lines in this area have always attracted various excursions both privately chartered or run by the railways themselves enabling day trippers to enjoy both the seaside and the magnificent coastal and inland scenery. Already mentioned are the ramblers' specials into Ryedale which continued until the lines closed altogether in 1964. During the 1950s the Scarborough-Whitby line was a notable venue for scenic tours from the West Riding and Hull, its severe gradients demanding that these 8-coach trains be double-headed. September 1972 marked the start of a new era for special traffic on the lines to Scarborough for this was when the first steam-hauled train for five years reached Scarborough after the lifting of BR's notorious ban on privately-owned steam locomotives over its lines. On that day, preserved LNER A4 Pacific No.19 *Bittern* ran a private charter from York to Scarborough and back and, with the turntable at the old Scarborough engine shed site removed some years before, it ran light

engine to Filey Holiday Camp where it turned on the triangle. Since then, Scarborough has been a popular destination for steam-hauled special trains. In May 1981, British Rail launched its own summer steam service - The Scarborough Spa Express, the name reflecting the reopening after refurbishment of the resort's famous Spa Pavilion and the contribution by Scarborough Borough Council towards the cost of reinstating a 60ft turntable(previously at Gateshead) and watering facilities at the engine shed site. The train was still being run in summer 2007 by the National Railway Museum and West Coast Railway after an interruption of several years during the BR privatisation process. In the early years of the 21st century, memories of the Scarborough Flyer were invoked by a once-a-month King's Cross-Scarborough train run by Hertfordshire Railtours. It used steam power between York and Scarborough and an electric locomotive between King's Cross and York.

A daily York-Scarborough parcels train once ran each way and some DMUs were authorized to haul tail vans. The summer 1960 working timetable listed the 6.35am Monday to Saturday and 6am summer Saturday York-Scarborough, and the 9.10am(4.30pm on Sats) Scarborough to York parcels trains, booked to call at Malton and at all other stations as required.

Freight traffic

Freight traffic was relatively light, chiefly agricultural and domestic in nature and services consisted mostly of the traditional local pick-up goods meandering from station to station, picking up and dropping off wagons of goods and coal as required. There were, however, some notable heavy freight flows: the chalk trains which ran during the 1950s from quarries on the Malton-Driffield line via Gilling to Thirsk for forwarding to Dorman Long's steel plants on Teesside - along with limestone from quarries at Thornton Dale and around Pickering. Incoming coal for depots at the various stations throughout the area made up a significant proportion of freight but Scarborough was an especially heavy consumer with its large gas works, loco shed and domestic merchants, and one of the most memorable freight trains to run on the York line has to be the Scarborough-Gascoigne Wood coal empties of the late 1940s and early 1950s, not least because it could be hauled by an ex-North Eastern Railway Atlantic. The cattle markets at Malton and Seamer generated livestock traffic throughout the area while the Associated British Maltsters grain silo at Knapton warrented a dedicated trip working from Malton.

The 1959/60 working timetable showed eight freight wo ings on the York-Scarborough line with the Hull line c tributing another two each way. The 5.30am York Branc Yard to Gallows Close class E express goods (with not than half the vehicles fitted with vacuum brakes) also c veyed livestock for Seamer from York and beyond, and li stock from Malton market(where it called 6.15 to 6.25 attach wagons) and then called where required. An extra minutes were allowed in its schedule for the guard to d off newspapers at Knapton, Heslerton and Weaverthorpe. line's only fully fitted class C express freight was the 5.45 Gallows Close to York Dringhouses which also convey fish and other perishables. It also attached vans and wage at Scarborough Central and Malton. The 5.15am Gallo Close to York Yard South and 10.35am York to Washb were class F partially fitted freights which also served M ton and likely as not conveyed the afore-mentioned coal t fic. Other workings on the York line were the 4.45am Y Branches Yard to Malton class H unfitted, 7.45pm Malton York Yard North class H unfitted, and the 1.55pm Y Branches Yard to Malton pick-up, timed to shunt Fl ton(2.30-40pm,) Barton Hill(2.50-3pm,) and Castle Howa Crambeck and Hutton's Ambo when required, due Malto 3.30pm. It was limited to 45 wagons maximum and on Thu days, if required, attached cattle wagons at Bur Lane(York.) The Knapton trip ran as a class E and was tim

Chalk and limestone from quarries on the Malton-Driffield line and around Pickering to the steel plants of Teesside provided Malton-Pilmoor branch with regular through freight hauls. No information is available to definitely identify this picture but Mal J39 0-6-0 No. 64938 is believed to be just east of Gilling with the afternoon stone empties from Thirsk in 1958.
Ken Hoole/Stephen Chapman archive.

The York-Scarborough line may have been busy with holiday traffic on summer Saturdays but the everyday business of freight and local traffic had to go on. This Through Freight passing Kirkham Abbey on 29th July 1961, hauled by Malton shed's J39 0-6-0 No. 64867, seems likely to have been the Monday-Saturday 7.45pm Malton to York Yard North unfitted. *PB Booth/Neville Stead collection*

leave Malton at 4.10pm and Knapton at 5.40.

The Hull line trains were the 4.30am Hull to Gallows Close class E and 7.15pm return(5.50 on Saturdays,) and the ?0am Bridlington-Gallows Close pick-up which returned when required.

The York District local freight workings book issued on 19th September 1955 gives a good indication of freight in the area at the time. Malton engines and men had six trip duties covering the various branches. Malton trip M1 was the Whitby pick-up. Booked to leave Malton at 7.45am, it was untimed for the rest of its journey. On the outward run it shunted Rillington and Marishes Road as required before making a booked call at Pickering to detach wagons. It then shunted Farworth Siding, Levisham, Raindale Sidings, Newton Dale Sidings and Goathland as required, called at Grosmont to detach, Woodlands Sidings(where it was also instructed to wait for milk traffic) to detach and pick-up, at Sleights as required, Ruswarp to detach and Whitby to detach and pick-up. On the return, it called Whitby gas works, Ruswarp, Sleights, Grosmont, Goathland, Levisham, Pickering, Black Bull Sidings, Marishes Road and Rillington as required. On Saturdays it also worked to Thornton Dale if required. The following quaint instruction also applied: "Stops at Newton Dale, Raindale and Farworth to take up platelayers wives every fourth Monday." The Whitby line's second freight was Trip M7 which ran Mondays and Wednesdays when required. Leaving Malton as an engine and brake van at 1.30pm, it shunted Levisham, Goathland Summit and Grosmont when required and

was booked to pick up wagons at Ruswarp from where it returned as a class H cattle train, shunting Pickering as required.

Trip M6 was a daily Malton-Thornton Dale working leaving Malton at 3.15pm and running as required. The loco also shunted Malton from 1.45pm and, if required, on its return. Trip M5 which ran when required on Mondays, Wednesdays and Fridays only, served local stone traffic. Booked to leave Malton at 10.55, it ran as an untimed class H mineral train to Burdale on the Driffield line(until the quarry's closure) or Pickering when required before proceeding to Thirsk yard with the loaded wagons and returning with the empties to Pickering or Burdale, pausing for water at Gilling. On Tuesdays and Thursdays, M5 did a grand tour of East Yorkshire, being the 10.10am Malton to Selby pick-up which ran via Driffield and Market Weighton. The Malton engine and men didn't have to work throughout, though. They swapped enroute with the Selby engine and men working the 10.30am Selby-Malton pick-up. Trip M2 also worked stone traffic. It left Malton as an engine and brake van at 7.20am but hauled the timetabled 7.20am Malton to Thirsk stone train as far as Scarborough Road. From there it continued untimed as engine and brake van to Thirsk, collecting wagons from Hovingham Spa when required. It returned, untimed, from Thirsk as a class H mineral train which also shunted Husthwaite Gate, Coxwold and Gilling(where it took water) as required. Trip M4 was the Kirbymoorside pick-up which shunted Amotherby, Barton-le-Street, Slingsby, Hovingham Spa, Gilling, Nunnington, Helmsley and Nawton as required on

Malton-based J27 0-6-0 No. 65844 trundles downgrade with the returning Malton-Whitby pick-up near Ellerbeck on Thursday 10 August 1961. *Neville Stead*

the way out, and Nawton, Helmsley, Gilling, Hovingham Spa, Slingsby and Amotherby on the return. Pickering, a sub-shed of Malton, had one trip duty, the 10am(1.30pm on Saturdays) to Thornton Dale.

The book listed just one trip working for Scarborough engines and men. This was the 8.35am Gallows Close to York Yard South pick-up. Running untimed, it shunted Ganton, Weaverthorpe, Heslerton, Knapton, Crambeck coal depot, and Haxby as required on the outward run as well as being booked to detach and pick up at Malton. On the return it shunted as required at Strensall, Kirkham Abbey, Malton(where it also took water,) Heslerton, Weaverthorpe, Ganton and Seamer before returning to Gallows Close. A pick-up served the Scarborough-Whitby line but no mention can be found in either local working books or the working timetable. Stations between Whitby and Grosmont were also served by the daily Whitby-Eaglescliffe(later Newport yard-Whitby) pick-up while Ruswarp and Grosmont were also visited by the 9.30am Wednesdays only Danby to Whitby cattle train which ran when required.

The story of freight traffic on all the lines in this part of Yorkshire from the start of the 1950s onwards can only be one of steady decline and eventual extinction. When the Seamer-Pickering passenger service was axed on 5th June 1950, the goods service was also withdrawn between Seamer and Thornton Dale and that section of line closed completely, the section from Pickering being retained mainly for quarry traffic. The next to go was the Grosmont-Beckhole branch which

had hung on by delivering coal and provisions to the ham of Esk Valley because there was no road. A road was laid 1951, and the fortnightly trip working was withdrawn a this remnant of the original Whitby & Pickering Railway cline route was no longer required. Falling output fr Burdale quarry on the Malton-Driffield line and its ultim closure in 1955 brought about a significant decline in sto traffic via Gilling but stone still came from Thornton Da Pickering and Hovingham Spa. Livestock traffic was also rapid decline as farmers switched to more convenient ro transport and gas making at Scarborough would cease in late 1960s with the switch to natural gas. Other freight ser ices withdrawn during the 1950s were those between Kirb moorside and Pickering(1953,) and Malton(Scarborou Road Junction)-Driffield(1958.) Through freight on Thirsk & Malton ended in 1962 when goods services we withdrawn from the Husthwaite Gate-Pilmoor section.

The spring and summer of 1964 saw the biggest cuts as Beeching axe lopped off stations and lines all over the cou try. From 27th April, local freight services between Pickeri and Grosmont were withdrawn, and all intermediate goo yards between Scarborough and Whitby except Rot Hood's Bay were closed from 4th May. The most savage c came on 10th August when not only was the surviving pic up(three days a week) withdrawn from the Ryedale bran between Amotherby, Gilling, Kirbymoorside and Hus waite Gate, but also all local goods yards on the York-Sc borough line were closed except for those at Scarborou

...lton, Knapton, Weaverthorpe andSeamer. On the same ..., goods services were officially withdrawn from the Scar-...ough-Whitby and Seamer-Bridlington lines upon the clo-...e of Robin Hood's Bay and Filey goods yards, and from ...ornton Dale. An outstanding contract with Amotherby ...ur Mill kept the Malton-Amotherby section of the Gilling ... going until 17th October when it too was axed.

...y the time the freight working timetable of 14th June 1965 ...s issued, the only goods traffic remaining in the whole area ...s between York, Scarborough and Pickering and between ...itby and Tees marshalling yard. The working timetable ...ws two York-Scarborough freights each way and they ran ...Mondays to Fridays only. They were 6K51, the 05.10 ...k Up Yard to Scarborough, booked to call at Malton and ...mer; 7K52, the 15.30 from York Up Yard which called ...y at Weaverthorpe as required; 7K57, the 09.00 Scarbor-...gh to York Up Yard which was booked to attach wagons at ...mer, attach and detach wagons at Malton, and shunt ...averthorpe, Knapton and officially closed Rillington as ...uired; and 4K58, the 17.45 Scarborough to Dringhouses ...ed which was booked to stand at Malton for 39 minutes ...1 run as class 5 thereafter. The afternoon trip between ...lton and the grain silo at Knapton still ran, leaving ...lton at 16.50 and Knapton and 17.25. Since the closure of ...lton shed in 1963, the local pilot was supplied by York, ...1 there were paths from York at 05.50 and from Malton at ...40 for the exchange of engines. A similar pair of workings

were still shown in the summer 1970 working timetable: the 05.35 from York Dringhouses, booked to call at Malton 06.27-06.53, and 08.22 from Gallows Close which was booked to shunt Knapton and also Weaverthorpe when required, and the 12.53 from Dringhouses(booked to call Malton 12.43-14.38) and 16.09 from Gallows Close which was also booked to shunt at Knapton. Running Monday to Friday, they were class 8 trains but the 05.35 was class 7 from Malton and the 08.22 class 7 from Knapton. Seamer traffic was often tripped by the Scarborough pilot.

Freight traffic between Rillington and Pickering(mainly quarry traffic) ended on 4th July 1966 but the Tees-Whitby goods soldiered on until 1983 by which time it was mainly serving coal merchants at Whitby and Sleights. After this, the only remaining regular freight train in the whole area was a York-Scarborough trip which left York in the early hours and returned by about 08.00. The main traffic was coal for merchants at Malton, Seamer and Scarborough, oil for Malton and Scarborough, steel for a stockholders at Weaverthorpe, occasional sand from Seamer and some agricultural traffic including fertilizer. The service was out of line with BR's freight policy which favoured bulk trains, and with BR eager to eliminate unbraked mineral wagons the coal had finished by 1985 when Gallows Close goods yard closed along with the last remnant of the Whitby line from Falsgrave. Freight traffic finally came to a complete end in 1992 when BR shut down its Speedlink wagonload network and the Scarborough

...tt Class 2 2-6-0 No. 46413 of Malton shed at Robin Hood's Bay with a rather short returning Scarborough-Whitby pick-up goods ...September 1962. *Rev. J. David Benson*

trip, which by then was serving only the oil terminal at Scarborough as and when required, ceased running. Freight can never be said to be at a permanent end as in these days of the privatised railway, it can always return and there are possibilites for the Whitby line, especially where timber traffic is concerned.

All change

On a local level, the railways in this part of the world served mostly scattered rural communities and were therefore vulnerable to competition from road transport at an early stage. The seasonal holiday traffic which proved their worth during the summer also came under threat as more families owned their own cars or opted for package holidays abroad. As a result, most changes took the form of closures and retrenchment - though not all. Even so, minerals and heavy summer traffic ensured that all the lines in the area covered by this book survived in whole or in part to the Beeching era of the 1960s.

Apart from the wholesale closure of small intermediate passenger stations on the York-Scarborough line in 1930, most-cutbacks began after nationalization and the formation of British Railways in 1948. The first casualty was the Seamer-Thornton Dale section of the Pickering line which was completely abandoned with effect from 5th June 1950 when the Scarborough-Pickering passenger service was withdrawn along with goods traffic between Seamer and Thornton Dale. Tiny Ampleforth station, midway between Gilling and Coxwold, closed later that year - Gilling was nearer to the school anyway. The Beckhole branch shut, as already mentioned, in 1951(going only as far as Esk Valley since floodwater cut

off the Beckhole end in 1931,) and the Pickering-Kirb moorside section on 2nd February1953 upon withdrawal the York-Kirbymoorside-Pickering passenger service. T next major changes came in 1958. The coastal line north Whitby West Cliff to Loftus and Teesside closed complete on 5th May when Scarborough-Whitby-Middlesbrou trains were re-routed via the Esk Valley line. Then, on 20 October, the Wolds line from Malton Scarborough Ro Junction to Driffield was shut down completely, leavi Scarborough Road as purely a reversing point for Gilling li trains. Soon after that, a new, if short, stretch of line was co sidered and a report to the British Transport Commission 1960 listed Seamer as one of several locations on Briti Railways where "major engineering work to provide add tional track facilities are at present in hand or planned." does not reveal what this work was but a curve was propos that would have allowed trains to run direct between Malt and Butlin's holiday camp at Filey. In the event, it was n built, presumably as all traffic could be accommodated existing lines via Hull and Market Weighton.

Whitby West Cliff station closed on 12th June 1961 a Scarborough trains began reversing at Prospect Hill Juncti to reach Whitby Town. Then, on 19th March 1963, t Gilling lines ceased to form any sort of through route wh the Pilmoor-Husthwaite Gate section was closed complete after track damage caused by a parcels train derailment the East Coast main line prompted abandonment of Sess Wood Junction at Pilmoor. The last summer Saturday trai ran this way in September 1962. As Beeching's closure pr gramme gained momentum, the rest of the Gilling branch was totally abandoned following the withdrawal of loc goods services in 1964,the Amotherby-Husthwaite Gate a

By the late 1970s, the York-Scarborough trip was one of only two regular freight workings left in the whole area covered by this boo There was still a fair amount of traffic but times were changing and before long there would be no freight on the railway at all. Bru Type 2 No. 31266 shunts Malton goods yard in 1981. *Malcolm Roughley/Stephen Chapman archive.*

e last day of the Ryedale lines. York's J27 0-6-0 No. 65894 prepares to take the last goods train away from Kirbymoorside on Friday
August 1964. The line closed completely with effect from the following Monday. Although this railway is gone, 65894 works on in
area, having been saved from the scrapman by the North Eastern Locomotive Preservation Group and is based on the North
rkshire Moors Railway. *Ken Hoole/Neville Stead collection*

ling-Kirbymoorside lines on 10th August and the Malton
st-Scarborough Road-Amotherby stretch on 17th October.
he closure of all lines into Whitby was proposed under the
eching plan and a sustained campaign to keep them open
s well under way. Not only did remote communities in an
a of poor roads often closed by bad weather depend on the
lways, but Whitby's very existance as a holiday resort was
eatened by the loss of its railways. Protests were swept
de by BR and the government of the day but the minister
transport did finally refuse close of the Esk Valley line
m Middlesbrough - although its long-term future was far
m assured. Before the 1964 General Election, Labour
der Harold Wilson was reported to have stated that the clo-
res would be rescinded should Labour win, but once
cted, they claimed that under the Transport Act 1962 they
d no power to overturn the previous government's deci-
n and withdrawal of the Malton and Scarborough services
uld go ahead. Early in 1965 a last ditch attempt was made
the member of Parliament for Scarborough and Whitby
overturn the closure decision when he tabled a private
mber's bill in Parliament. Around the same time, six
hitby businessmen formed a syndicate aimed at taking over
Malton service from BR. Nonetheless, the closures went
ead, the Whitby Bog Hall-Scarborough(Gallows Close)

and Grosmont-Pickering lines closing completely with effect
from 8th March 1965, the section from Pickering to Rillington Junction remaining open for freight until 4th July 1966
when it too closed.

The powers-that-be suffered an embarrassment in
November 1965 when all local roads were blocked by snow
and a passenger service had to be temporarily reinstated between Goathland and Whitby so that local children could get
to school, the then transport minister being forced to re-ex-
amine the closure. More embarrassments followed with numerous complaints about the substitute bus services. In
summer 1965 the Yorkshire Post reported that whereas the
mid-morning Saturday Whitby-York train in summer 1964
had regularly carried around 300 passengers, the replacement
bus carried just two beyond Goathland. In spring 1966 the
new transport minister, Barbara Castle refused to consider
reopening the Malton and Scarborough-Whitby lines but she
did agree to examine the prospect of retaining all or parts of
the lines so that standby winter services could be provided.
This did not of course materialise and would never have been
viable but the issue was far from over. After closure, both the
Malton and Scarborough lines became subject to preservation bids and 1967 saw the formation of the North Yorkshire
Moors Historical Railway Trust. By late 1968 the Trust had

23

After closure of the Malton and Scarborough lines in 1965, the only trains to Whitby were from Teesside. On 25th October 196❚ Metro-Cammell DMU passes Whitby signal box and the former engine shed as it enters Whitby Town station with a service fr❚ Middlesbrough. *Neville Stead collection*

agreed a £42,500 purchase price with BR for the whole 18 miles from Grosmont to Pickering including the track as far as Ellerbeck. It wasn't long before trains, mainly steam, were running again over this section but hard work and dedication by NYMR volunteers and staff was finally rewarded in 1973 when the whole Grosmont-Pickering section was officially reopened. In 2005, following the strengthening of bridges between Ruswarp and Whitby, the NYMR was able to start running steam trains into Whitby, albeit with a change at Grosmont until track alterations can be made to permit through running from Pickering. Reopening of the Pickering-Rillington section remains a long-term hope and in 1999 the North Yorkshire County Council included it in its local transport plan following a favourable consultants' report. Since then, plans for a supermarket which would have destroyed the route through Pickering have been rejected.

Various attempts to preserve all or parts of the Scarborough line have not proved successful. As recently as 1996 a 2ft gauge railway along the trackbed from Whitby to Robin Hood's Bay was proposed. Had it reached fruition it may well have been operated by ex-South African Garratt locomotives.

The first half of 1966 saw track and signalling at Malton simplified and modernised in the wake of the various closures. The York-bound platform was abandoned and with it the famous drawbridge used by passengers to reach it. The Up and Down lines were made bi-directional with all stopping trains using the Down(Scarborough-bound) line and platform, and non-stop trains using the Up(York-bound line.) Other work included the abolition of Malton and Malton West signal boxes and the installation of electric signalling controlled from Malton East which had to be retained for the level crossing, as well as the removal of surplus track

from the west end, the engine shed site and the Whitby b❚

In 1968, the York-Scarborough line's future became m❚ secure when the government awarded it a grant aid subsi❚ But it refused any subsidy for the Seamer-Hull line and❚ August 1969 BR proposed to withdraw the Scarborou❚ Hull service. Fortunately, the Hull line survived this and ot❚ threats and is thriving in the 21st century. Also in 1968, track was lifted between Gallows Close and Hawsker but ❚ 2.75-mile Hawsker-Whitby section was retained until 19❚ pending possible potash traffic which, alas, never materializ❚

By 1973 the rail network we have in this area in 2008 v❚ in place with the York-Scarborough, Seamer-Hull, Middl❚ brough-Whitby and Grosmont-Pickering lines remainin❚ Another threat arose in 1981, though, when as part of ❚ 'Branches on the brink" campaign, BR's Eastern Regi❚ named all three of its lines in the area as being at risk of c❚ sure unless government money was provided for investm❚ to replace clapped out trains and infrastructure. Thankful❚ the risk did not become reality. Some investment came d❚ ing the 1980s, owing partly to a new BR organisation bas❚ on business sectors rather than geographical regions but a❚ to rising passenger revenues. Various measures, especia❚ with local involvement, which improved the Esk Valley lin❚ viability are set out in Railway Memories No.18. So far as ❚ York-Scarborough line is concerned, a switch to quasi Int❚ City status in 1982 when it became part of the TransPenn❚ network with through trains to Manchester and Liverpo❚ has done a lot to develop healthier year-round business.

The layout at Scarborough has gradually been whitt❚ down since the early 1960s. Northstead carriage sidings a❚ the line connecting them to Gallows Close were abandon❚ in 1965 and Londesborough Road station officially close❚

24

66, having not been used since summer 1963. Gallows
ose goods yard closed in 1985 and with it the last remnant
the Whitby line from Falsgrave Junction. The several sig-
boxes and impressive semaphore signal gantries have
en reduced to just the one at Falsgrave, and Central station
dually reduced in size until it reverted to the original York
North Midland portion. The main catalyst for many of
se changes occurred at the end of the 1980s when Sprinter-
e diesel multiple units replaced loco-hauled trains on nor-
l services and fewer facilities were needed as a result.

1989, Malton's Y&NMR trainshed was demolished and
old Whitby bay roof used to provide a canopy on the one
tform. The unusual timber platform buildings and canopy
Seamer were done away with and replaced by a bus shel-
around the same time. Since the 1970s there has been talk
reopening Haxby and Strensall stations to meet popula-
n growth resulting from major housing development at
se two erstwhile villages but nothing has so far material-
d. Nor has a new station proposed in the 1970s at Bootham
serve the new York District Hospital and York City foot-
ll club who at that time were in the old second division.

it by bit, the Whitby-Middlesbrough line was stripped bare
the 1980s and 1990s. Whitby Bog Hall and Sleights signal
xes were closed in 1984 following the end of goods traffic,
Whitby-Sleights section singled, Whitby Town goods
rd abandoned and the station reduced to just one active

platform. In 1993, the remaining signal boxes(except Nunthorpe 4.5 miles out of Middlesbrough) were abolished when
a revolutionary "No signalman token system" of signalling
was commissioned. Beyond Nunthorpe, the line was divided
into three token sections: to Battersby, Battersby-Glaisdale
and Glaisdale-Whitby, drivers exchanging single line tokens
in lockers provided at Battersby, Glaisdale and Whitby " Remote token stations."

In 1998 Scarborough station received a £3.5 million refurbishment when the original Y&NMR grade 11 listed roof was
repaired after being found to be in such poor condition that
the platforms beneath it had to be closed despite a million
pounds worth of repairs five years earlier. Buildings were refurbished, platforms raised, new lighting installed and the
imposing clocktower illuminated.

Seamer was resignalled in 2000 during a staged project
which included the replacement of semaphore signals with
colour lights, and resignalling of the Hull line with track cir-
cuit block as far as Hunmanby. The 1911-built Seamer East
box was temporarily closed and Seamer West permanently
closed. A temporary box was used until November when East
box, refurbished, equipped with a new panel and renamed
just Seamer, took over control of the whiole area.

On a positive note - a new loco stabling point was opened by
the NYMR at Pickering in April 2006 - 47 years after closure
of the town's original small engine shed.

e changes which have overcome the railways to Scarborough are epitomized by this picture. Nowadays the doyen of trains on the
rk-Scarborough line has to be The Scarborough Spa Express, hauled by locomotives the likes of which were never seen there in
am days! Coronation Pacifics were the pride of the West Coast main line but No. 46229 *Duchess of Hamilton,* wearing the 'SSE'
adboard, charges a Scarborough-Sheffield special past Seamer West signal box and the junction with the Hull line on 7th October
95 as it had often done over the previous 15 years. Five years later, the box was abolished and the semaphore signals replaced by colour
hts controlled from a refurbished Seamer East box. *Stephen Chapman*

Above: The York-Scarborough line begins at Waterworks Junction at the north end of York station rather than in the centre of it, an in the incoming direction it terminates at what is today's platform 4. Pulling out of platform 15 with a heavy train for Scarborough 9.50am on 17th June 1961, Leeds Neville Hill original B16/1 4-6-0s 61429 and 61432 head towards the Waterworks diamond crossing that will take them across the East Coast main line and on towards the coast. There has been no access to the Scarborough line fr this side of the station since the diamonds were simplified in the 1970s. Branches Yard is on the right. *Robert Anderson*

YORK-SCARBOROUGH

Below: The spectacle of Malton G5 0-4-4T No. 67332 heading an express on the Scarborough line at Waterworks Junction in the 1950s. A likely explanat is that 67332 has the Whitby portion off a train from King's Cross, such as Scarborough Flyer.

Neville Stead collection

ove: A reminder of the beautiful engines that regularly graced the York-Scarborough line in days long gone. In the early 1900s, NER ss J 4-2-2 No. 1519, stunningly immaculate in lined-out green livery, waits patiently for its next run in York's Pumphouse Sidings ich were situated in the junction between the Scarborough and the East Coast main lines. *Neville Stead collection*

ow: Now back to earth! The English Electric Type 4s were associated with Scarborough line trains for the best part of 25 years from 0 onwards. Here, No. 40131, passes Haxby with the 18.58 Scarborough to Wakefield on 26th July 1982. The Down(Scarborough-nd) platform was on the left. *Stephen Chapman*

Above: A Brush Type 2 and a B1 4-6-0 head a special empty stock working near Haxby on 3rd August 1963. *David Holmes*

Although closed in September 1930, Haxby station remained opened for parcels traffic. The 1956 Stations Handbook lists goods yard as able to handle general goods, livestock, horse boxes and prize cattle vans but it had no permanent crane.

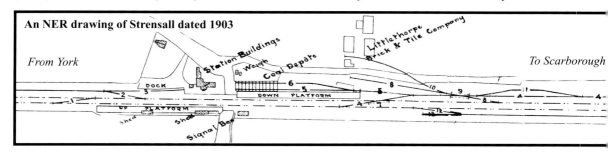

An NER drawing of Strensall dated 1903

From York

To Scarborough

Below: B16/3 4-6-0 No. 61444 storms past Strensall No.2 crossing with a Bradford-Scarborough train. The tiny Strensall Halt w opened by the NER in the early 20th century for use by a local railmotor service from York. The service was not advertized in timetable until 1926 but the halt closed along with all the other small stations on the Scarborough line in September 1930. *Neville Stead collection*

ove: The Scarborough-Gascoigne Wood coal empties, a class H unfitted express freight train, thunders past resleepering work at
xton in the late 1940s with an unidentified C7 class Atlantic in charge. Once prime NER East Coast main line power, these engines
e by this time working out their final years, often on relatively menial tasks. *Ernest Sanderson/Stephen Chapman archive*

ow: Barton Hill station, looking towards York, 11 miles 1050 yards away, viewed from the A64 road bridge in the 1950s. Spare
ches retained for summer excursions can be seen stored in the siding. Barton Hill closed to normal passenger services on 22nd
tember 1930 and to goods on 10th August 1964. *Ken Hoole/Neville Stead collection*

Left: Barton Hill lookin‡ towards Scarborough fro‡ the A64 road bridge on 28‡ July 1981 as a Brush Type ‡ (Class 31) passes the statio‡ site with the evening Sca‡ borough-Sheffield train.
The goods yard was on th‡ left while the modern sty‡ signal box replaced th‡ NER pitched-roof versio‡ in 1936.
The A64 crossed the line ‡ a level crossing until t‡ dual carriageway was bui‡ in the 1930s under a go‡ ernment scheme aimed ‡ creating work during t‡ Depression.
Stephen Chapman

Barton Hill goods yard consisted of only two sidings(bisected by the level crossing shown above) and a headshunt with a trailing crossover between the platforms. A loading dock and a small goods shed were situated on one siding while the headshunt went onto coal drops. There was no permanent crane. The 1956 Handbook of Stations listed the yard as able to handle general goods, furniture vans, carriages, motors cars, portable engines, machines on wheels, livestock, horse boxes, prize cattle vans, carriages and motor cars by passenger or parcels train, while the passenger station was still able to deal with parcels.

The BR 1960 North Eastern Region Sectional Appendix stated that road motor vehicles may be used in Barton Hill sidings for "placing of wagons and removing them from the coal depot."

Below: Brush Type 2 No. D5816, allocated to Wath depot near Barnsley, near Kirkham Abbey with the 13.50 Scarborough to Bristol in summer 1965. At the time, these were all Eastern Region engines but by the 1980s a number were allocated to York and working daily on the Scarborough line. *David Lawrence/Photos from the Fifties*

SHORT MEMORIES

August 1955: The York spur of the Sunbeck triangle is being used for storing surplus wagons.

16.8.55: B1 4-6-0 61053(50A) is on the Whitby Town-West Cliff shuttle.

Sept., 1955: BR Standard and LMS Class 4 2-6-4Ts take over most Scarborough-Whitby passenger services and Standard Class 3 2-6-0s are on goods trains. LMS 2-6-4Ts 42084 & 42085 are transferred to Scarborough and 42083 to Whitby along with BR Class 3 2-6-0s 77004/13/14.

21.9.57(period ending) G5 0-4-4T 67311 is transferred from Selby to Malton.

August 1958: D49 4-4-0 62745 *The Hurworth* is transferred from York to Scarborough.

6.4.59: DMUs replace steam on Malton-Whitby locals and Whitby shed closes as a result

Above: B1 4-6-0 No. 61066, all the way from 31B March shed, passes Kirkham Abbey's York-bound platform as it approaches the level crossing with the 11.45am York-Scarborough on Saturday 29th July 1961. The station had been closed to passengers since 22nd September 1930 but was still available for parcels and excursions.

Below: On the same day, B16/3 4-6-0 No. 61418 from 50A York shed, comes the opposite way with the 2.10pm Scarborough-King's Cross. As the board says, speeds were restricted to 40mph round the meandering curves.
In the 1940s the redundant waiting room in the station house on the right was used as an arts and crafts workshop by the sister of the legendary cricketer Sir Len Hutton. Since this picture was taken, the platforms have been removed and the station house sold into private ownership, screened from the railway by conifer trees, but not much else had changed in 2007. *Both PB Booth/N. Stead colln.*

The sheer beauty of Kirkham Abbey which remains largely unspoilt to this day, is shown to good effect in this view of York-based J2[?] 0-6-0 No. 65887 shunting there with the Malton-York pick-up in the late 1950s or early 1960s. Timber from trees felled on Brotherton[?] Kirkham Hall estate provided outward traffic for the railway and trunks can be seen awaiting loading on to bogie bolster wagon[s]. Inward domestic coal was among other traffic handled here as well as agricultural produce such as potatoes and sugar beet. As wi[th] most others, the yard closed on 10th August 1964. *Ken Hoole/Neville Stead collection*

It was on the twisting stretch of line between Kirkham Abbey and Malton that Bellcode Books proprietor Stephen Chapman first became acquainted with all things railway.

"My very first experience of a train close up was in 1952 or 53 at the age of two or three and it was awesome, an experience that has stuck with me. I was in my push-chair and we had come down the hill from the bus stop at Whitwell to find the gates shut across the road at Kirkham. It was around 6.30pm and dark. In a moment the earth shook and a huge monster roared by, white steam billowing from its small chimney which looked to me as if it was touching the stars. At the back of its black bulk was a hellish scene with two human forms engulfed in a firey glow, followed by a line of incandescent windows. I was too young to know one engine from another but from the outline I remember I would say it was a V2.

"A few years later a locomotive in the goods yard caught my eye because the engine was black and the tender green. There was an old goods van which always seemed to be in Kirkham yard, pale blue or grey with peeling paint.

"Sometimes I ventured beyond Firby woods and down to the river, very much against my parents' orders. Once a train came along headed by a rakish engine with splashers over the driving wheels - a B16/1. One Sunday, I got so far when I looked down to see a big steam crane and a line of carriages near Crambeck

sidings. I ran home to tell my mother I'd seen a train crash. S[he] told me they'd be working on the line, and so they were.

"My dad, the late Denis Chapman, told me how in the 194[?] he hauled tree trunks with horses from woods on the hillside [to] a makeshift sawmill by the river bank powered by a steam tra[c]tion engine. The sawn timber and sometimes trunks were tak[en] to the goods yard for loading onto rail wagons.

"I only travelled on the line once in steam days. On Easter Su[n]day 1961 after I'd moved away from the area. We left York [on] what I guess was a Wakefield-Scarborough train hauled by [the] first B1, No. 61000 *Springbok*. How I enjoyed watching the e[n]gine from my carriage window as it led us round the curves [at] Kirkham. I wanted to see the tank engines at Scarborough bu[t] was distracted by the huge gas works, a wagon being upturn[ed] in its coal tippler, and pretty well missed the engine shed on [the] other side, but a Standard 2-6-2T was on pilot duty at the statio[n].

"One Saturday in August I spent a short time back at Kirkha[m] crossing. The engines that passed were mainly B1s and B1[?] K3 2-6-0 61922, Jubilee 4-6-0 No. 45663 *Jervis* and Standa[rd] Class 5 73166. Class 3 2-6-2T 82026 pulled up in the York p[lat]form with parcels vans while the signalman, Mr. Batty, collec[ted] some envelopes from the guard. As is always the way, I was [on] my way away from the station when I looked back to see a Ro[yal] Scot heading towards Scarborough - too far off to see which o[ne]

...ve: Leeds Neville Hill-based B1 4-6-0 No. 61257 passes Kirkham Abbey with a Leeds-Scarborough service in the late 1950s or early ...0s. *Neville Stead collection*

... 1956 Stations Handbook listed Kirkham Abbey as equipped to handle parcels and all kinds of freight while the yard crane ...he picture opposite had a maximum capacity of 5 tons.

...w: The 8th June 1961 was a day never to be forgotten as it brought no less than three of the illustrious A4 Pacifics and the Royal ...in to Malton for the wedding of the Duke and Duchess of Kent(Catherine Worsley of Hovingham Hall) at York Minster. The hon- ... of working the Royal Train fell to King's Cross-based No. 60028 *Walter K. Wigham,* **seen here skirting Firby Woods as it winds its ... round to Kirkham Abbey on the return to London.** *Neville Stead*

Above: One of the York-Scarborough line's notable trains up to the early 1960s was the 5.30pm Scarborough to Swindon, seen pass[...]
Castle Howard with York V2 2-6-2 No. 60842 in charge on 29th July 1961. *PB Booth/Neville Stead collection*

Below: Castle Howard station, viewed here towards Malton in 1959, was just 1339 yards from Kirkham Abbey. It was built to serve the Castle Howard estate 2.5 miles away, hence the additional grandeur endowed on its G.T. Andrews-designed buildings - complete with a balcony where it is said the Howards and their guests could watch for their train approaching without having to wait on the platform. Even so, its status did not save it from closure in September 1930. Goods facilities consisting of the siding and loading dock on the left and a 5-ton yard crane were withdrawn on 2nd November 1959 after being reduced to a public delivery siding since July 1952. *Ken Hoole/Neville Stead collection*

The 1956 Stations Handbook listed Castle Howard as equipped to handle parcels, general goods, livestock, horse boxes and prize cattle vans.

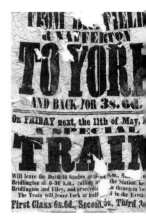

Above: Builders found [...] genuine poster advertising [...] excursion train from Driffiel[d] York via Scarborough on 1[...] May 1849, crumpled and h[...] eaten by mice beneath the fl[...] of a house near Kirkham Ab[...] Besides the sights of York [...] advertised excercises by the [...] Regiment Royal Horse Guar[...] The train left Driffield at 5.45 [...] and the third class fare wa[...] 6d, the first class 6s 6d.

ove: B1 4-6-0 No. 61218 from Leeds Neville Hill eases through Castle Howard station with a train for the coast in the late 1950s. *ı Hoole/Neville Stead collection.*

ow: The preserved A4s are a familiar sight on the Scarborough line nowadays. LNER No. 4498 *Sir Nigel Gresley,* rounds the curve t Crambeck, 732 yards east of Castle Howard station, with the newly introduced Scarborough Spa Express from York on 4th gust 1981. A coal depot was situated here and the two sidings, one with coal drops, were immediately to the left, sandwiched between railway and the river. *Stephen Chapman*

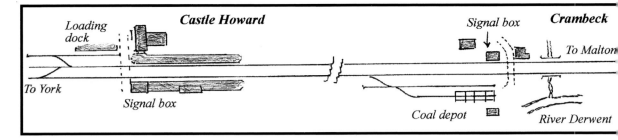

Loading dock

Castle Howard

Signal box

Crambeck

To Malton

To York

Signal box

Coal depot

River Derwent

Below: Hutton's Ambo station(Hutton until 1885) looking towards Malton and the bridge over the River Derwent by which the line crossed from the North Riding of Yorkshire to the East Riding. The squat station buildings are probably due to the elevated location demanding reduced weight. *Ken Hoole/Neville Stead collection*

Top: The layout at Cas Howard and Crambeck c and sand siding. *Not to scale*

Hutton's Ambo goods ya was listed in the 1956 Statio Handbook as able to hand general goods, livestock, ho boxes and prize cattle vans. had no permanent crane. T station was open for parc traffic. The 1960 BR Section Appendix stated that ro motor vehicles may be used move wagons from the loa ing dock to the buffer stop.

Below: Viewed from the hi loading dock in the small goo yard, English Electric Type No. D349 takes the 12.30p Scarborough-Leeds throu Hutton's Ambo on 29th Ju 1961. *PB Booth/N Stead colln.*

ove: It's summer 1981 and traditional freight traffic is still alive and well at Malton. Coal wagons stand on the bank to the coal ps as a three-car Class 110 Calder Valley DMU, bathed in early morning light, passes on its way to Scarborough.

e 1956 Handbook of Stations showed Malton as able to handle all kinds of traffic and equipped with a maximum craneage lity of 10-tons. There were in fact two cranes, one in the yard shown in the picture below and another by the goods shed at east end of the station. Goods facilities were withdrawn on 3rd September 1984 after being reduced to public delivery ing status for some years. The site is now a housing estate.

ow: A general view of Malton goods yard on the same day as above showing, from left, the oil fuel depot, the former cattle dock and coal drops. A large warehouse situated in the right background was destroyed by fire in 1956.
h Malcolm Roughley/Stephen Chapman archive.

Above: Malton goods yard buildings, water tank, pump house and stables, and the base of the yard crane on 2nd August 1991, shortly after removal of the track. *Stephen Chapman*

Below: The west end of Malton station in summer 1981 with Brush Type 2 No. 31266 ready to leave on the returning York-Scarborough pick-up after shunting the goods yard which is just visible on the left. *Malcolm Roughley/Stephen Chapman archive*

Pope's visit to York 31st May 1982: 32 extra loco-hauled trains were run to York which meant finding somewhere to stable the empty stock until the return workings that evening. Two trains were stabled at Malton: the 8-coach 08.21 arrival in York from Hull, and the 11-coach 10.12 arrival from Huddersfield. They stayed there until leaving for their return workings at around 19.00 and 18.00 respectively.

"Trips to Malton were a delight. Entering town on the bus from the York direction I could see the carriage sidings down below, a large tank engine usually present. Across from the bus station, the tantalising top of an engine simmering in the Whitby bay protruded above a wall, its tall dome signifying a G5.

"I was enthralled by the walk into town. First the bridge over the river, small cabin boats moored below. Built by the NER in 1870 the bridge replaced a wooden one and once carried a siding to Derwent Mill, which by my time was the BATA animal feed mill where I watched sacks of grain being winched from lorries to a high floor. Across the road was Wise's, an agricultural implements dealers whose yard was always full of fascinating and colourful contraptions. One day in 1956 we returned to find the big goods warehouse next to the station a smouldering shell after being on fire." *Stephen Chapman*

Private Sidings in the area covered by this book, 1956

Amotherby: Amotherby Flour Mill.
Gas works sidings at Pickering, Scarborough and Whitby
Gilling: Ampleforth College
Goathland: Goathland Whinstone.
Grosmont: Balcony Slag Works/Eldon Brickworks
Grosmont: Hodsman & Sons.
Grosmont-Sleights: Harrison's Woodlands siding.
Helmsley: Duncome Park Estate Siding.
Knapton: Associated British Maltsters.
Malton: Esso Petroleum oil store.
Malton: Malton Manure Co./Yorkshire & Northern Wool Growers
Malton-Amotherby: Pye Pits Lime Works.
Nawton: Ministry of Agriculture, Fisheries & Food.
Norton: Yorkshire Farmers Bacon Factory.
Pickering: Chadwick Bros., New Bridge Lime Works
Pickering: Chadwick Bros.,Windle Bone Mills.
Pickering: General Refractories.
Ravenscar: Ravenscar Brickworks.
Scarborough: Chadwick Brothers
Scarborough: Shell-Mex & BP oil store.
Strensall: United Tile Manufacturers.
Whitby West Cliff: Whitby Urban District Council.

Above: B16/1 4-6-0 No. 61431 of Leeds Neville Hill calls at Malton's Up platform with a Scarborough-Leeds service on 5th April 1958. This platform was completely removed during major remodelling in 1966. *PB Booth/Neville Stead collection*

Below: A superb view showing the workings of the trolley bridge which connected the Down and Up platforms at Malton and how its flanged wheels ran on standard bullhead rails to be tucked away underneath the platform, doubtless with some bumping over the running line. 15th July 1957. *MH Walshaw/Photos from the Fifties.*

Above: Malton station buildings looking east on 2nd August 1991 with the station master's house boarded up. The second two-sto[r]y building houses the station's private cafe which at the time(and maybe still does) included rhubarb and custard on its menu - a far [cry] from bog standard fast food outlets usually found at railway stations these days! *Stephen Chapman*

Below: The Whitby bay platform at Malton's east end and BR Standard 2-6-4T No. 80119 waiting to leave with a local to Whitby To[wn] on 15th July 1957. In 1989 the roof from the bay was removed and used to make a canopy for the remaining platform upon demolit[ion] of the overall roof seen in the distance. The engine shed can just be seen on the left while on the right is a goods shed and another ya[rd] crane. *The late Rev. John Parker/Photos from the Fifties*

Malton passenger train departures summer 1960

am

6.3	4.30	York-Scarborough
6.20	5.20	Malton-Whitby
7.20SO	7.20	Malton-Scarborough light engine
7.37	6.35	York-Scarborough parcels
(7.33SO)		
9.34	8.15	Leeds-Scarborough DMU
(9.28SO)		
9.55SX	9.25	York-Whitby DMU *4 July-26 August*
10.24SO	9.55	York-Whitby DMU
10.25SX	8.17	Sheffield Victoria-Scarborough
		18 July-12 August
10.35	8.17	Sheffield Victoria-Scarborough
		SO 9/7-10/9/SX 11-15/7 & 15/8-2/9
10.35SX	8.42	Bradford Forster Square-Scarborough
		8 July-12 August
10.48	10.15	York-Scarborough *15/7-12/8*
10.48SO	8.42	Bradford Forster Square-Scarborough
		SX15 July-15 August
11.0	10.28	York-Whitby(From Leeds SO)

pm

12.15SX	11.45	York-Scarborough
12.49	12.13(12.20SO)	York-Scarborough DMU
(12.44SO)		
1.24	12.16	Leeds-Scarborough DMU
1.46SO	10.45	Newcastle-Scarborough* *Until 27 Aug.*
2.5	12.50	Leeds-Scarborough DMU
2.15	1.45	York-Whitby DMU
2.20SO	8.5	Glasgow-Scarborough* *2-30 July*
2.52SO	1.45	Leeds-Scarborough DMU
3.24SO	1.32	Bradford F. Square-Scarborough DMU
3.49SX	2.40	Leeds-Scarborough DMU
3.59SO	9.27	Glasgow-Scarborough*
		Until 27th August
4.8	4.8	Malton-Whitby
		From York SO & Fridays 22/7-19/8
5.17SO	4.45	York-Scarborough
5.36	4.30	Leeds-Scarborough DMU
6.4	5.35	York-Whitby DMU
6.44	5.30	Leeds-Scarborough DMU
7.46	6.12	Leeds-Scarborough DMU
9.4	7.55	Leeds-Scarborough DMU.
10.31FSO	10.0	York-Scarborough *10 June-3 Sept.*

* *Via Gilling. Reverse at Malton.*

am

7.45	7.15	Scarborough-Leeds DMU
8.13	7.2	Whitby-York DMU
8.28	8.2	Scarborough-Leeds DMU
8.50SO	7.50	Filey Holiday Camp-Newcastle*
		25 June-20 August
9.10SO	8.40	Scarborough-Glasgow* *9 July-20 Aug.*
9.40SO	9.8	Scarborough-Newcastle* *23 July-20 Aug.*
9.57SX	9.10	Scarborough-York parcels
10.12SO	8.55	Whitby-York
10.30SX	9.11	Whitby-Malton*(To York Fris 22/7-19/8)*
10.38SO	10.5	Scarborough-Leeds
10.47SO	9.33	Whitby-York
10.44SX	10.10	Scarborough-York
10.54SO	10.25	Scarborough-Glasgow* *Until 3 Sept.*
11.20SO	10.50	Scarborough-Newcastle*
11.37SX	11.10	Scarborough-York DMU
11.39SO	10.25	Whitby-York DMU *23 June-3 Sept.*

pm

12.35SX	12.5	Scarborough-Leeds DMU
12.47	11.36	Whitby-York DMU
1.0SO	12.30	Scarborough-Leeds
1.37SX	1.10	Scarborough-Leeds DMU
2.44	2.17	Scarborough-Leeds DMU
3.26SO	2.10	Whitby-Leeds
3.35	3.5	Scarborough-Leeds DMU
4.24	3.15	Whitby-York DMU
4.35	4.5	Scarborough-Leeds DMU
5.20SO	4.38	Scarborough-York parcels
5.38	5.10	Scarborough-Bradford F. Square DMU
6.41	6.15	Scarborough-Leeds DMU
6.58SX	6.30	Scarborough-York *11 July-2 Sept.*
		To Leeds 18 July-19 August
6.58SO	6.30	Scarborough-York DMU
		To Doncaster 2 July-3 September
7.17SX	6.5	Whitby-York *4 July-26 August*
8.25	7.3	Whitby-Malton *To York 11 July-27 Aug.*
8.26	8.0	Scarborough-York
9.44SX	9.15	Scarborough-York *(SO 23 July-3 Sept.)*

NB: Besides these, 16 trains passed through non-stop to Scarborough and 15 towards York on Saturdays. The small number of non-stop trains during the week included the Down Scarborough Flyer on Fridays and the 5.30pm Scarborough-Swindon.

Malton station signal box. The provisions of Rule 96(where under certain conditions a train is allowed to enter a platform already occupied by another train or vehicles-*sic*) may be applied on the Up and Down platform lines. In fog or falling snow, arrangements will be made for a competent man to meet the second train at the platform and conduct it to the rear of the first train.
North Eastern Region Sectional Appendix 1960.

Right: A reminder of how Malton-Whitby services used dedicated rakes of coaching stock. Until tight curves were eased by the LNER to allow larger engines and standard coaches, Whitby trains needed specially built short coaches. *Maurice Burns*

Above: Malton station looking towards York as it was in the 1950s. Taken from the Up platform - isolated from the rest of the sta... as the trolley bridge is retracted - it shows Malton signal box and the engine shed. Two lines once ran through the trainshed but was later moved to the outside position on the left, enabling the platform on the right to be widened.

The overall roof is typical of those designed by the York architect G.T. Andrews for the York & North Midland Railway and there w... others at Scarborough, Whitby, Pickering and Rillington. This one was demolished in 1989 but those at Scarborough survive along w... others at Filey, Beverley and Pocklington. Being south of the river Derwent, Malton station is actually in the adjoining town of Nor...

Coded 50F in BR's York District, Malton locomotive depot consisted of a two-road shed first built in the 1850s to house four engi... and lengthened in the 1860s to take 12. Facilities included a turntable and coal stage.

Its role was to provide engines for local goods and passenger work, especially on the Whitby, Gilling and Driffield branches, and... pilot duties which in the summer included assisting holiday trains between Scarborough and the north to and from the Gilling line. ...

York District freight working book issued on 19th September 1955 showed Malton as covering two winter pilot duties. No. 1 wor... 5.20am to 7.30pm Monday to Saturday shunting as required. No. 2 worked 1.45pm to 3.15pm Monday to Saturday followed by ... 3.15pm trip to Thornton Dale and back, then shunting as required.

Malton shed closed on 22nd April 1963 and its engines were sent to York where they were put to work, stored, withdrawn or transfer... away. From then on, Whitby trains were generally worked by York B1s or diesels.

Locomotives allocated to Malton on 1.5.1960 were: Ivatt Class 2 2-6-2T: 41247/51/65; J39 0-6-0: 64867/928/47; J27 0-6-0: 65844/9/8... A8 4-6-2T: 69861/86; BR Class 3 2-6-2T: 82027/9. Total: 14

Below: Malton shed on 5th April 1958 with G5 0-4-4T 67248 looking in respectable condition despite being very close to the end o... days which would come in December. J39 0-6-0 64928 stands on the left and a J27 0-6-0 on the right. *Both Neville Stead collection*

Above: Snowplough-fitted J27 No. 65827 stands alongside Malton shed on 16th April 1958. This engine was withdrawn in July 1959. *David Holmes*

Below: Stanier LMS-design 2-6-4T No. 42639 passes Malton East signal box with the York to Scarborough parcels consisting of a completely random mixture of vehicles on 1st April 1961. Since 1966 Malton East has been the only signal box, simply called Malton. The level crossing is the only link between the twin towns of Malton and Norton and while the river forms the official boundary between the two, psychologically the railway has always been more of a demarcation line. On the right is the former Russell's brewery, famous for its 1953 Coronation stout. *Peter Cookson/Neville Stead collection*

Above: East of Malton, with the line up to Scarborough Road Junction going away left, V2 2-6-2 No. 60820 of 34E New England s (Peterborough) heads for Scarborough with the 8.20am from Sheffield Victoria on 29th July 1961. *PB Booth/Neville Stead collection*

The 1960 BR NE Region Sectional Appendix showed the York(Waterworks Junction)-Scarborough line as signalled by Absolute Block signalling.

Signal boxes(mileages are from the previous box) were at: Burton Lane(1 mile 97yds and junction with the Foss Islands branch,) Bootham(919yds, junction with the Beverley line,) Haxby(2m 1036yds,) Strensall(2m 732yds,) Flaxton(2m 1170yds,) Barton Hill(2m 616yds,) Kirkham Abbey(3m 692yds,) Crambeck(1m 411yds,) Huttons Ambo(2m 264yds,) Malton West(2m 841yds,) Malton(553yds,) Malton East(473yds and junction with the Gilling line,) Houlbeckfield(1m 949yds,) Rillington(2m 954yds and junction with the Whitby line,) Knapton(2m 48yds,) Heslerton(1m 1583yds,) Weaverthorpe(3m 774yds,) Ganton(1m 1034yds,) Seamer West(4m 622yds and junction with the Hull line,) Seamer East(747yds,) Gas Works(1m 1717yds,) Washbeck(473yds,) Falsgrave(574yds and junction with the Whitby line,) and Scarborough station(315yds.)

Some boxes had limited opening times as shown in the BR manual of signal box opening hours issued on 16th September 1957. Haxby was only a block post during shunting, being otherwise a gatebox. Crambeck was opened as required, being otherwise a gatebox. Huttons Ambo was open only during shunting as required; Malton West was open Monday-Saturday from 4.40am until after departure of the 7.45pm class H freight to York. Knapton was only a block post for passing the 4.30am from York and as required, being otherwise a gatebox. Heslerton and Ganton were open only during shunting, being otherwise gateboxes. It also showed Houlbeckfield as closed, and showed Castle Howard box(1339yds from Kirkham Abbey) open only for attaching and detaching wagons, it presumably closed permanently with the goods yard in 1959.

The maximum permitted line speeds were: 70mph York-Barton Hill; 60mph Barton Hill-Houlbeckfield; 70mph Houlbeckfield-Seamer East and 60mph Seamer East-Scarborough. Permanent speed restrictions included 40mph Kirkham Abbey-Hutton's Ambo.

Additional running lines were: Up Goods Malton East-West(permissive block signalling;) Down Slow Seamer West-East; two bi-directional passenger lines Washbeck-Falsgrave, and one bi-directional passenger line Falsgrave-Scarborough stn. Down refuge sidings were at Haxby, Strensall, and Weaverthorpe, Up refuge sidings at Kirkham Abbey, Barton Hill(used for storing coaches,) Flaxton, and Strensall.

ht: Closed Rillington ~~ion~~ looking east with the ~~itby~~ line going away left beyond the platforms. ~~overall~~ roof was stripped ~~he~~ steelwork in the early ~~0s~~ and had all gone by ~~5.~~ The gate cabin was abol-~~d~~ when a new signal box opened in 1959. A bay ~~form~~ was originally ~~vided~~ on the left for ~~itby~~ trains. *Ken Hoole/ ~~ille~~ Stead collection.*

1956 Stations Hand-~~k~~ listed Rillington as ~~able~~ of handling parcels all types of goods but it no permanent crane.

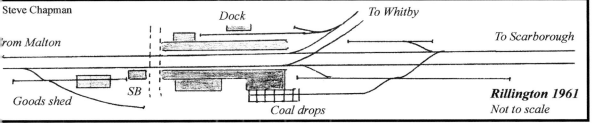

Steve Chapman

Dock

To Whitby

From Malton

To Scarborough

Goods shed　　SB

Coal drops

Rillington 1961
Not to scale

~~w:~~ Knapton station looking towards York in 1959. The huge bulk of the Associated British Maltsters silo looms high above the rail-~~·~~ buildings. The rather basic dutch barn-style goods shed is typical of those at small stations between Malton and Scarborough. ~~ipton~~ was also equipped to handle parcels and all kinds of freight but had no permanent crane. Eventually it served only the grain ~~and~~ that ceased in 1979. The signal box has since been abolished, the level crossing replaced by automatic half barriers, and the plat-~~ns~~ and sidings all cleared away. *Ken Hoole/Neville Stead collection*

45

Above: Heslerton station looking towards York - a similar prospect to Knapton but without the grain silo and with an unusual tra
verse signal box. This station has also been wiped out, the signal box gone and crossing replaced by automatic barriers.

Below: Platforms were retained at closed Scarborough line stations for parcels traffic and excursions. One such event was on
October 1956 when York shed's stalwart B1 4-6-0 No. 61002 *Impala* and its Scarborough-Blackpool special were forced onto the 'wr
line' at Weaverthorpe(originally Sherburn and then Wykeham) by what appears to be the local pick-up goods whose wagons
occupying the Up line. The station is now gone along with the goods yard which lasted until 1981, but the transverse signal box rem
in use along with a crossover - the only ones in the 18 miles between Malton and Seamer. *Both Ken Hoole/Neville Stead collection*

ove: Ganton, pictured looking towards York, was the only small intermediate station with a brick-built goods shed as seen opposite
 signal box. On the right was the cattle dock and two-road coal drops. This station had a one-ton crane and was equipped to handle
 kinds of parcels and goods except furniture vans, carriages, motor cars and machines on wheels. In September 1949 Ganton was
 pened to passengers for five days when the Ryder Cup was staged at the nearby golf course.

ow: Now just three miles from the sea, B16/3 4-6-0 No. 61461 approaches Seamer West with the 6am parcels from York in the late
 0s. The space on the right is where the branch from Pickering used to come in.
 m 1944 onwards, 17 of the original 3-cylinder NER B16/1s were rebuilt to the design of LNER chief mechanical engineer Edward
 ompson with standard B1 boilers and Walschaerts valve gear and were classified B16/3. Another seven rebuilt from 1937 onwards
 he design of Sir Nigel Gresley with double Walschaerts valve gear and derived motion to the inside cylinder were classified B16/2.
 h Ken Hoole/Neville Stead collection

Above: B1 4-6-0 No. 61035 *Pronghorn* brings a 1950s Leeds-Scarborough service past Seamer West box. Coaching stock experts v doubtless find the ex-Great Central Railway 'Barnum' coach behind the engine of interest. The signal box was abolished in 2000 wl signalling was modernised and the junction with the Hull line brought under the control of Seamer East.
Ken Hoole/Neville Stead collection

Below: A truly classic 1950s scene at Seamer West junction. As farm workers manually hoe crops in the adjacent field, their he covered from the blazing sunshine, Selby's D20 4-4-0 No. 62381 and Ivatt Class 4 2-6-0 No. 43096 take the Hull line with a sumn Saturday service to Liverpool via Filey and Bridlington. *Ken Hoole/Neville Stead collection*

Above: Seamer station with its wooden platform canopy and buildings, viewed towards York, summer 1981. A bridge has since replaced the level crossing. *Malcolm Roughley/ Stephen Chapman archive*

Centre: Seamer was notable for its two signal boxes alongside the station. The original(right) was replaced by the larger box on the left in 1911 but still stood until being demolished in 1994. The larger Seamer East box was refurbished and renamed Seamer when it took over control of the whole area under the 2000 resignalling. *Neville Stead collection*

Below: The layout at Seamer in 1961. Seamer was listed in the 1956 Stations Handbook as able to handle all types of traffic but it had no permanent crane. The Dutch barn type goods shed was situated on the right of the top picture until demolished in 1978. Just visible beyond the station is a warehouse used by animal feed merchants Brandsby Agricultural Trading Association(BATA.)

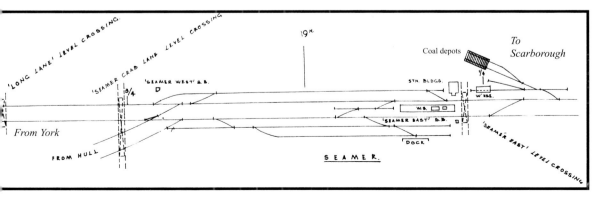

Above: Early on a bright morning in summer 1981, Brush Type 2 No. 31266 on the York-Scarborough pick-up, shunts Seamer siding. Seamer East signal box is in the background. *Malcolm Roughley/Stephen Chapman archive*

Below: Following a spell at York shed, BR Standard Class 5 4-6-0s 73167-70 were allocated to Scarborough from December 195 June 1959. Here, No. 73167 climbs away from the outer limit of Scarborough's railway complex to pass Mere Road level crossing the 4.19pm to Bradford on 13th June 1959. A DMU can just be seen reposing in the Gas Works Down carriage sidings on the left. *Neville Stead*

…ve: On hectic summer Saturdays when everything that could turn a wheel would be needed, goods engines would be pressed into …senger service . Here 8F 2-8-0 No. 48078 passes the engine shed with a service from Sheffield Victoria on 3rd August 1957. Gas …ks Down carriage sidings are beyond the back of the train and the sidings to the gas works itself are on the left. Gas Works signal …, closed in 1965, is hidden behind the train. *Both pictures on this page Ken Hoole/Neville Stead collection*

…en Gas Works signal box is closed the signals applicable to Nos.1 and 2 Reception lines will be lowered for the Up and Down di-…ions to enable movements between Washbeck and Gas Works Down carriage sidings.....The hand points connecting the loco yard … No.2 Reception line must be clamped in the normal position....to prevent their use during the time Gas Works box is closed....Dur-…this period locomotives must use the connection worked from Washbeck signal box..... *BR NE Region Sectional Appendix 1960*

…ow: Coming the other way, past Washbeck signal box, is another goods engine, this time it is WD 2-8-0 No. 90578 on empty stock …. On the right, wagons are being shunted to or from the gas works sidings. Washbeck box was abolished in 1970.

Above: A general view of Scarborough's eight-road straight shed on 13th June 1959. Engines present, from left, are: V2 2-6-2 No. 608 **B1 4-6-0 No. 61315, B16/2 4-6-0 No. 61421, Stanier Class 5 4-6-0 No. 44826 and BR Standard Class 5 4-6-0 No. 73168. The shed ev** **tually suffered from subsidence, hence the two huge supports holding up the gable ends and, in fact, the half covering the four ro** **nearest the gas works had to be demolished shortly after this scene was recorded. The monolithic gas plant looming above was a** **nificant source of freight trafffic until superseded by North Sea gas in the 1960s. It was demolished in 1970.** *Neville Stead*

The first engine shed at Scarborough was established by the York & North Midland Railway and was a two-road building o site later occupied by Londesborough Road station. The second shed, built by the NER in 1882, was a rather cramped rou house situated roughley behind the photographer who took the above picture; the big straight shed was added just eight ye later. The roundhouse was then used for storing locomotives while others, including some redundant Pacifics, were brou from York for storage in the straight shed as closure approached.

Coded 50E in BR's York District, Scarborough shed provided engines for express and local passenger, local goods and p duties until the introduction of diesels in 1959/60 after which its allocation was reduced to cover just local goods and pilot wo It closed on 18th May 1963 when its allocation was sent to York to be stored, scrapped, re-used at York or transferred aw Facilities were retained for servicing visiting steam locomotives until 1967. The straight shed was demolished in 1966 and roundhouse in 1971.

Locomotives allocated to Scarborough

January 1957: Fairburn Class 4 2-6-4T: 42084/5; B16/1 4-6-0: 61445; D49 4-4-0: 62726 *The Meynell*, 62735 *Westmorland*, 62739 *The Badsworth,* 62751 *The Albrighton,* 62756 T*he Brocklesby,* 62769 *The Oakley,* 62770 *The Puck-eridge*; J72 0-6-0T: 69016; A8 4-6-2T: 69867. Total: 12

May 1962: Stanier Class 3 2-6-2T: 40117; Ivatt Class 2 2-6-0: 46409; BR Class 3 2-6-0: 77004/13; BR Class 3 2-6-2T: 82026/7. Total: 6

Other classes allocated to Scarborough at times in the late 1950s and early 60s were B1 and BR Standard Class 5 4-6-0s, ex-LMS 3F 0-6-0T No.47403 and J39 0-6-0 No. 64904.

Seven bell pushes are provided near the connection from the shed line to No.2 Reception line. Operation of the appropriate plunger indicates in Washbeck signal box the direction in which the locomotive(leaving the shed *sic*) requires to proceed. If locomotives do not turn out in the proper order for working trains when there is more than one train for a certain direction at about the same time, locomen must verbally inform the signalman on passing the box of the train they are about to work. *BR NE Region Sectional Appendix 1960*

The BR York District local freight working b issued on 19th September 1955 showed t Scarborough shed provided engines for th local pilot duties during the winter, besides main line rosters. No.1 passenger station p shunted 8.55am to 2.35pm each weekday required and at this time of year was the o pilot booked to work the station. More were quired in the summer. Gallows Close No.1 p shunted as required from 6am to 12.30pm e weekday. No.2 pilot worked 6.20am to 7pm M day to Friday(6pm on Saturday.) Its duties we "Shunting in goods yard. Attaching and deta ing loaded and/or empty wagons. Shunts c wagons in Gallows Close carriage sidings, G Works Down sidings; Falsgrave coal ya Station coal yard; Gas Works loco yard; Wa beck Yard coal sidings; Gallows Close and Sh Mex sidings; trips to Scalby when required. "

The next few pictures aim to demonstrate the amazing variety of locomotives to be found on Scarborough shed, especially during the summer.

Above: D20 4-4-0 No. 62387 rests outside the shed in June 1957 having been spruced up and brought out of store to help with summer traffic. This engine is shown as allocated to Selby until May 1957 and then Tweedmouth until being withdrawn in September so is perhaps working its passage north. *Ken Hoole/Neville Stead collection*

Below: J11 0-6-0 No. 64302, simmering on shed on 30th July 1955, had probably brought an excursion in from Barnsley for that was its home depot. *Neville Stead collection*

Above: Caught outside the shed in the 1930s was D49/3 4-4-0 LNER No. 322 *Huntingdonshire* with Lentz oscillating cam poppet valve hence the unusual shape of the cylinders. These engines were rebuilt with piston valves from 1938 onwards and reclassified D49/1, being converted before nationalization in 1948. *Neville Stead collection*

Below: Ex-LMS 4F 0-6-0 No. 44108 visiting from Saltley shed, Birmingham, on 5th July 1958, was not on Scarborough Flyer duty - headboard was put there as a touch of humour. *Ken Hoole/Neville Stead collection*

above: With the coal stage behind it, Midlands-based Jubilee 4-6-0 No. 45636 *Uganda* **takes water in front of the old roundhouse while** ~~on~~ **obvious private charter duty.** *Ken Hoole/Neville Stead collection*

below: Another ex-LMS express passenger 4-6-0 visiting on 7th June 1959, Patriot No. 45509 *The Derbyshire Yeomanry* **from Newton** ~~He~~**ath shed, Manchester.** *Ken Hoole/Neville Stead collection*

Above: This veteran caught on s
in LNER days was ex-Great Nor
ern D3 4-4-0 No. 4079. *Cecil C
Neville Stead collection*

Centre: Stored alongside the c
stage are ex-LMS 3F 0-6-0Ts 47⸱
47462 and 47581. They were tra
ferred to York when their ho
50D Starbeck, closed in Septem⸱
1959 and put into store at Scarb
ough before being sent on to Ge
where, from 1960, they again c
ried the 50D shedplate. No. 47
also came from Starbeck
worked at Scarborough until be
withdrawn in September 1961.
Below: Pacifics were not unc
mon at Scarborough and here
No. 60074 *Harvester* stands in
yard after bringing in a troop tr
from Birtley, County Durham,
18th July 1954.
Both Ken Hoole/Neville Stead co

Above: Scarborough and Malton sheds were both home to a variety of main line tank engines and Scarborough's were especially noted for their slick pilot work moving empty trains between station and carriage sidings. Here on 18th May 1963, BR Class 3 No. 82027 prepares to tow withdrawn Ivatt Class 2 No. 41265 and Stanier Class 3 No. 40117 away to York for storage following Scarborough shed's closure. No. 40117(withdrawn in December 1962) languished in York South shed until it was demolished that autumn and was then inside the north shed, cleaned up, during February 1964 before eventually being sent for scrap. Their place was taken at Scarborough by Class 03 and 08 diesel shunters from York but nowadays any arriving locos(often steam) have to reverse their own coaches out to the remaining sidings. *Ken Hoole/Neville Stead collection*

Below: Ugly but efficient, that's visiting Stanier Class 5 4-6-0 No. 44756, equipped with Caprotti valve gear, Timken roller bearings and double chimney, coming on shed with 4F 0-6-0 No. 44552 on 5th September 1959. *Ken Hoole/Neville Stead collection*

Above: York A1 Pacific No. 60138 *Boswell* backs onto shed after bringing in the 10.45am from Newcastle via Gilling on 9th July 19 The A1 was too long for Scarborough's turntable and returned light to York. *Ken Hoole/Neville Stead collection*

Below: A summer Saturday in the mid-1950s and the yard is packed with engines. This line-up includes D49/1 4-4-0 No. 62 *Huntingdonshire* - notice the different shaped cylinders from how it appeared on page 54 - K3 2-6-0 No. 61842, and D49s 62775 *Tynedale* and 62730 *Berkshire*. *Ken Hoole/Neville Stead collection*

ve: No. 61429 shows off the elegant lines of the original B16s as her crew grapple with the shed's 60ft turntable in front of the old
ndhouse. The turntable was reinstated with a 70ft-long deck in 1981 and must be one of the very few places, if not the only place on
national rail network, where a turntable is still used for turning steam locomotives. *Ken Hoole/Neville Stead collection*

ow: Adding its classic Great Northern lines to the variety on 13th August 1960 was K2 2-6-0 No. 61756.
Hoole/Neville Stead collection

Above: On 10th December 1958 a test was carried out to see if Britannia Pacifics could be turned on Scarborough's 60ft turntable. 70053 *Moray Firth,* recently allocated to Leeds Holbeck, was the guinea pig and as can be seen it fit - but with only inches to spare *Ken Hoole/Neville Stead collection*

Below: At the end of the 1962 summer timetable York sent some of its Pacifics, made redundant by diesels on the East Coast main l for storage at Scarborough shed until their future was settled. Here, on 13th September, B16/3 4-6-0 No. 61434 has just arrived w A2/3 No. 60522 *Straight Deal* and A2 No. 60526 *Sugar Palm. Straight Deal* went on to work again in Scotland but *Sugar Palm* was w drawn in December and sent for scrap. *Ken Hoole/Neville Stead collection*

60

Above: After the introduction of diesel multiple units on the Whitby line, redundant A8 4-6-2Ts were stored in the roundhouse. Nos.(from left) 69867, 69877 and 69885 were photographed there on 13th June 1959. *Neville Stead*

Below: Londesborough Road station was opened by the NER on the site of the York & North Midland loco shed to help accommodate the ever increasing numbers of summer holiday excursion trains descending on Scarborough. In this 1950s scene, Ivatt Class 4 2-6-0 No. 43052 prepares to pilot D49/2 4-4-0 No. 62755 *The Bilsdale* away from the bay platform at the head of a summer Saturday train to Liverpool as A8 No. 69885 looks on. The through platform could accommodate 14 coaches and the bay platform 11. *K Hoole/N Stead colln.*

Above: The Liverpool train again but this time on 4th September 1954 with D20s 62378 and 62374 in charge. As the D20s are Sc
engines, it seems likely that this train was routed via Bridlington, Market Weighton and Selby and would be handed over to a Lon
Midland Region engine at Gascoigne Wood. *TG Hepburn/Neville Stead collection*

Below: B16/3 No. 61454 makes a rousing start from Londesborough Road with a 1950s summer Saturday service to Manchester.
Ken Hoole/Neville Stead collection

Just to show how well the 2003 scene on the back cover recreated the 1950s - the very same engine, V2 No. 60800 *Green Arrow,* the resident of King's Cross shed, storms past Londesborough Road with the London-bound Scarborough Flyer on 23rd August 19
The Londesborough Road buildings were demolished after official closure in 1966 but the platform survives in 2008.
Ken Hoole/Neville Stead collection

THE SCARBOROUGH FLYER

REFRESHMENT CAR EXPRESS

(with Through Carriage to and from Whitby)

LONDON (King's Cross), GRANTHAM, YORK,
SCARBOROUGH (Central) and WHITBY (Town)

			A	B				SO	SO	C
			am	am				am	am	am
LONDON			**11 28**	**11 28**	**SCARBOROUGH**				**10 42**	**10 35**
(King's Cross)	..	dep.	pm	pm	(Central) ..	..	dep.	..		
GRANTHAM	..	dep.	1 39	1 38	MALTON ..	..	arr.	....	....	11 1
YORK	..	{ arr.	3 14	3 14	WHITBY (Town) ..	dep.	9 33	..		9 30
		{ dep.	3 22 3 40	3 22 3 40	MALTON ..	..	arr.	10 43	....	10 42
MALTON	..	{ arr.	.... 4 8	.... 4 8	MALTON	..	.. dep.	10 47	..	11 9
							arr.	11 20	....	11 37
MALTON	..	dep.	.... 4 15	.... 4 15	**YORK**	..	{ dep.	11 44		11 45
WHITBY (Town)	..	arr.	.... 5 28	.... 5 28				pm		pm
MALTON	..	dep.	....	....	**GRANTHAM** ..	..	arr.	1 18		1 26
SCARBOROUGH					**LONDON**					
(Central)	..	arr.	4 14	4 14	(King's Cross)	..	arr.	3 28		3 40

A—Runs Fridays only 26th July to 23rd August.

B—Runs Saturdays only. Not after 7th September.

C—Sundays only. Commences 14th July.

SO—Saturdays only.

Seats are reservable in advance for passengers travelling from London (King's Cross) and Scarborough and Whitby, on payment of a fee of 1s. 0d. per seat.

In summer 1957 an ordinary Scarborough to King's Cross 2nd class return fare cost £3 12s 6d. The first class fare was £5 8s 10d. The return fare from Whitby Town was £3 6s 10p 2nd class and £5 15s 4d(first class.)

The 1957 summer timetable listed Scarborough Central as having refreshment rooms serving teas and lunches. Malton had a private buffet serving lunches.

Left: The Scarborough Flyer page from the summer 1957 timetable.

SHORT MEMORIES

February 1960: Malton loan J27 65844 to Scarborough fo snowplough work. It is als used on Scarborough-York mi eral trains and deputises on pil duty for 3F 0-6-0T 47403 whi is out of action.

Summer 1960: D49 4-4-brought out of store in Hull f summer traffic diagrammed work the Saturday 8.35am Hul Scarborough and 6pm retur 12.45pm Hull-Scarborough ar 4.30 return, and the 11.15a Scarborough-Liverpool as far Goole. The weekdays 1.20p Hull-Scarborough and 6pm r turn are often a D49 instead the booked K3 2-6-0.

18.6.60: 2-6-2Ts 82027/8 tran ferred to Scarborough fro West Hartlepool

ove: It wasn't always about summer excursions, Scarborough football club have had their share of cup exploits and here York B1
0 No. 61337 storms past Londesborough Road with a football special to Wembley. *Ken Hoole/Neville Stead collection*

ow: Setting off from Central station in splendid style with a 1950s service to Leeds, BR Standard Class 5 4-6-0 No. 73066 passes Fals-
ve signal box, tunnel and platform 1A. In 2007 the grade 11 listed box underwent major renovation and external restoration to BR
0s style while the signal gantry is the only one left at Scarborough. *Ernest Sanderson/Stephen Chapman archive*

Above: Scarborough Central station as it looked in summer 1981. Beneath the clocktower is the original Y&NMR station and sta▮ signal box. The hipped trainshed on the right, behind the Brush Type 2 locomotive, is the Y&NMR goods shed converted in 190▮ passenger use covering platforms 8 & 9 while the hipped roof immediately left of it over platforms 6 & 7 links it to the original stat▮ Platforms 6 to 9 were closed in the early 1980s and are now a car park. *Malcolm Roughley/Stephen Chapman archive*

Left: A Brush Typ▮ (Class 31) stands▮ platform 4 with an▮ rival from York ▮ summer 1982. L▮ hauled trains on n▮ mal services have b▮ a thing of the past s▮ the late 1980s.
Stephen Chapman

Platform 1 on the ▮ of the top pict▮ could(and presum▮ still can) accommo▮ 13 bogie coaches ▮ the others betwee▮ and 10. The 1960 S▮ tional Appendix st▮ that the longest tr▮ allowed into the sta▮ were 13 bogie or 2▮ wheel vehicles. Tr▮ over 7 vehicles ha▮ have a brake vehicl▮ each end.

Scarborough Central Station. When a passenger train drawn by two locomotives is brought to a stand at any of the platfor▮ and one locomotive has to be detached, or both locomotives are detached, and are required to leave singly, the station insp▮ tor, foreman or other person in charge of the platform concerned, must advise the signalman at Falsgrave in the case of platfo▮ 1 and 2, and Station box in the case of platforms 3 to 9, of this arrangement.

The signalman at Falsgrave or Station......must, as a precautionary measure, put a lever clip on the signal controlling the entra▮ to the platform line concerned, until the leading locomotive has been disposed of and the platform line is again clear.

Electric starting bells and visual indicators are provided on Nos. 1 and 2 platforms. A push-button operates the bell and i▮ minates the visual indicator...which shows the letter 'S' when the bell is rung. *BR NE Region Sectional Appendix 1960*

Above: Brush Type 2 No. 31266 shunts the York-Scarborough pick-up in the station sidings in June 1981. The station signal box, which closed in 1984, is on the left and the former Y&NMR goods shed extension to the station is behind the loco. Until 1959 there were coal drops off the picture to the right. *Malcolm Roughley/Stephen Chapman archive*

Below: On 23rd April 1959, B16/3 4-6-0 No. 61434 was on pilot duty removing the stock of an arriving parcels train, which consisted of one non-corridor passenger brake and a fish van, from platform 6. *Ken Hoole/Neville Stead collection*

Above: A Derby Works DMU for Middlesbrough via Whitby stands in platform 2 on 6th March 1965, the last day of this service. Now days platform 3 is the main platform. A Cravens DMU stands in platform 5 on the right with a Hull service. The impressive clocktow was added in 1884 and renovated in 1996 along with the station frontage and remaining platform canopies at a cost of £2 million.

Below: The board on the porter's barrow proclaims the destination for the 3-car Metro-Cammell DMU in platform 2 on 6th March 196 All this part of the station has been in the open since the roofing was removed in 1971. *Both Maurice Burns*

SCARBOROUGH-WHITBY

...ght: Having left Central station and reversed at Londes-...ough Road, a Whitby-bound Metro-Cammell DMU is ...ut to enter Gallows Close Tunnel on 6th March 1965. ...is section of the Whitby line closed in 1985 along with ...llows Close goods yard. *Maurice Burns*

...ssenger trains may be propelled between Scarborough ...ntral and Falsgrave under the following conditions: ...rains must not exceed two coaches. 2) The brake com-...tment must be leading, in which the guard must ride and ...e access to the automatic brake. 3) The speed must not ...eed 10mph. 4) When propelling out of the station, the ...n must be routed at Falsgrave signal box to the Middle ...e or Londesborough Road station No.1 platform line. In ...er case, the line must be clear throughout. When pro-...ing into the station, the platform line must be clear to the ...fer stops...*BR NE Region 1960 Sectional Appendix.*

...ferring to restrictions on coaching stock through Gal-...vs Close Tunnel, the Appendix also stated that certain ...mer LNER and LMR(Midland Division) short buffered ...k may work through the tunnel for stabling in the goods ...d or carriage sidings provided the personal authority of ...station master or person in charge at the time is given. ...eed must not exceed 5mph.

...ght: At Gallows Close signal box, ...driver of a Whitby-bound DMU ...lects the token for the single line ...ad to Cloughton. *...urice Burns*

SHORT MEMORIES

8.6.60: As English Electric ...ype 4 diesels start taking over ...carborough line services, ...254 works the 10.28 King's ...ross-Scarborough.

5.6.60: D253 is on the 'Down' ...carborough Flyer while ...anier 2-6-4T No. 42477 ...orks the Whitby portion.

...8.60: K2 2-6-0 61760(41A) ...rings an excursion from the ...heffield area to Scarborough ...d then runs light to Bridling-...n shed.

...2.8.60: D49 62727 *The Quorn* ...on the 6pm Scarborough-...ull.

Two views of Gallows Close goo[ds]
yard at sunrise in August 1978.
Looking towards Whitby(Le[ft])
and(below) towards Scarborou[gh]
with the mechanised coal depot left [of]
the tunnel and the NER 1902 goo[ds]
shed just visible behind the mode[rn]
shed on the right. A supermarket h[as]
occupied the site since 1994.
Malcolm Roughley/Stephen Chapm[an]
archive

Bottom: Stockton-based A5 4-6-[2]
69835 approaches Gallows Close w[ith]
a train from Middlesbrough in spri[ng]
1958, shortly before being replaced [by]
DMUs. The line on the left is an in[de]
pendent single line to Northstead ca[r]
riage sidings. *Neville Stead collectio[n]*

ove: There were 4 miles of carriage sidings plus a 60ft turntable and loco stabling facilities at Northstead. This is the sidings in 1965, king north after closure of the Whitby line which is on the right. Lifting of the sidings was in progress at the north end.
ille Stead collection

ht: Scalby station complete with camping coaches that provided iday accommodation at a number stations along the Whitby lines. lby closed to passengers on 2nd rch 1953 and the goods yard was uced to a public delivery siding, some trains still called there until mer 1964 for the benefit of holimakers using the camping ches.

Hoole/ Neville Stead collection

SHORT MEMORIES

9/20.5.62: Four overnight rains convey Bertram Mills Circus from Hull to Scarborough. Three go to Gallows Close for unloading(booked to rrive at 2.9, 5.9 and 7.9am) nd one to Londesborough Road(due 5.29am.)

.5.63: Class 3 2-6-0 No. 7004 works the 4pm Malton Whitby.

rborough Gallows Close was ed in 1956 as having a 10 ton eage capacity and able to han-general goods, livestock, furni-e vans, carriages, motor cars and chines on wheels.

Right: From the summer 1957 BR NE Region timetable

The BR NE Region Sectional Appendix stated that empty coaches or freight wagons may be propelled with or without a brake van in the Down direction between Gallows Close and Northstead carriage sidings.

Above: Cloughton station, 5 miles from Scarborough was the first on the Whitby line with a crossing loop. A Derby Works DMU for
ing the 11.45 Scarborough-Middlesbrough calls there on 6th March 1965. *Maurice Burns*

The canopied goods shed is on the left. The 1956 Handbook of Stations listed Cloughton as able to handle general goods, livesto
horse boxes and prize cattle vans. It had a 1 ton 10 cwt permanent crane.

Below: The single platform passenger halt at Hayburn Wyke, with the 11.45 Scarborough-Middlesbrough arriving, 7 miles into
journey, on 6th March 1965. Hayburn Wyke had been unstaffed since March 1955. *Maurice Burns*

.9.62: B16 No. 61421 works the last passenger train between Husthwaite Gate and ilmoor, the last Scarborough-Newcastle service of the summer season.

.5.64: The last passenger train o use Kirbymoorside and Nawton stations is the last ramlers excursion.

7.7.64: Two DMU sets, one -car and one 7-car operating unday school excursions from Helmsley and Gilling to Scarorough and back are the last Ryedale line passenger trains.

4.8.64: B1 4-6-0 61319(50A) s on the Malton-Whitby oods.

Above: Stainton Dale station, 8 miles north of Scarborough, looking south as trains hauled by Fairburn tanks cross on 27th June 1957. The northbound one appears to be 42083, the only one allocated to Whitby at the time while the one hauling the photographer's train is probably 42084 or 42085, one of the two Scarborough examples at that time.
The small goods yard containing the camping coach on the right was listed in 1956 as able to handle general goods, livestock, horse boxes and prize cattle vans but there was no permanent crane. *Hugh Davies/Photos from the Fifties*

ow: Fairburn 2-6-4T No. 42085(a York engine by this time) and B1 4-6-0 No. 61131(a 56A Wakefield engine) pound through inton Dale on 20th August 1961 with the last scenic special to run over the line, train No. 1Z04 from Wakefield.
Hoole/Neville Stead collection

73

Above: Ravenscar station, 631ft above sea level, was at the top of a steep climb from both north and south and until 1895 was appropriately named Peak. In this wintry view looking north, the summer holiday camping coach sits in the yard undeterred.
David Lawrence/Photos from the Fifties
The 1956 Handbook of Stations listed Ravenscar as only able to handle general goods and there was no yard crane.

Below: A short distance north of Ravenscar station was Whitaker's brickworks, situated on the site of old alum workings which proliferated along the coast all the way to north of Whitby. The siding was listed in the 1956 Stations Handbook but by the time this undated photo was taken the works appeared shut and the siding disused.
Notice how the main running line appears to just fall off the edge where it drops away at **1 in 39.** *Ken Hoole/Neville Stead collection*

Ravenscar station siding. Wagon from the Scarborough direction must attached next to the engine. The eng and wagons must run through crosso road No.12, then propel the wagons the Up platform line, and when th have been brought to a stand and pr erly braked, the engine must uncou and move forward to the Whitby sid No.9 points, and the wagon or wag pushed into the siding. Any wagons be attached must be pushed out of siding to the Up platform line with engine at the tunnel side of No.9 poi then picked up by the engine and pla on the train.

If wagons cannot be pushed in or ou hand, the train must be left standi properly secured on the piece of le line at the Scarborough side close No.6 points, and the wagons then dra on to the loop and run round.

Wagons from Whitby direction must next to the engine. The train must to the Down platform line, and after guard has secured the train, the eng or engine and wagons, may leave siding via the Up platform line, a No.9 points have been set for the s ing. *BR Sectional Appendix 1960*

74

**ve: The severe climb up to Ravenscar was hardest for southbound trains, a harsh 1 in 39 for almost three miles from Fyling Hall.
dlesbrough-based L1 2-6-4T No. 67764 has no problems though with its winter service load of two coaches.** *Hoole/Neville Stead collection.*

**w: Heavier trains such as the scenic tours which came from the West Riding had to be double headed. With the North Sea way below
n, B1 4-6-0 No. 61383 (of 56F Low Moor shed,) assisted by Malton's BR Standard Class 3 2-6-2T No. 82029, heads an eight-coach
al from Laisterdyke, Bradford, on 14th June 1959.** *Ken Hoole/Neville Stead collection*

Above: The view southwards as the 11.45 Scarborough-Whitby DMU calls at the single platform Fyling Hall station on 6th March 1965. This station became an unstaffed halt in May 1958 when the small goods yard was reduced to a public delivery siding. It was listed in 1956 as equipped to handle general goods and livestock only with no permanent crane.

Below: Robin Hood's Bay, 15 miles from Scarborough and six from Whitby, was undoubtably the most important intermediate station on the line. It is much busier than usual in this view of the 14.18 from Whitby, however, and that's because it is Saturday 6th March 1965, the extra passengers being the inevitable hordes that turned out during the 1960s for a last ride on a service about to fall under the Beeching axe. There was no Sunday service at this time of year and there would be no trains on Monday - or ever again.
Both Maurice Burns

ve: Robin Hood's Bay station looking north. The mile and a half 1 in 43 climb away from the station is easily visible in the distance. *ole/N Stead collection* The goods yard here was listed in 1956 as having a 1.5-ton crane and able to handle all kinds of freight.

w: The closure of the lines to Whitby was marked by the Whitby Moors Rail Tour run by the Stephenson Locomotive Society and Manchester Locomotive Society. Hauled by preserved LNER K4 2-6-0 No. 3442 *The Great Marquess* and York shed's K1 2-6-0 2005 it appears besieged while pausing for water at the north end of Robin Hood's Bay station. As chief mechanical engineer of North Eastern Locomotive Preservation Group, the photographer who took this picture with a Praktica camera at the age of 18, d be involved in ensuring that 62005 keeps running to this day - and in the North Yorkshire Moors. *Maurice Burns*

Above: The two or three-car diesel multiple units on Scarborough-Whitby services had to consist of at least two power cars(600h[...] order to cope with the steep gradients. Here a 3-car Derby Works set on a Scarborough-Middlesbrough service begins the 1 in 4[...] of Robin Hood's Bay and heads for Whitby in September 1962. *Rev. J. David Benson*

Below: Hawsker station looking south on the last day, 6th March 1965. The small goods yard on the left was listed in the 1956 Sta[...] Handbook as being equipped for only general goods, livestock, horse boxes and prize cattle vans and it had no permanent crane. I[...] closed from 4th May 1965 but the track from here to Whitby was left in situ until 1973 pending potash traffic which, alas, di[...] materialise. *Maurice Burns*

ve: A scenic tour on 1st June 1958 presents its passengers with the breathtaking vista of the Esk Valley 120ft below as it blasts
)ss Larpool Viaduct on its way out of Whitby and on to the 1 in 43/58 slog up to Hawsker, which even included a short stretch at
38. The train engine, B1 4-6-0 No. 61010 *Wildebeeste*, is being assisted by A8 No. 69861. It is said that five million bricks were used
he construction of Larpool Viaduct. It still stands in 2008, carrying a footpath and cycle track. *Ken Hoole/Neville Stead collection*

w: Prospect Hill Junction, half a mile south of Whitby West Cliff station was where the line from Scarborough met the line from
tus to Whitby Town. This 1960s view looking north shows a 3-car Metro-Cammell DMU leaving for Scarborough, the line to Whitby
rn descending on the left. The elevated signal box survived, disused, until 1971 when it was destroyed by fire.
id Lawrence/Photos from the Fifties.

SCARBOROUGH(FALSGRAVE) - WHITBY(WEST CLIFF) 1960

Signalling: Electric token block

Maximum speed on single line: 35mph

Signal boxes with distance from previous box

Gallows Close (691yds from Falsgrave)
Cloughton(4 miles 339yds)
Stainton Dale(2 miles 1671yds)
Ravenscar(2 miles 784yds)
Robin Hood's Bay(4 miles 1584yds)
Prospect Hill(5 miles 1248yds)
West Cliff(1223yds)

Crossing Loops with lengths

Gallows Close(26 wagons, engine & brake van)
Cloughton(15 wagons, engine & brake van)
Stainton Dale(16 wagons, engine & brake van)
Ravenscar(14 wagons, engine & brake van)
Robin Hood's Bay(17 wagons, engine & brake van)
Prospect Hill(14 wagons, engine & brake van)
West Cliff(15 wagons, engine & brake van)

Whitby Prospect Hill - Bog Hall

Length: 1485yds. Signalling: Electric token block.
Maximum speed on single line: 20mph

Above: Whitby West Cliff station looking south in the 1950s and Fairburn Class 4 2-6-4T No. 42085 is stood in the northbound platform with a two-coach local. Scarborough-Whitby Town trains reversed here until June 1961 when the station closed to both passengers and goods, after which they reversed at Prospect Hill. No. 42085, a Whitby engine from June 1958 to April 1959, still runs today at the Lakeside & Haverthwaite Railway in Cumbria. *Neville Stead collection*

...ove: A 3-car Derby Works unit has just passed beneath Larpool Viaduct and is tackling the 1 in 54 climb from Whitby Town to ...spect Hill with a 1960s Scarborough service. Down below on the right is the River Esk and, out of sight on the near bank, the Esk ...ley line to Pickering and Middlesbrough. *David Lawrence/Photos from the Fifties*

...ow: Whitby Town in the 1950s. Scarborough-based A8 4-6-2T No. 69881 stands at the buffers after bringing in what appear to be ...ough coaches to London. Such is the scale of rationalization at Whitby that the line on which 69881 is standing is the only one ...aining in 2008. *Neville Stead collection.*

Above: A grand entrance at the start of the Whitby & Pickering Railway reflecting the time when Whitby was a much more import
railway centre than it is today. Beautifully restored, this was how the side entrance looked in July 1996 - and there's another two-a
portico of the same design on the end, round the corner on the right. *Stephen Chapman*

WHITBY - RILLINGTON

Below: A busy scene at Whitby Town with DMUs and parcels vans present on Sat
day 6th March 1965 but things would be a lot quieter from Monday onwards when
Scarborough and Malton lines have closed. *Maurice Burns*

The 1960 BR NE Region Sectional Appendix stated that one vehicle with continuous brake and having a tare weight plus l
not exceeding 17 tons could be attached to Malton-Whitby two or three-car DMUs of minimum 600hp.

It also stated that passenger trains may be propelled from Bog Hall to West Cliff provided they consisted of no more than t
coaches, that the brake compartment must be leading in which the guard must ride and have access to the continuous brake,
that the speed must not exceed 10mph.

Whitby Town weekday departures summer 1957

9(6.51SO)	Middlesbrough via Battersby	12.30	West Cliff
	Middlesbrough via Loftus	12.35	Goathland
	Malton *To York Mons & Sats only*	1.55	Scarborough
8	Goathland	2.10 SO	Leeds via Malton & York
2	Scarborough	3.15	Malton
5 SO	York via Malton	4.5	Battersby(to Middlesbrough SO)
SO	West Cliff	4.20	Scarborough
0 SX	Malton.	5.35	Middlesbrough via Battersby
	To York Fridays 26th July to 23rd August	5.58 SX	Middlesbrough via Loftus
3 SO	York via Malton		*22nd July to 16th August*
	Through carriages to King's Cross	6.10 SX	York via Malton *15th July-23rd August*
5	West Cliff	6.33	Middlesbrough via Loftus
12	West Cliff *29th June to 7th September*	6.57	York via Malton *15th July to 31st August*
26 SO	York via Malton *29th June to 7th September*	7.13	West Cliff *29th June to 7th September*
44	West Cliff	7.30	Scarborough *Not after 31st August*
27 SX	Malton	7.35	Middlesbrough via Battersby
36 SO	York via Malton		*15th July to 17th August*
		8.5	West Cliff
		8.35	Middlesbrough via Battersby
5	Middlesbrough via Battersby	9.5 SO	Glaisdale

...er trains between Scarborough and Middlesbrough via Loftus ran from Whitby West Cliff

...ow: Whitby's A8 No. 69864 awaits departure with a 1950s local service. 69864 was withdrawn in October 1958.
...ille Stead collection

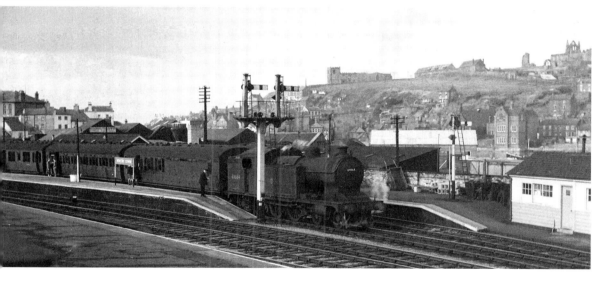

...he early 1960s, Mr Ron Hollier worked on the diagramming of Whitby-Scarbor-
...h line diesel multiple units at North Eastern Region headquarters in York.

...had been to meeting at Middlesbrough with a colleague who was in charge of the
...senger section at York and he suggested we return via Whitby - appropriate since
...had been finalising with the Middlesbrough district the DMU drivers' diagrams for
...: line to work the service with no more than 30 DMU vehicles. Not easy with the
...straints on timing through single line sections.

...he DMUs(blue square) had to be either twin power cars or two power cars and one
...ler to cope with the gradients between Whitby and Scarborough. Even so, there
...e occasions in the control log during the peak summer(when trains from Middles-
...ugh were heavily loaded) of the engines being overheated and trains delayed while ra-
...ors were topped up. There must have been supplies of water at intermediate stations."

SHORT MEMORIES

24.6.67: BR Standard Class 5 4-6-0 No. 73045 arrives at Scarborough with the 08.28 from Manchester Victoria.

January 1969: The York-Scarborough line is awarded £383000 grant aid.

Above: Most of the rationalization at Whitby came after the withdrawal of freight services in 1983. With the signal box and various go... sheds beyond it, Brush Type 2 No. 31153 waits the road in platform one while working the freight trip from Tees Yard in May 1982. ... signal box was closed and the semaphore signals removed when a new signalling system was installed in 1993.

Below: No. 31153 at work in Whitby Town goods yard in May 1982 by which time the traffic was mainly coal for local merchants. *Both Malcom Roughley/Stephen Chapman archive*

Whitby Town goods yard was listed in the 1956 Handbook of Stations as having a maximum crane capacity of 5 tons and ... ability to handle all classes of freight. The yard closed in 1983 when coal traffic ceased. A private siding leaving the main ... underneath Larpool Viaduct served coal drops at the gas works.

Whitby Gas Works Siding: When shunting wagons on to the coal store not more than 4 wagons may be propelled up ... gradient and they must remain coupled to the locomotive until they are on the cells. *BR Eastern Region Northern Area Sectio* ... *Appendix 1969.*

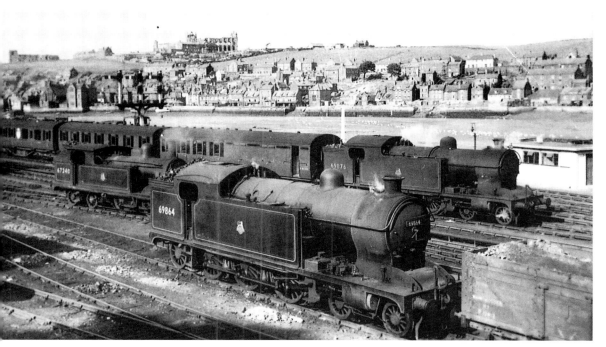

itby engine shed, coded 50G in BR's York District, provided mainly locomotives to work the passenger services that radiated south, rth and west from the busy fishing port and closed on 6th April 1959 when services from the Malton direction were turned over to sels. The shed was still standing in 2007, having been used as a chandler's store. This 1950s view shows A8 4-6-2T No. 69864 and G5 -4T No. 67240 simmering in the yard as A8 No. 69876 passes on a local passenger. Beyond them is the River Esk and on top of the is Whitby Abbey, the inspiration for Bram Stoker's Dracula. *Neville Stead collection*

ht: In LNER days
e Hull & Barnsley
lway 0-6-0s found
ir way onto
itby's books and
rked passenger
ins to Malton. Bear-
its pre-1946 LNER
nber, J23 No. 2522
nds in the shed yard.
ille Stead collection

comotives allocated to Whitby
gust 1950
0-6-0: 65621/24/27/28. G5 0-4-4T: 67302/35. A8 4-6-2T: 69858/60/61/64/65/88/90. Total: 13
closure 6.4.59
rburn Class 4 2-6-4T: 42083/84/85. BR Class 3 2-6-0: 77004/13. Total:5

Above: A8 No. 69888 shunts coaching stock in the sidings opposite the engine shed during the 1950s. The A8 4-6-2 tanks(rebuilt in 1930s from NER 4-4-4Ts) were introduced to the Whitby coast line services after a change of northern destination from Saltburn Middlesbrough, along with new Runabout tickets, in 1933 brought a big increase in passengers and the need for heavier trains. Before that, services were more usually worked by smaller A6 4-6-2Ts. Along with the Great Central-design A5s, the A8s were staple power the Whitby lines until replaced in the 1950s by LMS-design and BR Standard 2-6-4Ts. *Neville Stead collection*

Below: The once commonplace thrill of watching a big steam locomotive being turned can only be enjoyed at a handful of preserv railways and museums nowadays - and of course at Scarborough! Here, B1 4-6-0 No. 61319 has just been turned ready for working goods back home to York on 24th August 1964, through freight still running for a time after closure of local yards between Pickeri and Grosmont. The signal box at Bog Hall, junction with the line up to Prospect Hill, stands in the background. *Neville Stead colln.*

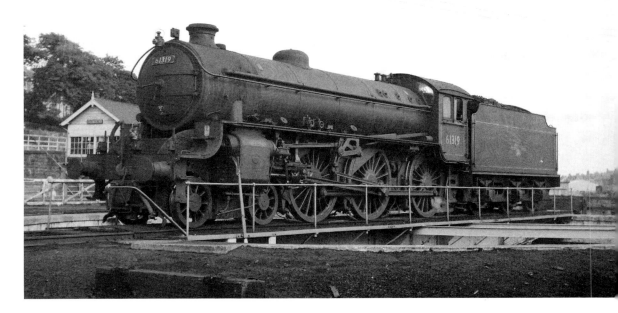

Above: A Middlesbrough-Scarborough 2-car Metro-Cammell DMU passes Bog Hall and the turntable on its way into Whitby Town on Saturday 6th March 1965. From Monday these trains will go no further than Whitby before returning to Teessside. *Maurice Burns*

Below: Brush Type 2 No. 31153 working the Whitby-Tees Yard pick-up waits at the signal by Bog Hall box in May 1982. The line up to Prospect Hill went off to the right in the far left of the photo. The train will also shunt the coal sidings at Sleights on its way home to Teesside. *Malcolm Roughley/Stephen Chapman archive*

Above: BR Class 3 2-6-2T No. 82028 makes a stirring sight as it storms past Bog Hall box and a classic NER slotted post signal with **Whitby to Malton local on 27th June 1962.** *Neville Stead collection*

Below: Ruswarp station, a mile and a half out of Whitby on the Pickering line, as seen in May 1982 from 31153 on the Whitby-Tees Ya **goods just before it goes onto the fine lattice girder bridge over one of the line's many crossings of the Esk. The level crossing has sin** **been converted to automatic barriers and the box abolished.** *Malcolm Roughley/Stephen Chapman archive*

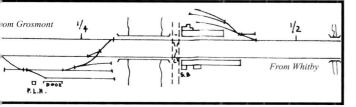

Left: The layout at Ruswarp station and Sneaton Siding in 1961.

The small goods yard at Ruswarp was listed in 1956 as equipped to handle only general goods, livestock, horse boxes and prize cattle vans. Sneaton public siding handled coal and minerals in wagonloads only. There was no permanent crane and they closed with effect from 2nd August 1965.

...ve: A rustic scene at Sleights in May ... as 31153 places loaded 16-ton min-... wagons in the coal yard. *Malcolm ...ghley/Stephen Chapman archive*

...t: What remained of Sleights sta-... on 26th July 1999 - just one active ...form and, thankfully, the Tudor-... buildings while at least the station ... has a train service. The layout ...w shows what used to be there in ... The sidings, which in 1956 were ...d as equipped to handle the same ...ic as Ruswarp and had no crane, ...ained in use for coal traffic until ... . *Stephen Chapman*

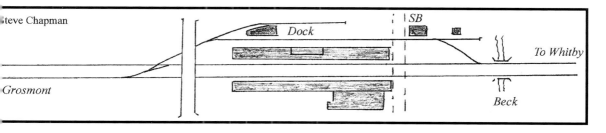

89

Above: The scene at Grosmont on a rather murky 1st October 1963. A B1 4-6-0 is in the Pickering line platform on the left with w
looks like a railtour from the Pickering direction while another B1 stands light engine in the Battersby line platform. Camping coac
can be seen in winter storage behind the light engine. Since the late 1960s, the platforms on the left have been part of the North Yo
shire Moors Railway while that on the right remains part of the national network being used by Middlesbrough-Whitby trains.
Neville Stead collection

Below: The weather varied a good deal on 6th March 1965, the last day of Whitby-Scarborough and Malton services. Snowfall star
the day as if to warn of the difficulties to come once the railway was gone. York-based English Electric Type 4 No. D259 en
Grosmont with the 08.55 Whitby to York on which the photographer travelled to Malton. *Maurice Burns*

ve: Grosmont station looking towards Whitby on 6th March 1965.
rice Burns

smont goods yard was listed in the 1956 Handbook of Stations as
ng no crane and able to handle only general goods, livestock, horse
es and prize cattle vans. Goods facilities were withdrawn from 2nd
ust 1965. See Page 38 regarding private sidings around Grosmont.

LINGTON JUNCTION-WHITBY TOWN 1960

alling: Absolute Block(Permissive Block Pickering Bridge Street-
h Mill and Electric Token on single line New Bridge-Levisham.)

imum line speed: 60mph Rillington-New Bridge
35mph New Bridge-Whitby Town

al boxes with distance from previous box: Marishes Road(3 miles
yds from Rillington,) Mill Lane(3 miles 141yds & junction with
rnton Dale branch,) Pickering Bridge Street(603yds,) Pickering High
(416yds,) Pickering New Bridge(1198yds,) Levisham(5 miles
yds,) Goathland Summit(6 miles 830yds,) Goathland(2 miles 96yds,)
smont(3 miles 728yds and junction with Battersby line,) Sleights(2
s 1232yds,) Ruswarp(1 mile 951yds,) Bog Hall(1 mile 248yds and
tion with the West Cliff line,) Whitby Town(284yds.)

itional running lines: Down Refuge siding for 21 wagons, engine
ake van at Levisham; Down Refuge siding for 33 wagons, engine &
e van at Goathland Summit.

r the withdrawal of passenger services the Rillington-Pickering
ion was worked according to "One engine in Steam" (only one train
wed on the line at a time)regulations.

Assistance to freight trains. The double heading
of Down freight trains from Levisham to Goathland Summit signal box and of Up freight trains
from Grosmont to Goathland Summit signal box
is prohibited unless there is also an assistant locomotive in the rear.

When an assistant locomotive is necessary in
either direction it must be in rear, and on arrival at
Summit box it must be taken off the rear and, if
neccessary, placed in front. In the case of an Up
train, if the assistant locomotive is required only
as far as Goathland station signal box it may be
detached there. It may, however, when necessary,
be used to assist in starting a train from Goathland
station, in which event it must not proceed beyond
the Up Advanced starting signal.
BR NE Region Sectional Appendix 1960

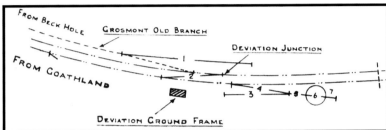

Above: Deviation Junction looking towa[rds] Grosmont on a gloomy day in the 1950s, [the] signal box long since downgraded t[o a] ground frame
Ken Hoole/Neville Stead collection

Left: The layout at Deviation Junctio[n in] 1946. *Not to scale.*

Below: Climbing up the 1 in 49 from Grosmont to Goathland during the 1950s, Malton-based Ivatt Class 2 2-6-2T No. 41251 assists [B1] 4-6-0 No. 61218 on the 2.10pm Saturdays Only Whitby-Leeds. *Ken Hoole/Neville Stead collection*

ove: The scene at Goathland on 28th June 1962 with a Whitby-bound 3-car DMU in the station. A camping coach is all that occu-
s the mineral sidings, the siding behind the water tower once reaching to a loading chute coming down the bank on the right from a
nway up on the top which brought whinstone from quarries about 2.5 miles away. The 1956 Handbook of Stations listed Goathland
aving a 2-ton crane and able to handle general goods, livestock, horse boxes and prize cattle vans. *Neville Stead colln.*

ow: The old lady looks a little perplexed by an 08.55 Whitby-York train that has pulled into Goathland's Up platform on 6th March
5 packed with excited but heavy-hearted gricers taking a farewell ride on the last day of Whitby-Malton services. *Maurice Burns*

Above: The 08.55 Whitby-York passes Goathland Summit signal box which was right on the 19 milepost from Rillington. There v two trailing crossovers and a Down siding here. Just over a quarter of a mile further on was Ellerbeck ground frame contro connections to an Up siding once used by the North Riding County Council. *Maurice Burns*

Below: Another one of Malton's Ivatt Class 2 2-6-2Ts, No. 41265, and York B1 No. 61053, double-head a heavily-loaded service Ellerbeck on 10th August 1961. *Neville Stead*

ve: G5 0-4-4T No. 67255 heads a Malton to Whitby local north of Levisham during the early 1950s. *Neville Stead collection*

w: The view from the 11am Malton to Whitby as it heads north from Levisham hauled by BR Class 4 2-6-4T No. 80120 on 16th il 1958. Thanks to the North Yorkshire Moors Railway, it is still possible to make this same journey behind the same class of loco 008. *David Holmes*

Above: The 08.55 Whitby-York train hauled by English Electric Type 4 No. D259 on 6th March 1965 approaches Levisham station, [...] miles from Rillington. *Maurice Burns*

The small goods yard, which was on the left beyond the station, was listed in the 1956 Handbook of Stations as having no perman[...] crane and able to handle general goods, livestock, horse boxes and prize cattle vans. A mile north of Levisham was Raindale pu[...] siding which was listed as equipped to handle only wagonload mineral traffic.

Left: On the evening [...] 6th March 1965 the '[...] man' of an English E[...] tric Type 4 holds out [...] arm to collect the to[...] for the single line to P[...] ering as the last Whit[...] York via Pickering tr[...] enters Levisham stat[...] watched by a few onlo[...] ers come to pay their respects.

The engine carries [...] wreath or headboar[...] could it be that pe[...] knew it would not be [...] last train between Wh[...] and Pickering, at least [...] *Maurice Burns.*

Below: The layouts [...] Levisham and Rainda[...] 1961. *Not to scale*

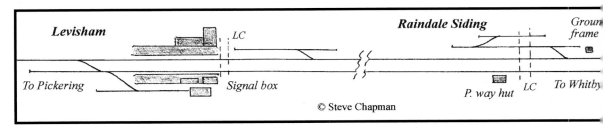

© Steve Chapman

ve: **D259 threads its way through the wintry landscape south of Levisham with the 08.55 Whitby-York on 6th March 1965. The line
veen Levisham and Pickering New Bridge was singled during the first world war so that the track could be used in France. Alas,
ship carrying it was lost at sea.**

w: **The 08.55 Whitby-York entering Pickering station on 6th March 1965**. *Both Maurice Burns*

Above: The relaxed scene at Pickering station on arrival of the 08.55 Whitby-York. That evening when the last York train arrived platform was absolutely packed with people saying farewell to their service. From Monday they would have to rely on buses but w a few years the platforms would be thronged with passengers again, only the trains can go no further than this and the bus is needed to reach Malton - for the time being. The signal box at Bridge Street level crossing is just beyond the train. *Maurice Burns*

Pickering departures summer 1950

am
5.44	5.20 Malton-Whitby
7.10	7.10 to York via Helmsley
8.0	7.2 Whitby-Malton. *To York Mons & Sats Only*
10.15	10.15 to York via Helmsley
10.23	9.25 Whitby-Malton *To York Mons & Sats Only*
10.58 SO	10.5 York-Whitby
11.25	10.30 Whitby-King's Cross *Mons & Sats Only*
	Not after 9th September
11.31	11.10 Malton-Whitby
	From York on Mondays, Leeds on Saturdays

pm
12.37	11.40 Whitby-Malton
2.37	2.20 Malton-Whitby
3.8 SO	2.10 Whitby-Leeds
4.20	4.0 Malton-Whitby
	From York Mon, Fri, Sat Only. Through carriages Kings Cross-Whitby FSO until 9th Sept.
4.25	3.20 Whitby-Malton
6.0	6.0 to York via Helmsley
6.19	6.0 Malton-Whitby
7.50	6.50 Whitby-Malton

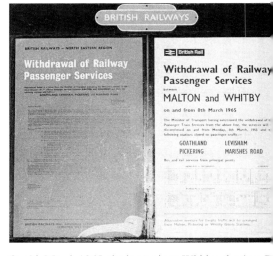

On 6th March 1965, the last train to Whitby, the 4pm L from York, had to be strengthened by three cars to ac modate the extra passengers saying their farewells.

The Whitby Moors railtour began from Manchester. C *Marquess* took over at Wakefield and from there the ran via Market Weighton, Bridlington and Scarboroug

Left: Pickering station from the Malton end when still under British Rail stewardship. Nowadays the line ends here. The station had an overall roof until 1952. *David Lawrence/ Photos from the Fifties*

Below: Preserved LNER K4 2-6-0 No. 3442 *The Great Marquess* at Pickering with the returning Whitby Moors Railtour carrying 340 enthusiasts on 6th March 1965. Behind it is K1 2-6-0 No. 62005. Both engines have revisited this spot and 62005 is a regular. *Maurice Burns*

ckering Bridge Street-High Mill signal boxes. Drivers of empty coaching stock trains leaving Beck Sidings or the Down dings for the Up line must run cautiously on all occasions and be prepared to stop short of any obstruction between Beck dings or the Down Sidings and Bridge Street signal box. *British Railways North Eastern Region Sectional Appendix 1960.* e Appendix also stated that wagons with or without a brake van may be propelled on both Up and Down lines between High ll and New Bridge in daylight and clear weather. They may also be propelled between High Mill and Mill Lane but if the length ceeded 5 wagons signalmen must only accept them with their block instruments showing 'Line Clear.'

Above: J25 0-6-0 No. 65656 has just crossed Hungate level crossing and is passing Pickering engine shed on the right and the raised co[al] drops on the left with a short goods in the 1950s. The goods shed is in the left background. The 1956 Handbook of Stations listed Pick[...]ering as having a permanent crane facility of up to 5 tons and the ability to handle all types of freight. Black Bull public siding, one a[nd] three quarter miles south of Pickering, was able to handle coal, mineral and 'side to side' wagonload traffic only. *JW Hague/N Stead col[...]*

Left: Pickering engine shed lookin[g] north, was a sub-shed of Malton b[...] closed in 1959. Engines outbased the[...] in 1950 were Class Y3 Sentinel lo[...] No. 68157 for local shunting a[nd] D49/2 4-4-0 62774 *The Staintonda[...]* With two-speed gears and vacu[um] brake, the Y3 was also able to do li[...] work and at one time deputise for t[...] Sentinel railcar on the Seamer servi[...] On the right are remains of the co[...] stage on which was mounted a ha[...] crane for lifting coal in buckets fr[...] wagons to engines. The shed s[...] stands in private use.

Ken Hoole/Neville Stead collection

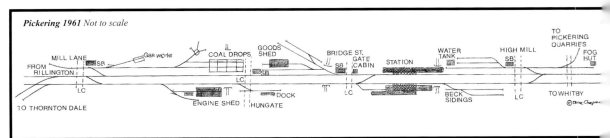

Pickering 1961 *Not to scale*

ove: Mill Lane crossing and junction looking towards Malton in the1950s and it's menial work for a one-time express engine. D49/1 -0 No. 62730 *Berkshire* from York shed comes off the Thornton Dale branch with a pick-up goods as the signalman collects the token m the fireman. The truncated remains of the Kirbymoorside branch on the right are acting as a headshunt for the gas works siding. *ille Stead collection*

Left: Upper Carr level crossing at Black Bull Siding had gates which opened outwards across the road and not across the railway when no train was due. This board signal was a usual feature at such crossings on the North Eastern network. It showed approaching loco drivers whether or not the gates were closed across the road. The crossing keeper is Mrs. Brewer.
H. Walshaw/Photos from the Fifites

Below: The layouts at Marishes Road(left) and Black Bull Siding (right) in 1961
The 1956 Handbook of Stations listed Marishes Road as equipped to handle general goods, livestock, horse boxes and prize cattle vans. It had no permanent crane.The goods yard closed on 10th August 1964.

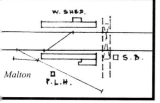

101

Above: An English Electric Type 4 calls at Marishes Road with the 08.55 Whitby-York during the 1960s. *Neville Stead collection*

Below: The 08.55 Whitby-York with English Electric Type 4 No. D259 in charge joins the Scarborough-York line at Rillington on (
March 1965. The overall roof is long gone but the station remains. The trackless bay platform originally meant for Whitby trains is
the right and the new 40-lever signal box commissioned in 1959 is beyond the station. This box was finally abolished in 1993 when (
level crossing was converted to automatic half barriers. *Maurice Burns*

Above: In this 1950s view of Scarborough Road Junction, Norton, facing towards field, G5 0-4-4T No. 67248 prepares to guide a Scarborough-bound summer urday express, which has just arrived from the north via Gilling, down to ton station. *AL Brown/Neville Stead collection*

Below: Supreme motive power at Scarborough Road. A4 Pacific No. 60017 *Silver*, has just arrived from King's Cross with a special for Ampleforth College on April 1963. Another engine will take the train forward to Gilling. The view oking west and the headshunt marks the private sidings serving the York-e Farmers' Bacon Factory. *Ken Hoole/Neville Stead collection*

THE BRANCHES
TO
RYEDALE

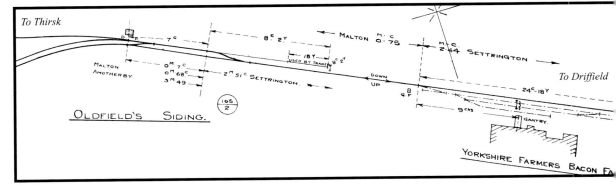

To Thirsk

MALTON
AMOTHERBY

OLDFIELD'S SIDING.

MALTON M.C. 0.75

SETTRINGTON

To Driffield

YORKSHIRE FARMERS BACON FA

Above: The layout at Scarborough Road in 1921.

Below: Apart from drawing summer Saturday expresses between Malton station and Scarborough Road, the local pilots also gave them a start up the gradient away from Scarborough Road when setting off towards Gilling. One of Malton's Ivatt Class 2 2-6-2Ts has just completed this task and has come to a rest on the bridge over the River Derwent as an express from Scarborough to the north gets away from it. Slip couplings for automatic release of the assisting engine were kept at Malton shed.
PB Booth/N Stead colln.

MALTON-PILMOOR/GILLING-KIRBYMOORSIDE 1960

PILMOOR-MALTON EAST

Signalling: Electric token on single line(no token Pilmoor-Sunbeck Jn.)
Absolute Block Scarborough Road-Malton East)

Maximum speed on single line: Pilmoor-Gilling 20mph. Gilling-Scarborough Rd: 30mph
Maximum speed on Up & Down lines: Scarborough Road-Malton East: 25mph

Signal boxes with distances from previous box: Sunbeck(695yds from Pilmoor,) Coxwold(miles 1537yds,) Gilling(5 miles 45yds,) Hovingham Spa(1 mile 1353yds,) Slingsby(1 mi 1399yds,) Amotherby(3 miles 637yds,) Scarborough Road(3 miles 949yds,) Malton East(904yds

Additional running lines: Crossing loop for 71 wagons, engine & brake van at Coxwold; cros ing loop for 13 wagons, engine & brake van at Gilling; Up refuge siding for 28 wagons, engi & brake at Gilling(available for use in both directions;) Down refuge siding for 32 wagons, e gine & brake at Slingsby(available for use in both directions;) Crossing loop for 7 wagons, engi & brake van at Scarborough Road.

GILLING-KIRBYMOORSIDE

Signalling: Electric token Gilling-Helmsley. One engine in steam Helmsley-Kirbymoorside

Maximum speed on single line: 30mph

Signal boxes: Helmsley(6 miles 1240yds from Gilling;) Kirbymoorside(5 miles 601yds.)

Additional running lines: Crossing loop at Helmsley

3.5.81: The BR-sponsored Scarborough Spa Express makes its inaugural run hauled by Class 8P Pacific No. 46229 *Duchess of Hamilton.*

10.8.99: Freight operator English Welsh & Scottish Railway runs two freight trains conveying scrap cars from Pickering New Bridge to Liverpool via Tees Yard hauled by Class 66 locomotives - the first commercial freight on the North Yorkshire Moors line since 1965.

Above: As some of the pictures in this book testify, Saturday 29th July 1961 was a heavily overcast day. Here, with assistance from the rear, York B16/3 4-6-0 No. 61461 heads Scarborough-Glasgow train 1S52 away from Scarborough Road and towards Gilling.
PB Booth/Neville Stead collection

Below: The layout at Amotherby Flour Mill Siding as it was in 1921.
The 1956 Handbook for Stations showed Amotherby goods yard equipped to deal with general goods, livestock, horse boxes and prize cattle vans. It had no permanent crane. The station was open for parcels traffic. Amotherby closed to all traffic on 17th October 1964, the section from there to Malton being the last stretch of the Ryedale lines to close.

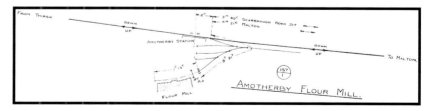

Assisting of trains from the rear. When it is necessary for a locomotive in the rear to give a start to a train from Scarborough Road towards Gilling, it must not go beyond the bridge crossing the York & Scarborough line, and the signalman at Scarborough Road must not give the "Train out of Section" signal to Malton East signal box or foul the loop line until the locomotive returns and is shunted clear. *BR North Eastern Region Sectional Appendix 1960*

Above: The cloud has broken and produced a hint of sunshine on 29th July 1961 as York B1 4-6-0 No. 61176 passes Slingsby with tr
1N13 from Glasgow to Scarborough. The goods yard here was listed in 1956 as having one-ton crane capacity and able to handle
types of freight except furniture vans, carriages, motor cars and machines on wheels. There was also a large two-storey granery wh
can be seen on the left of the picture. The station was still available for parcels traffic.

Below: The next station going towards Gilling was Hovingham Spa, seen here with 52D Tweedmouth-allocated V2 2-6-2 No. 60°
heading the 8.35am Scarborough-Glasgow, also on 29th July 1961. The signalman is ready to hand over the token for the next sect
of line and has his arm out ready to(hopefully) collect the token from the previous section as the train thunders through non-stop. T
station was listed in 1956 as having a 10cwt crane and able to handle all types of goods including parcels. *Both PB Booth/N Stead co*

ve: Gilling, 10.5 miles from Malton, 12 miles from Pilmoor and 19 miles from Pickering. Gateshead V2 2-6-2 No. 60929 heads
ugh with the 7.40am Filey Holiday Camp to Edinburgh on 29th July 1961. Although appearing to be double track, the line beyond
points is in fact the parallel single lines from Malton on the right, and Kirkbymoorside on the left. Note the water column at the
orm end - some summer Saturday trains stopped here for water. *P.B. Booth/Neville Stead collection*

w: Gilling station looking east. The cattle dock is visible beyond the station while the goods shed is hidden by the buildings. Gilling
listed in the 1956 Stations Handbook as having a 15cwt crane capacity and able to handle all types of freight while the station, like
on the Ryedale lines, was open for parcels and excursions despite being closed to regular passenger services.
lle Stead collection

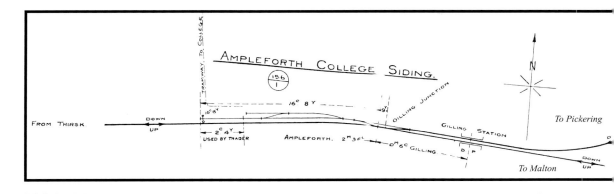

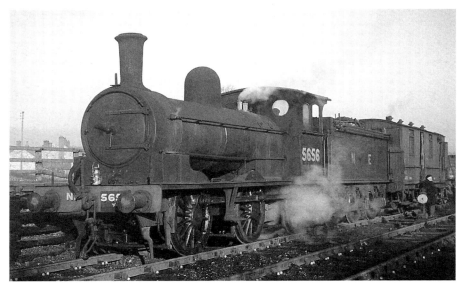

Top: A short distance wes
Gilling station were two
ings, an extension of one d
necting with the Amplefo
College tramway. This is
layout in 1921.

Centre: A relaxed scene
Coxwold station altho
there appears to have b
some spillage from the
drops onto the platform.
JW Hague/N Stead collectic

Bottom: LNER J25 0-6-0
5656 from York shed on e
neers duty at Coxwold
1948. *Ernest Sander*
Colour-Rail NE131
Coxwold was listed in 195
having a one ton crane
able to handle all types
freight.

ve: The tiny station at Husthwaite Gate was the last one on the **Thirsk & Malton** before it joined the **East Coast main line** just **of Pilmoor.** The station remained open for parcels traffic while the 1956 Stations Handbook listed the small goods yard as **g no permanent crane and being equipped to handle general goods only.** *JW Hague/Neville Stead collection*

w: Helmsley was the most important intermediate station served by the **Ryedale lines.** Six and a half miles east of **Gilling,** the sta-**was** better appointed than the others, being built to the requirements of the **Earl of Feversham** at nearby **Duncombe Park** estate, **oasted** a glazed platform canopy when regular passenger services were running. After regular services were withdrawn in 1953, **sley** and other stations continued to be served by occasional excursions bringing ramblers into the area and taking local people **day out. This long DMU formation with a Birmingham Railway Carriage & Wagon Co. set nearest, was such an excursion **d for Leeds.** *JW Hague/Neville Stead collection*

Above: Helmsley on 31st January 1953, the last day of regular passenger services. D49/1 4-4-0 No. 62730 *Berkshire* is on the 10.2[...] Saturdays only York-Pickering. The glazed canopy can just be seen above the train with the signal box at the far end and the coal d[...] beyond that. *JW Hague/Neville Stead collection*

Helmsley was listed in the 1956 Handbook of Stations as having a permanent crane of one ton 10cwt and able to handle par[...] and all types of freight. There was also a public siding at Harome Gate for coal, minerals and 'side to side' wagonload tra[...] and a long siding for timber traffic serving Duncombe Park estate plantations.

Below: Passengers mingle with locals who have turned out in force to witness the arrival this Railway Correspondence & Tr[...] Society railtour at Kirbymoorside(5.25 miles beyond Helmsley and since 1953 the end of the line) on 23rd June 1957. The engine is D[...] 4-4-0 No. 62731 *Selkirkshire* which was transferred from York shed to Selby that month. *Ken Hoole/Neville Stead collection*

ve: Sinnington was the last station before Pickering. On Saturday 31st January 1953, D49/1 4-4-0 No. 62730 *Berkshire* **calls there** **the 10.23am Saturdays Only York-Pickering. From Monday 2nd February this station and the line between Kirbymoorside and** **ering was closed altogether.** *JW Hague/Neville Stead collection*

w: Thornton Dale station looking towards Pickering on 30th October 1962, still intact despite being closed to passengers since **0.** *Neville Stead collection* **The 1956 Handbook of Stations listed Thornton Dale as having no permanent crane and equipped to** **dle coal, minerals and 'side to side' wagonload traffic only.**

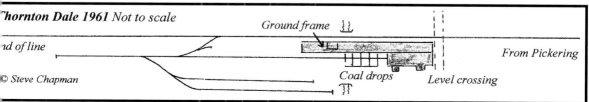

Thornton Dale 1961 Not to scale

nd of line

Ground frame

Coal drops

Level crossing

From Pickering

© Steve Chapman

Top: In the late 1940s, G5 0-4-4T No. 67286 is near Ebberston with a typical Pickering to Scarborough train. *Ernest Sanderson*

Centre: Ebberston station, 5.75 miles from Pickering, after closure. It was called Wilton until 1903. *Neville Stead collection*

Bottom: Three miles beyond Ebberston was Snainton, a two-platform station and the only one on the branch with a crossing loop. It is seen here after conversion to a private dwelling. *David Lawrence/ Photos from the Fifties.*

The single track goods branch from Pickering Mill Lane Junction to Thornton Dale was 2 miles 1069 yards long.

Its main purpose was to serve quarries at Thornton Dale, traffic which ensured its survival for 14 years after the rest of the branch to Seamer was closed.

It was operated according to "One Engine in Steam" regulations with no signalling beyond Mill Lane limits. The five level crossings, at Eastgate, Haygate Lane, Hugton, Westfield, and Broadmire had to be opened and closed by the train crew.

The maximum speed was 25mph.